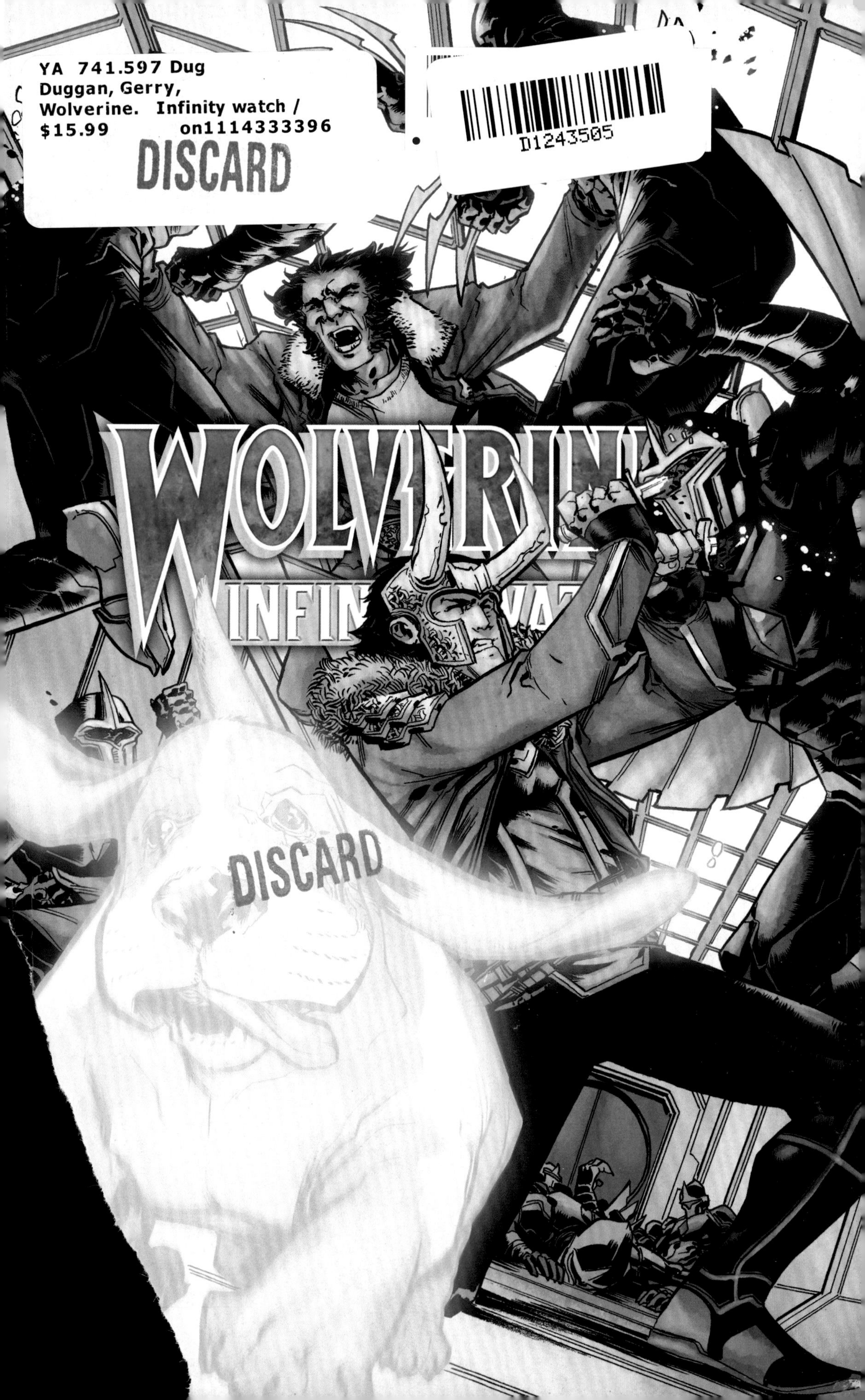
WOLVERIN
INFIN
WAT

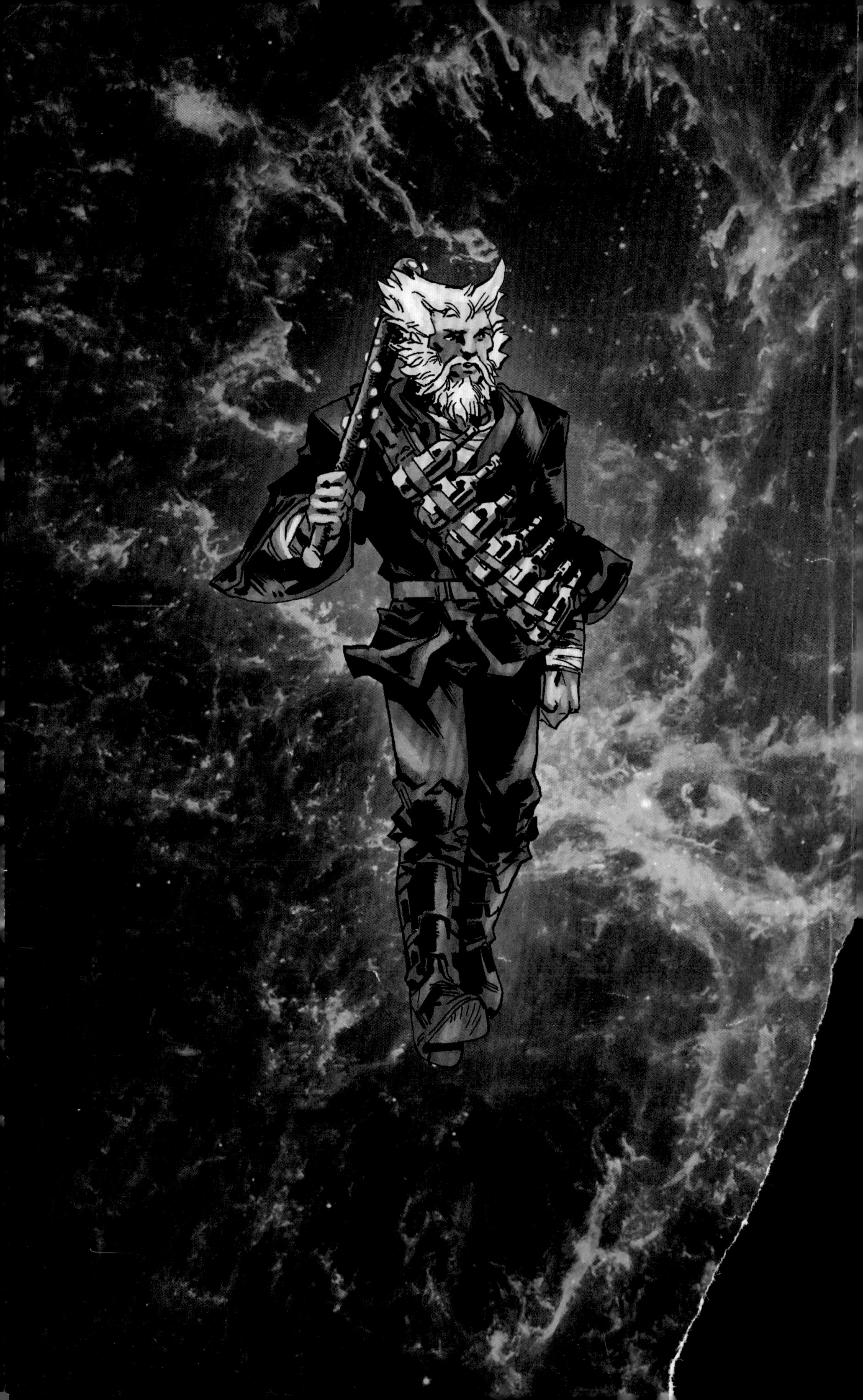

WOLVERINE
INFINITY WATCH

GERRY DUGGAN
WRITER

ANDY MacDONALD
ARTIST

JORDIE BELLAIRE
COLOR ARTIST

VC's CORY PETIT
LETTERER

GIUSEPPE CAMUNCOLI, ROBERTO POGGI & DEAN WHITE
COVER ART

ANNALISE BISSA
ASSISTANT EDITOR

JORDAN D. WHITE
EDITOR

COLLECTION EDITOR **JENNIFER GRÜNWALD**
ASSISTANT EDITOR **CAITLIN O'CONNELL**
ASSOCIATE MANAGING EDITOR **KATERI WOODY**
EDITOR, SPECIAL PROJECTS **MARK D. BEAZLEY**
VP PRODUCTION & SPECIAL PROJECTS **JEFF YOUNGQUIST**
BOOK DESIGNER **ADAM DEL RE**

SVP PRINT, SALES & MARKETING **DAVID GABRIEL**
DIRECTOR, LICENSED PUBLISHING **SVEN LARSEN**
EDITOR IN CHIEF **C.B. CEBULSKI**
CHIEF CREATIVE OFFICER **JOE QUESADA**
PRESIDENT **DAN BUCKLEY**
EXECUTIVE PRODUCER **ALAN FINE**

WOLVERINE: INFINITY WATCH. Contains material originally published in magazine form as WOLVERINE: INFINITY WATCH #1-5. First printing 2019. ISBN 978-1-302-91581-0. Published by MARVEL WORLDWIDE, INC., a subsidiary of MARVEL ENTERTAINMENT, LLC. OFFICE OF PUBLICATION: 135 West 50th Street, New York, NY 10020.

Printed in Canada. DAN BUCKLEY, President, Marvel Entertainment; JOHN NEE, Publisher; JOE QUESADA, Chief Creative Officer; TOM BREVOORT, SVP of Publishing; DAVID BOGART, Associate Publisher & SVP of Talent Affairs; DAVID GABRIEL, SVP of Sales & Marketing, Publishing; JEFF YOUNGQUIST, VP of Production & Special Projects; DAN CARR, Executive Director of Publishing Technology; ALEX MORALES, Director of Publishing Operations; DAN EDINGTON, Managing Editor; SUSAN CRESPI, Production Manager; STAN LEE, Chairman Emeritus. For information regarding advertising in Marvel Comics or on Marvel.com, please contact Vit DeBellis, Custom Solutions & Integrated Advertising Manager, at vdebellis@marvel.com. For Marvel subscription inquiries, please call 888-511-5480. **Manufactured between 7/5/2019 and 8/6/2019 by SOLISCO PRINTERS, SCOTT, QC, CANADA.**

10 9 8 7 6 5 4 3 2 1

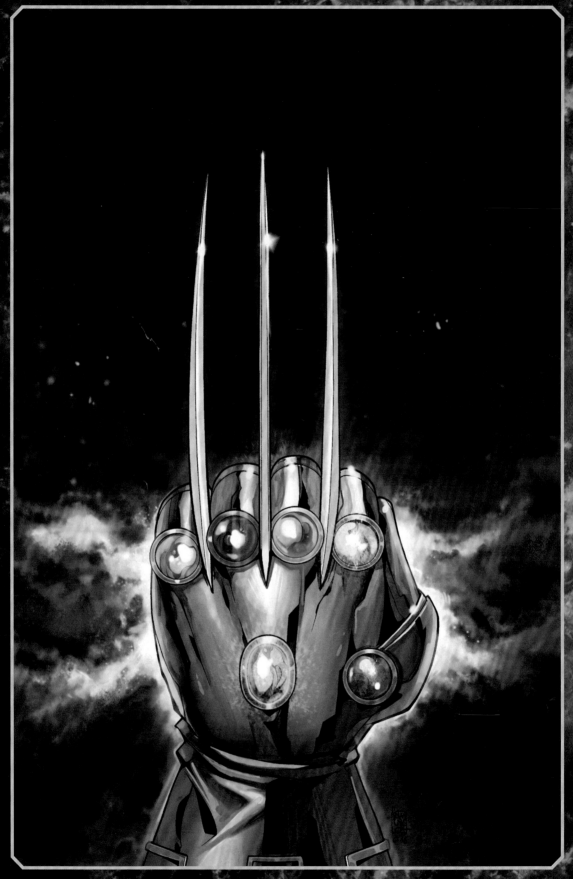

ONE

I'VE LOST TRACK OF THE NUMBER OF WINTERS...

...BUT I'VE LIVED MANY LIVES...

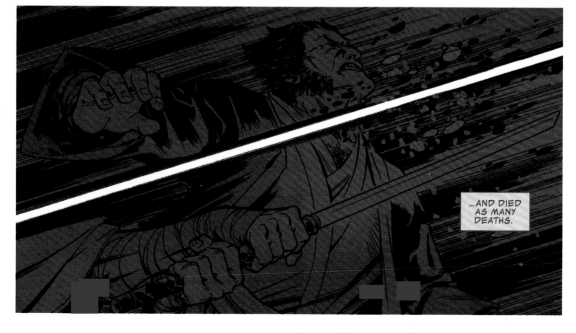

...AND DIED AS MANY DEATHS.

SOME DEATHS WERE SPIRITUAL...

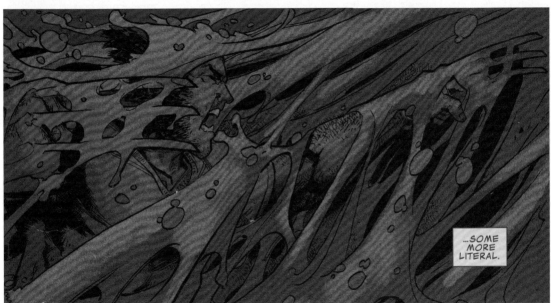

...SOME MORE LITERAL.

BUT MY HEART IS PUMPING AGAIN NOW.

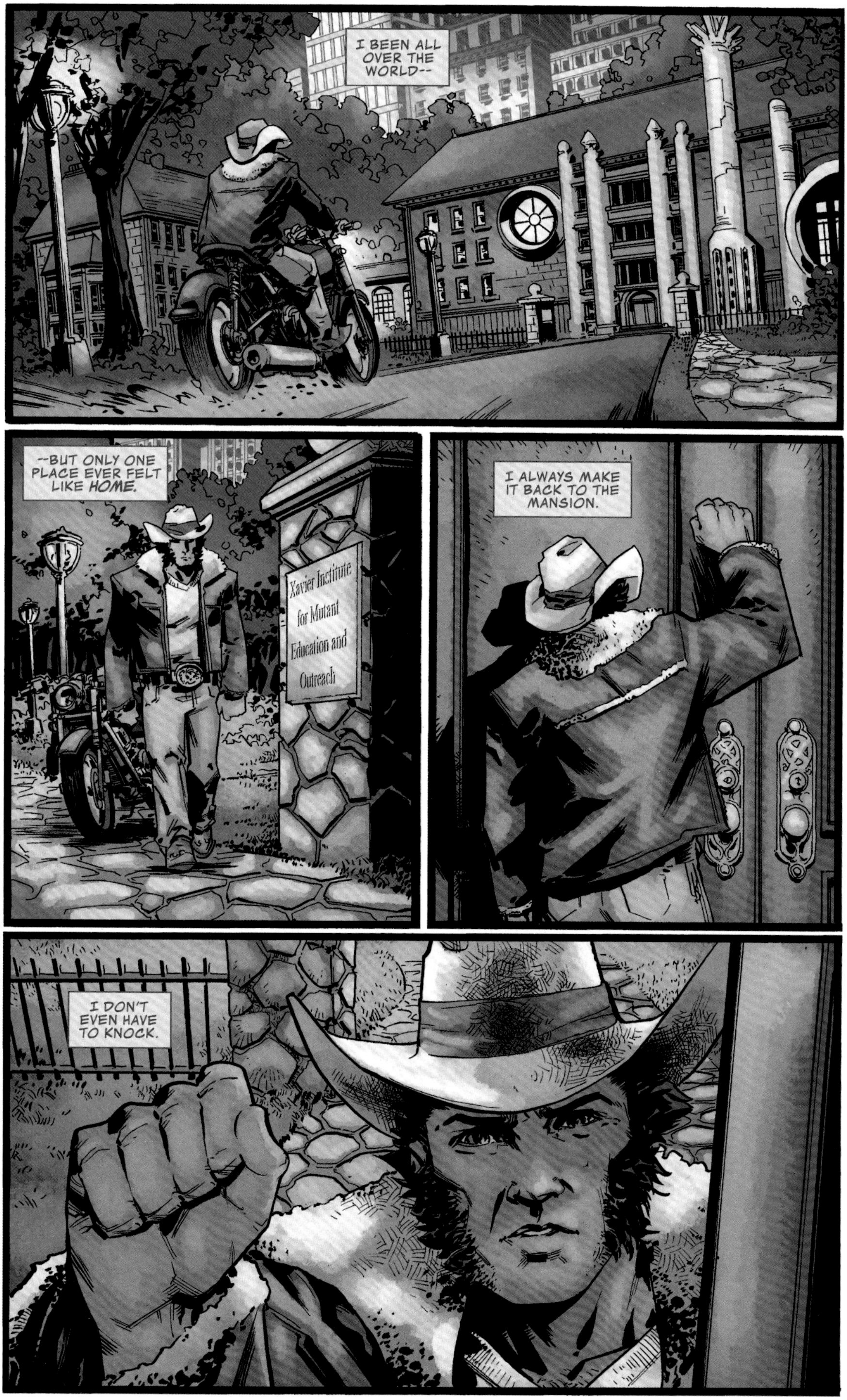
I BEEN ALL OVER THE WORLD--
--BUT ONLY ONE PLACE EVER FELT LIKE HOME.
Xavier Institute for Mutant Education and Outreach
I ALWAYS MAKE IT BACK TO THE MANSION.
I DON'T EVEN HAVE TO KNOCK.

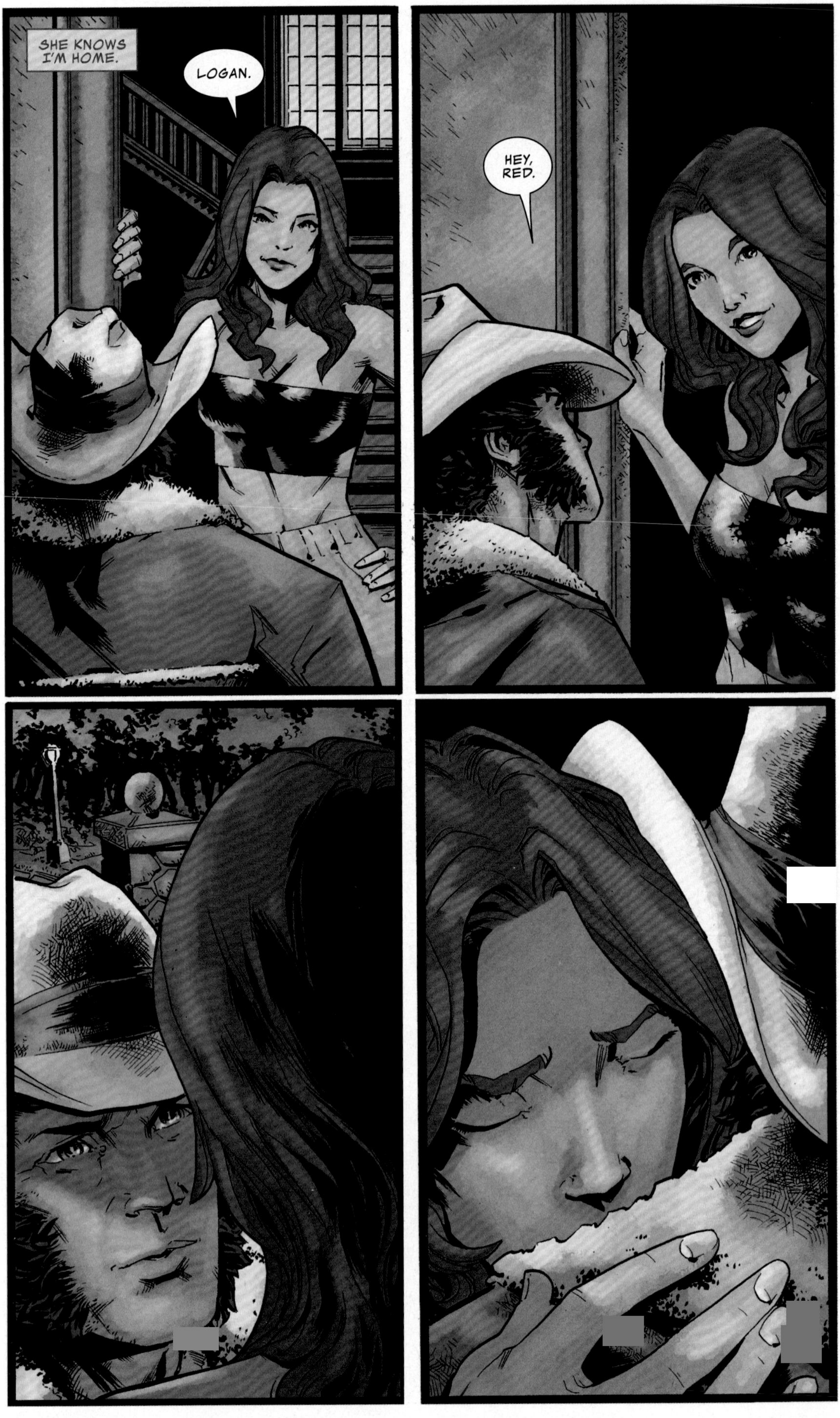
SHE KNOWS I'M HOME.
LOGAN.
HEY, RED.

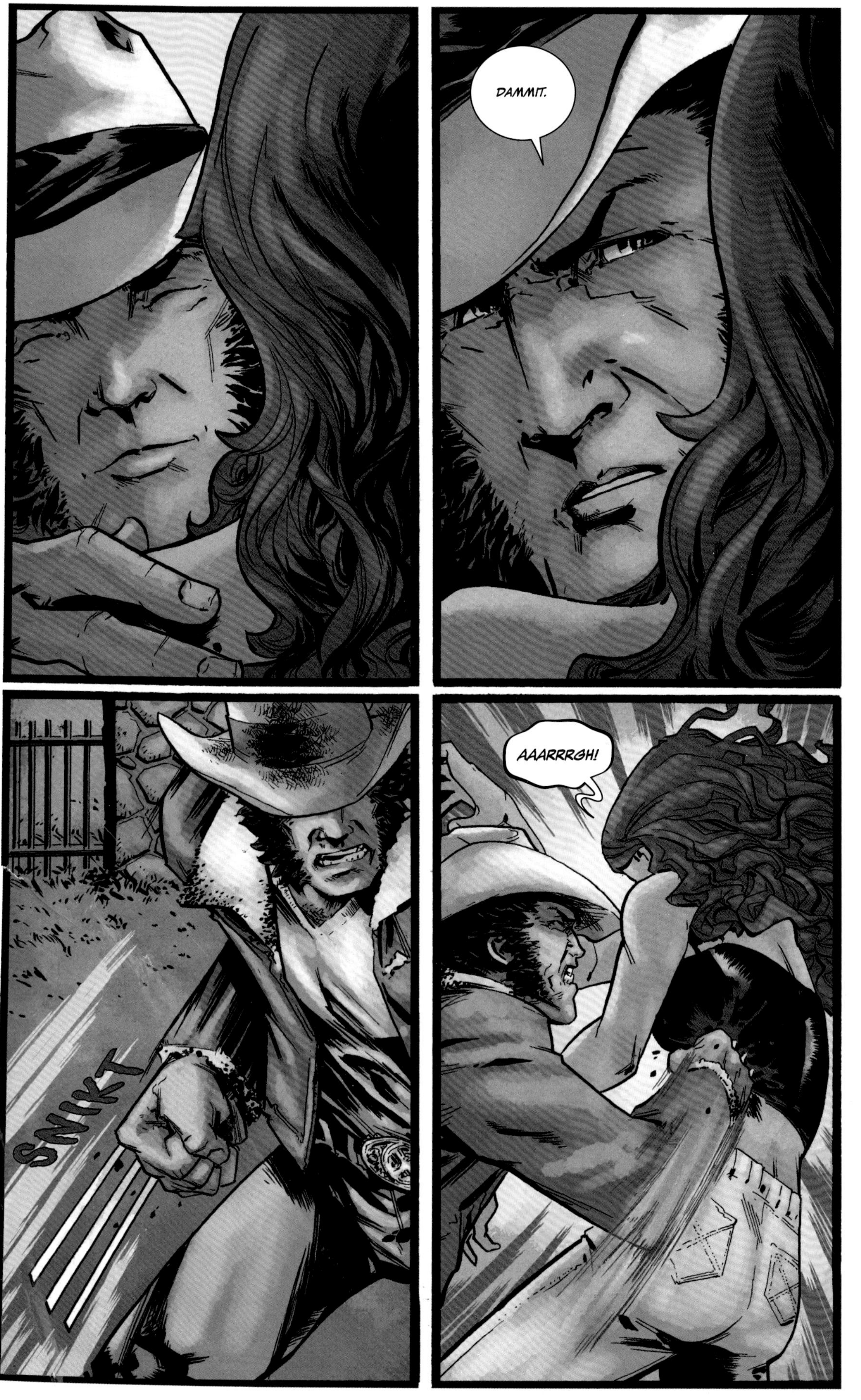
DAMMIT.
SNIKT
AAARRRGH!

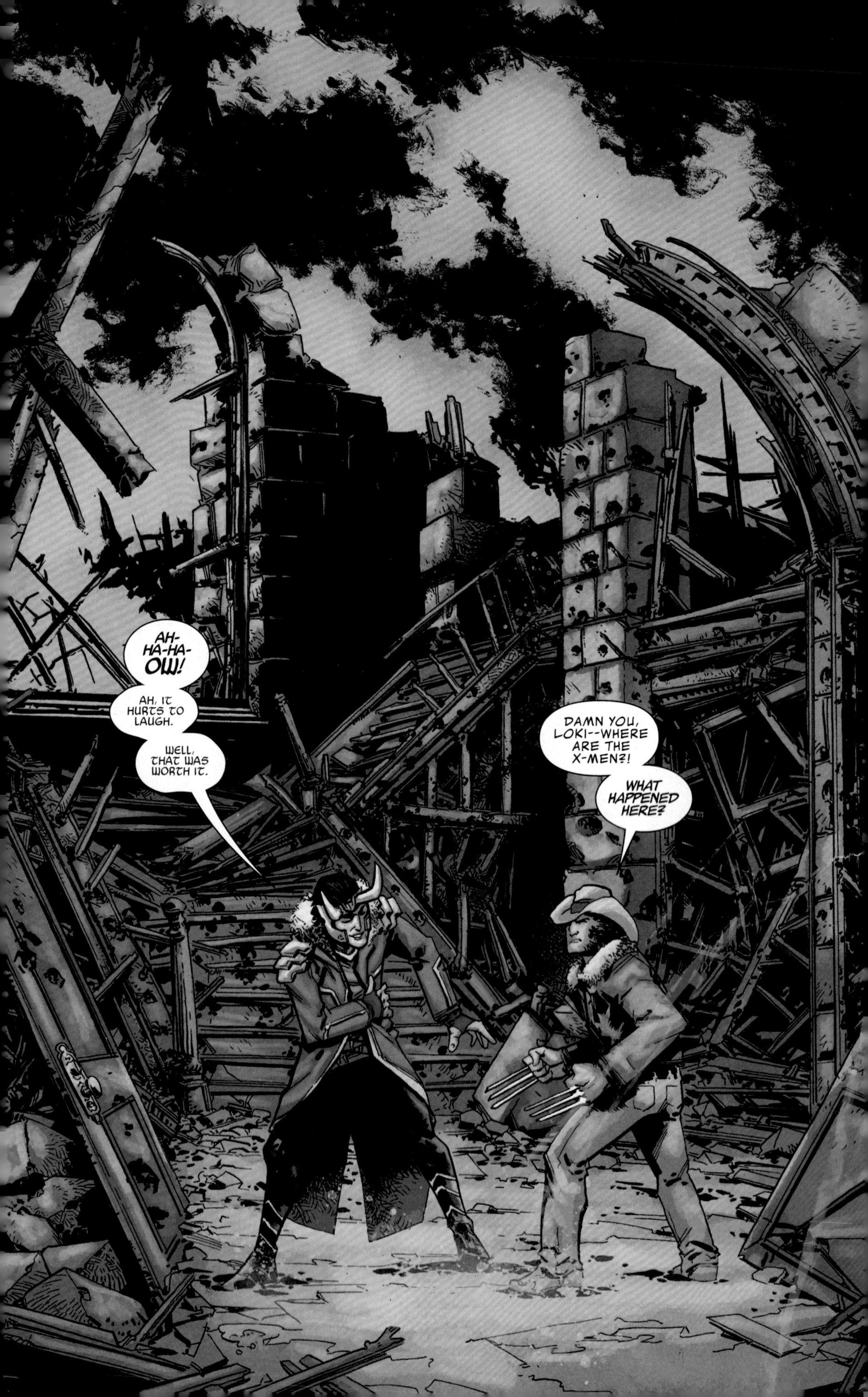
AH-HA-HA-OW!
AH, IT HURTS TO LAUGH.
WELL, THAT WAS WORTH IT.
DAMN YOU, LOKI--WHERE ARE THE X-MEN?!
WHAT HAPPENED HERE?

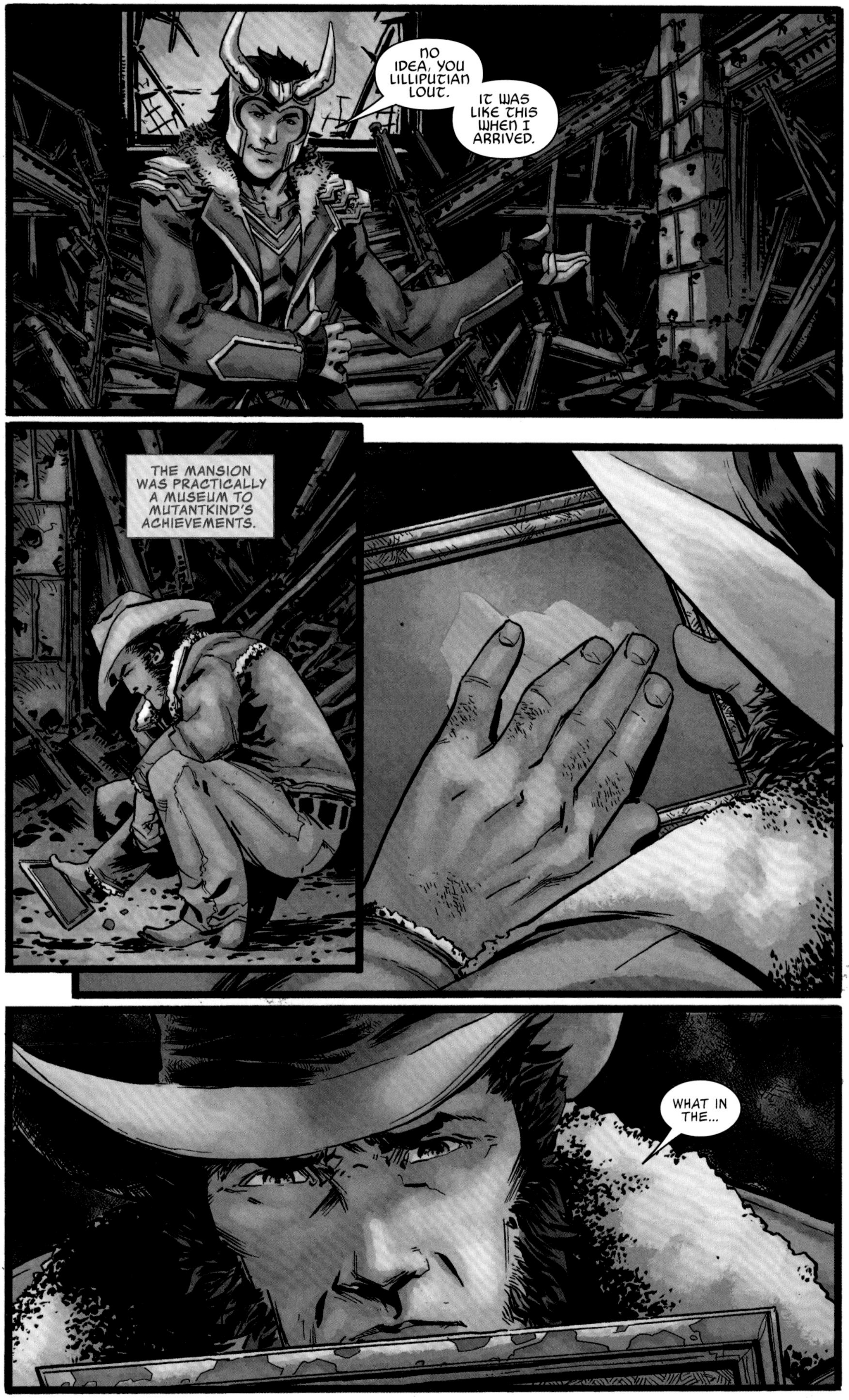
NO IDEA, YOU LILLIPUTIAN LOUT.
IT WAS LIKE THIS WHEN I ARRIVED.
THE MANSION WAS PRACTICALLY A MUSEUM TO MUTANTKIND'S ACHIEVEMENTS.
WHAT IN THE...

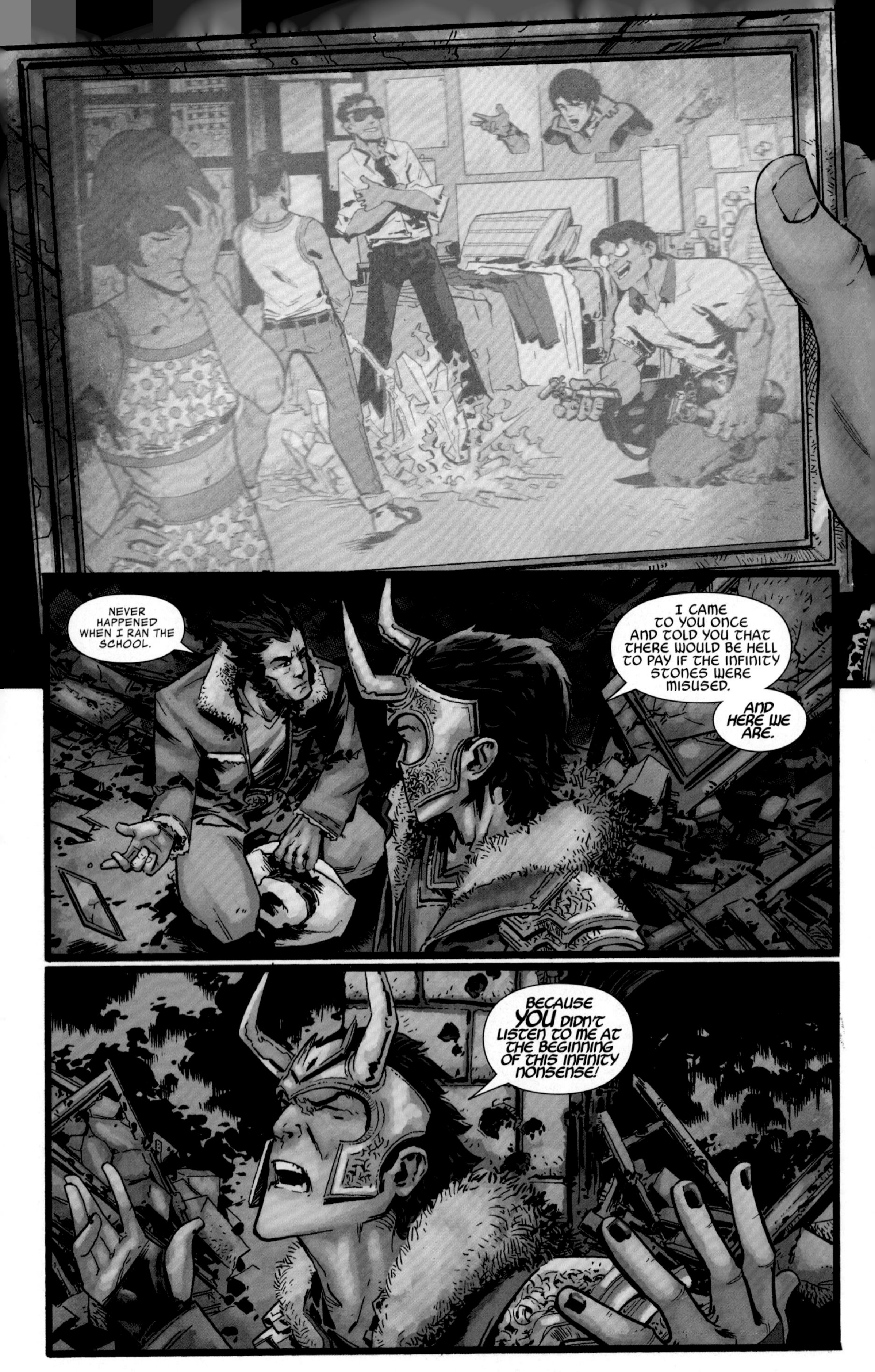
NEVER HAPPENED WHEN I RAN THE SCHOOL.
I CAME TO YOU ONCE AND TOLD YOU THAT THERE WOULD BE HELL TO PAY IF THE INFINITY STONES WERE MISUSED.
AND HERE WE ARE.
BECAUSE YOU DIDN'T LISTEN TO ME AT THE BEGINNING OF THIS INFINITY NONSENSE!

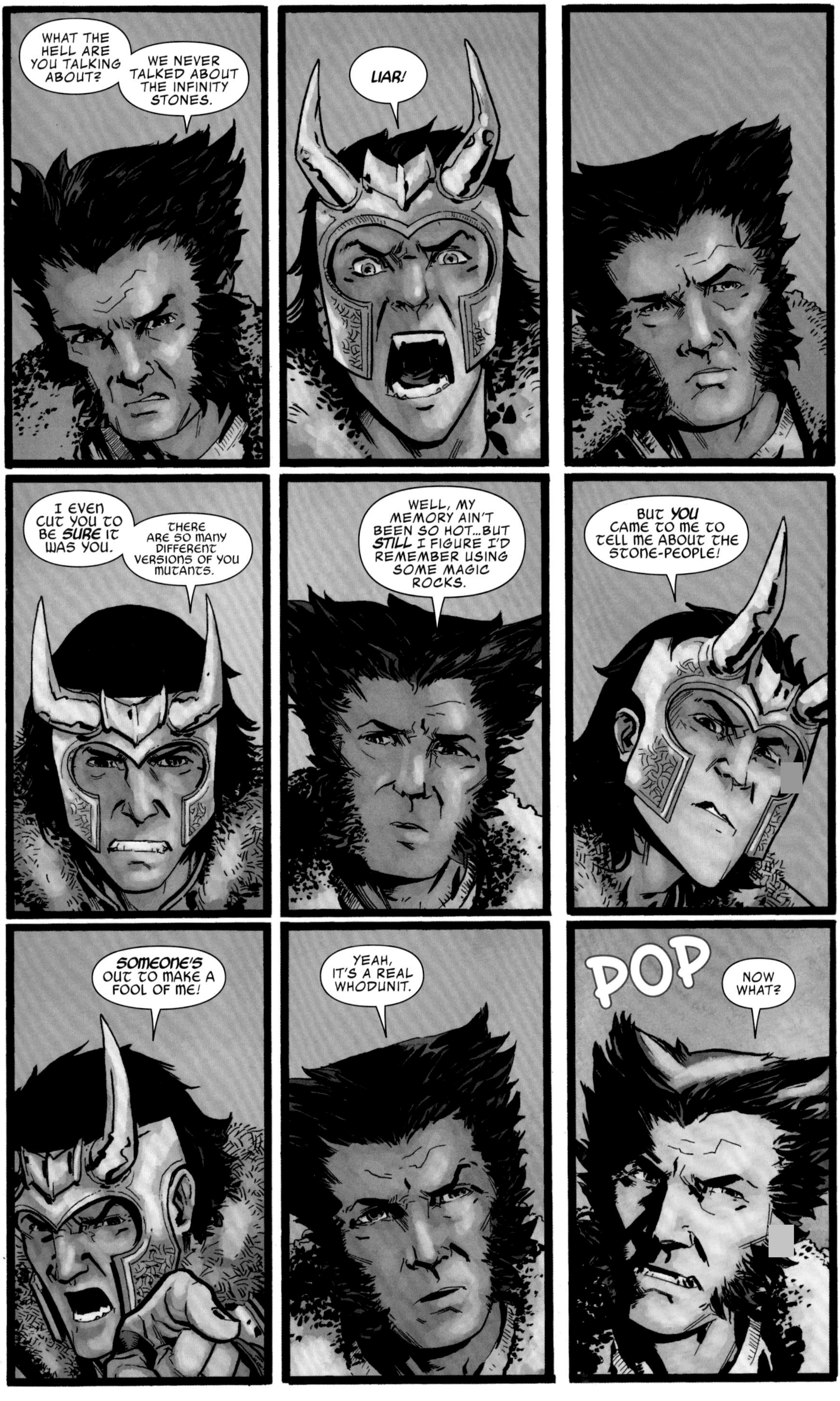
WHAT THE HELL ARE YOU TALKING ABOUT?
WE NEVER TALKED ABOUT THE INFINITY STONES.
LIAR!
I EVEN CUT YOU TO BE SURE IT WAS YOU.
THERE ARE SO MANY DIFFERENT VERSIONS OF YOU MUTANTS.
WELL, MY MEMORY AIN'T BEEN SO HOT...BUT STILL I FIGURE I'D REMEMBER USING SOME MAGIC ROCKS.
BUT YOU CAME TO ME TO TELL ME ABOUT THE STONE-PEOPLE!
SOMEONE'S OUT TO MAKE A FOOL OF ME!
YEAH, IT'S A REAL WHODUNIT.
POP
NOW WHAT?

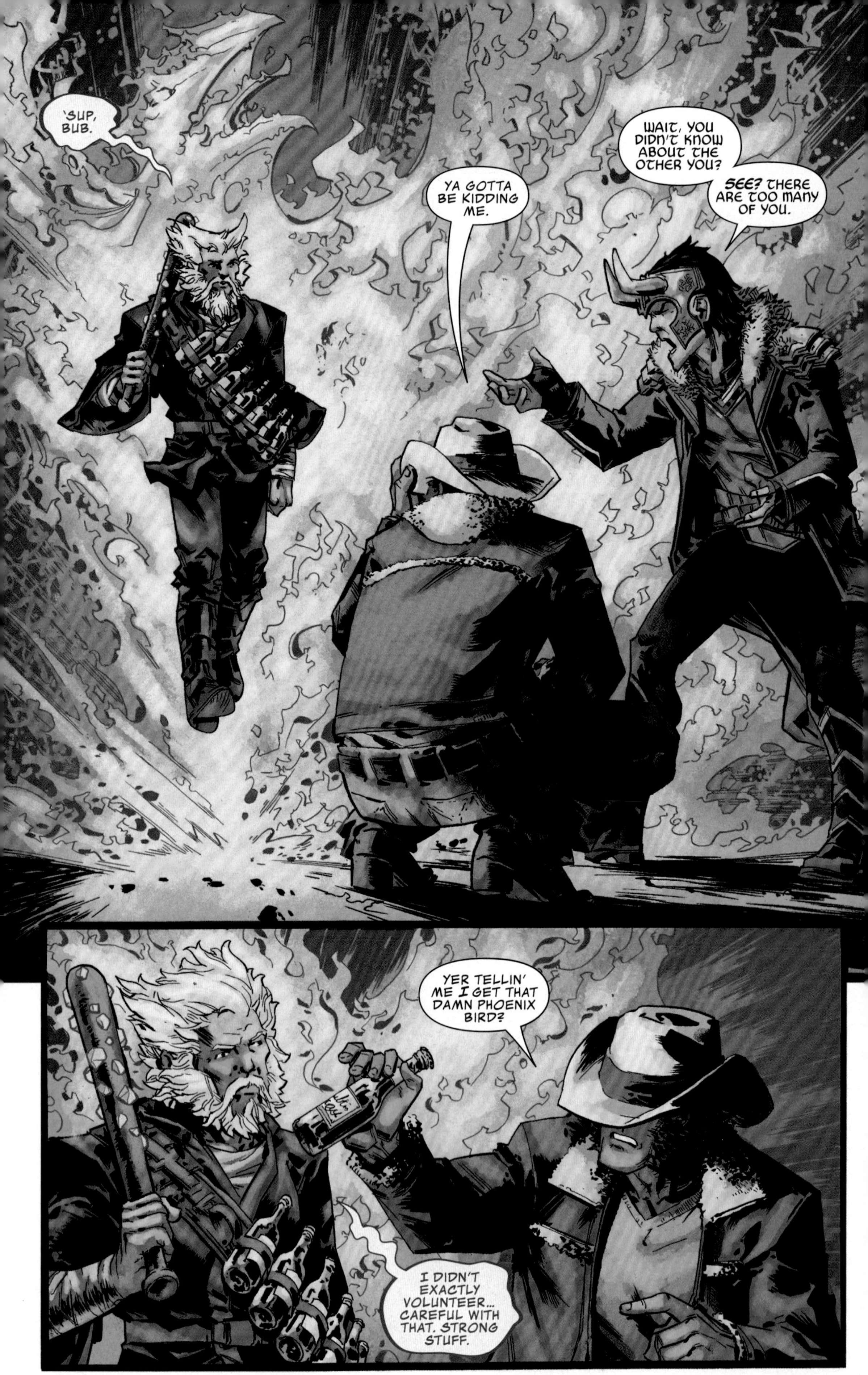
'SUP, BUB.
YA GOTTA BE KIDDING ME.
WAIT, YOU DIDN'T KNOW ABOUT THE OTHER YOU?
SEE? THERE ARE TOO MANY OF YOU.
YER TELLIN' ME I GET THAT DAMN PHOENIX BIRD?
I DIDN'T EXACTLY VOLUNTEER... CAREFUL WITH THAT. STRONG STUFF.

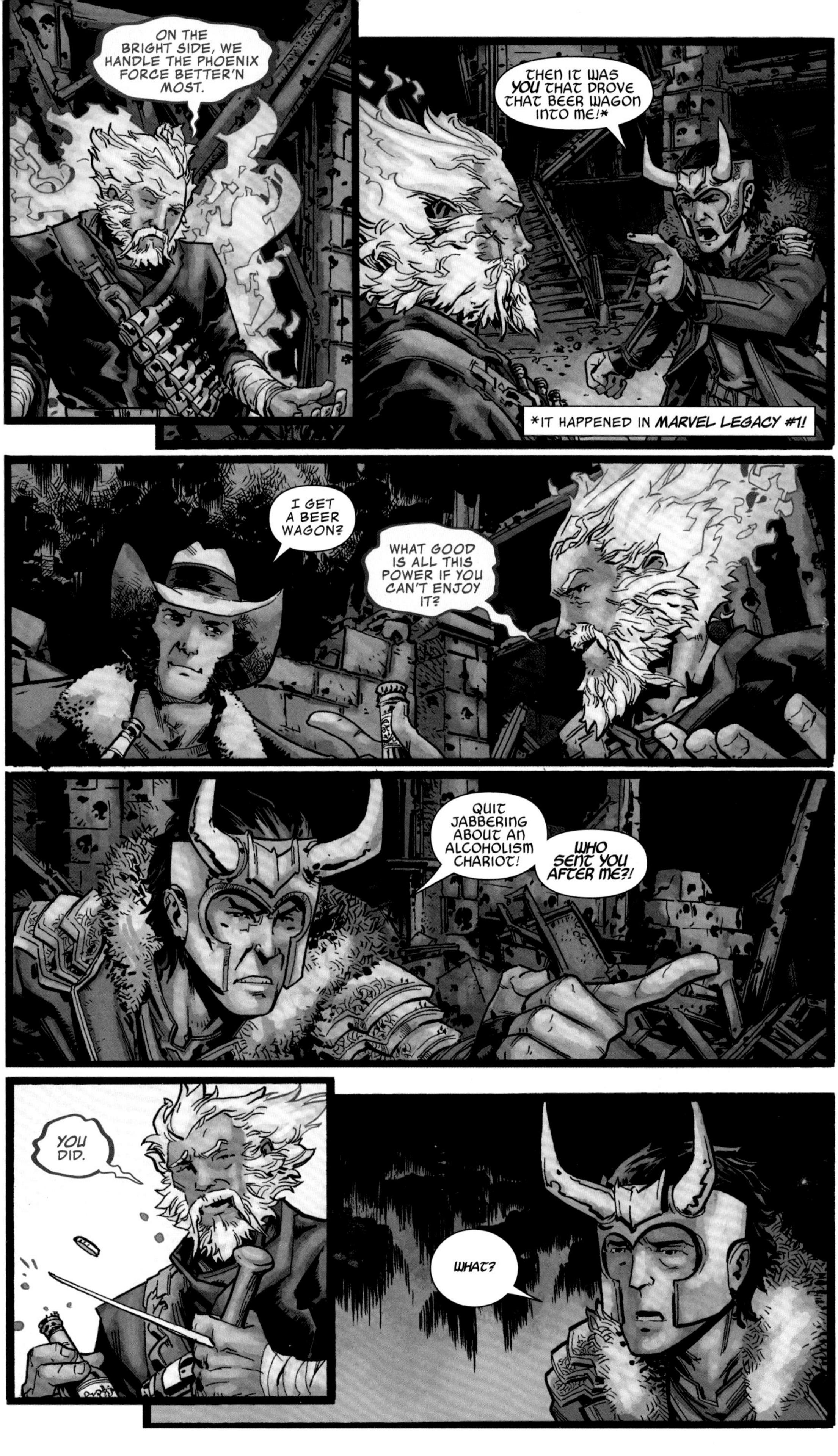
ON THE BRIGHT SIDE, WE HANDLE THE PHOENIX FORCE BETTER'N MOST.
THEN IT WAS YOU THAT DROVE THAT BEER WAGON INTO ME!*
*IT HAPPENED IN MARVEL LEGACY #1!
I GET A BEER WAGON?
WHAT GOOD IS ALL THIS POWER IF YOU CAN'T ENJOY IT?
QUIT JABBERING ABOUT AN ALCOHOLISM CHARIOT!
WHO SENT YOU AFTER ME?!
YOU DID.
WHAT?

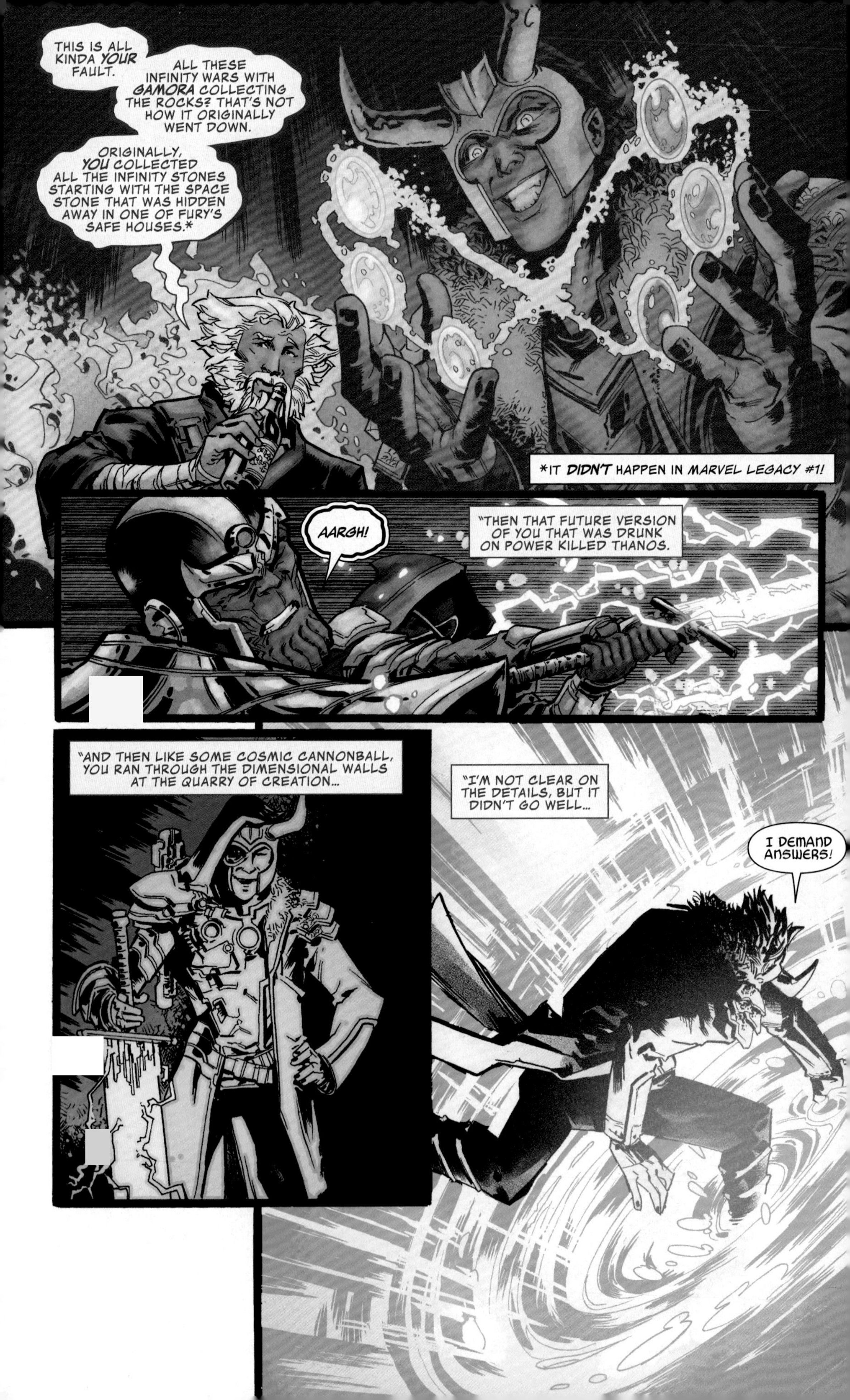

THIS IS ALL KINDA YOUR FAULT.
ALL THESE INFINITY WARS WITH GAMORA COLLECTING THE ROCKS? THAT'S NOT HOW IT ORIGINALLY WENT DOWN.
ORIGINALLY, YOU COLLECTED ALL THE INFINITY STONES STARTING WITH THE SPACE STONE THAT WAS HIDDEN AWAY IN ONE OF FURY'S SAFE HOUSES.*
*IT DIDN'T HAPPEN IN MARVEL LEGACY #1!
AARGH!
"THEN THAT FUTURE VERSION OF YOU THAT WAS DRUNK ON POWER KILLED THANOS.
"AND THEN LIKE SOME COSMIC CANNONBALL, YOU RAN THROUGH THE DIMENSIONAL WALLS AT THE QUARRY OF CREATION...
"I'M NOT CLEAR ON THE DETAILS, BUT IT DIDN'T GO WELL...
I DEMAND ANSWERS!

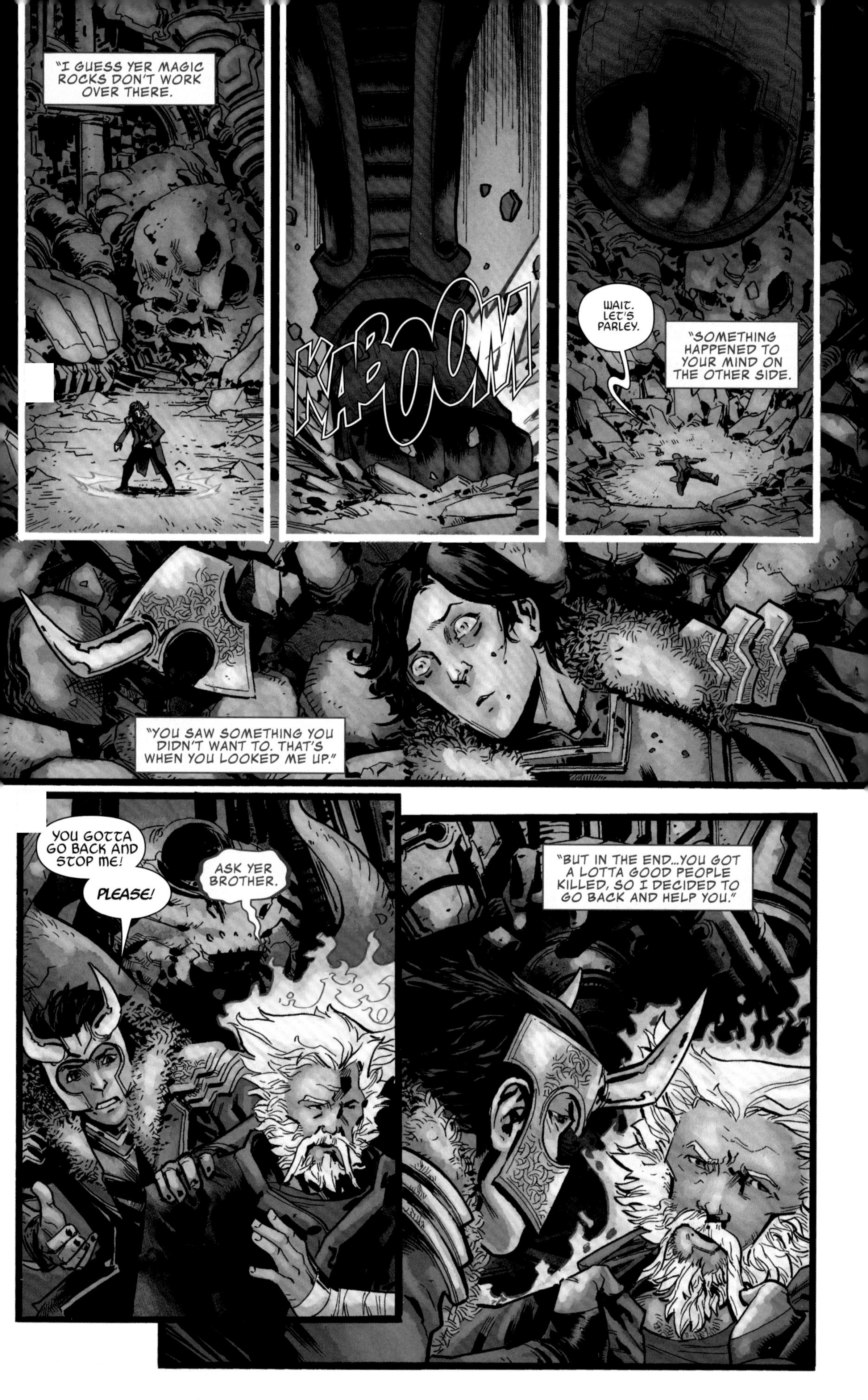
"I GUESS YER MAGIC ROCKS DON'T WORK OVER THERE.
KABOOM
WAIT. LET'S PARLEY.
"SOMETHING HAPPENED TO YOUR MIND ON THE OTHER SIDE.
"YOU SAW SOMETHING YOU DIDN'T WANT TO. THAT'S WHEN YOU LOOKED ME UP."
YOU GOTTA GO BACK AND STOP ME!
PLEASE!
ASK YER BROTHER.
"BUT IN THE END...YOU GOT A LOTTA GOOD PEOPLE KILLED, SO I DECIDED TO GO BACK AND HELP YOU."

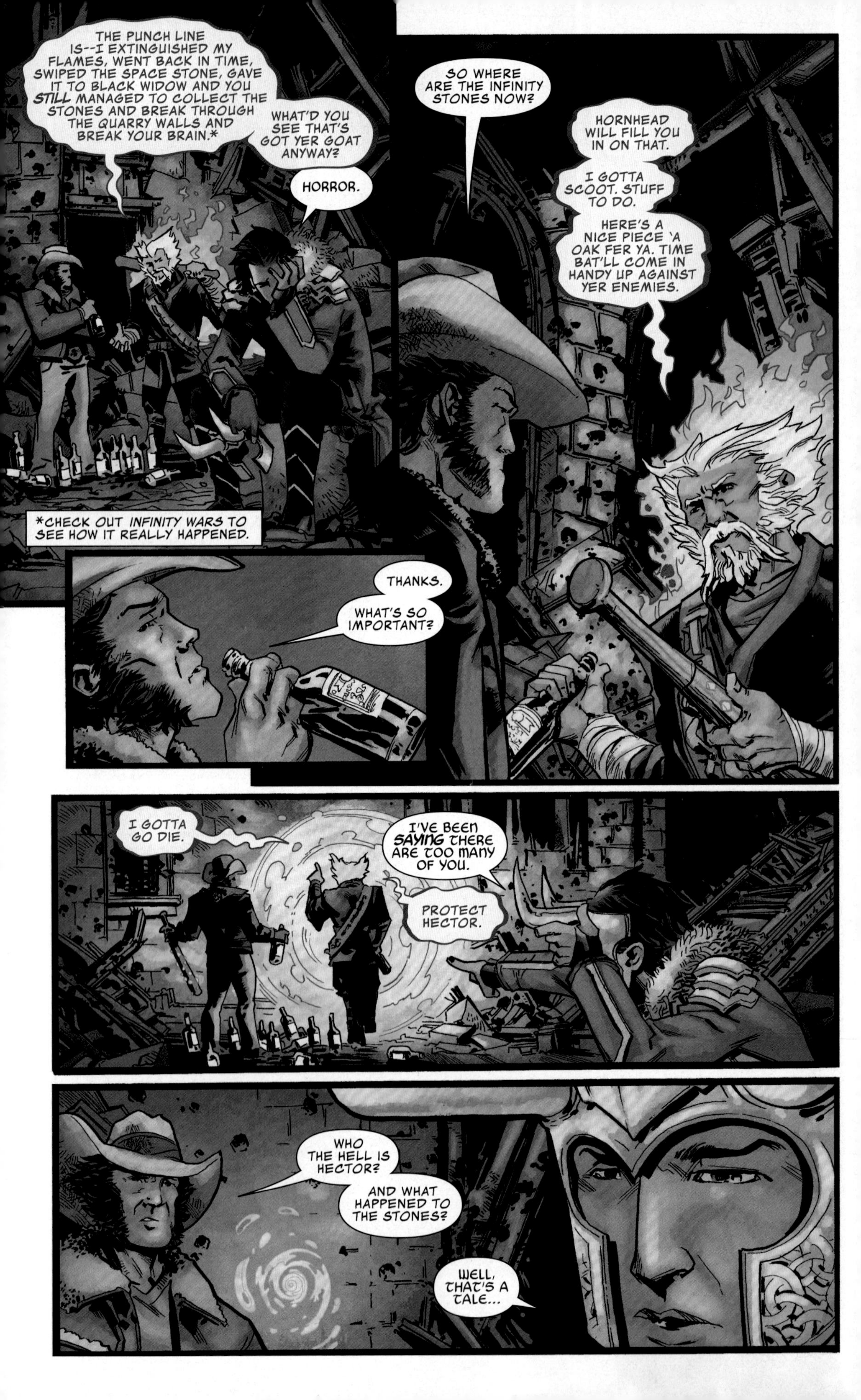
THE PUNCH LINE IS--I EXTINGUISHED MY FLAMES, WENT BACK IN TIME, SWIPED THE SPACE STONE, GAVE IT TO BLACK WIDOW AND YOU STILL MANAGED TO COLLECT THE STONES AND BREAK THROUGH THE QUARRY WALLS AND BREAK YOUR BRAIN.*
WHAT'D YOU SEE THAT'S GOT YER GOAT ANYWAY?
HORROR.
*CHECK OUT INFINITY WARS TO SEE HOW IT REALLY HAPPENED.
SO WHERE ARE THE INFINITY STONES NOW?
HORNHEAD WILL FILL YOU IN ON THAT.
I GOTTA SCOOT. STUFF TO DO.
HERE'S A NICE PIECE 'A OAK FER YA. TIME BAT'LL COME IN HANDY UP AGAINST YER ENEMIES.
THANKS.
WHAT'S SO IMPORTANT?
I GOTTA GO DIE.
I'VE BEEN SAYING THERE ARE TOO MANY OF YOU.
PROTECT HECTOR.
WHO THE HELL IS HECTOR?
AND WHAT HAPPENED TO THE STONES?
WELL, THAT'S A TALE...

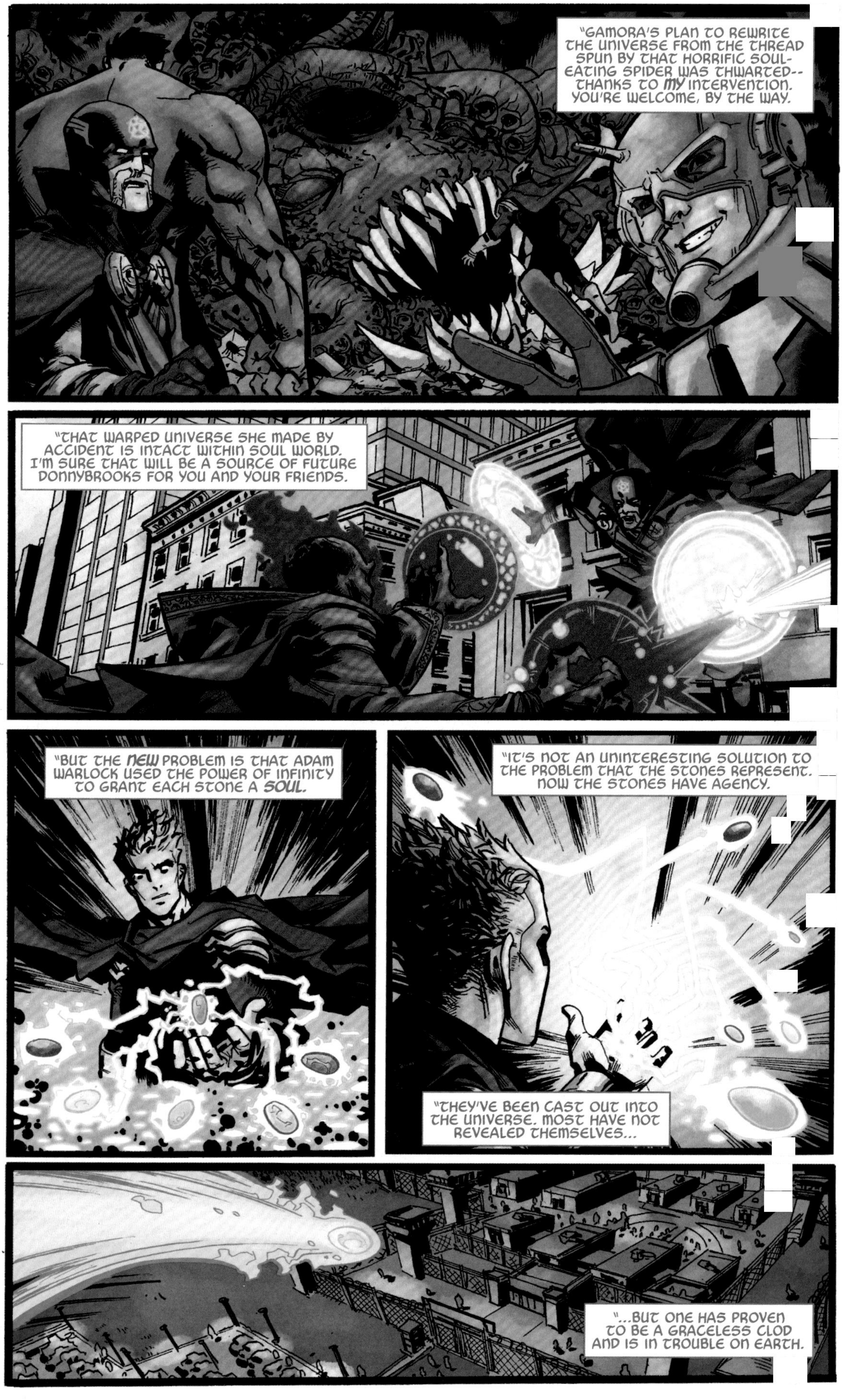
"GAMORA'S PLAN TO REWRITE THE UNIVERSE FROM THE THREAD SPUN BY THAT HORRIFIC SOUL-EATING SPIDER WAS THWARTED--THANKS TO MY INTERVENTION. YOU'RE WELCOME, BY THE WAY.
"THAT WARPED UNIVERSE SHE MADE BY ACCIDENT IS INTACT WITHIN SOUL WORLD. I'M SURE THAT WILL BE A SOURCE OF FUTURE DONNYBROOKS FOR YOU AND YOUR FRIENDS.
"BUT THE NEW PROBLEM IS THAT ADAM WARLOCK USED THE POWER OF INFINITY TO GRANT EACH STONE A SOUL.
"IT'S NOT AN UNINTERESTING SOLUTION TO THE PROBLEM THAT THE STONES REPRESENT. NOW THE STONES HAVE AGENCY.
"THEY'VE BEEN CAST OUT INTO THE UNIVERSE. MOST HAVE NOT REVEALED THEMSELVES...
"...BUT ONE HAS PROVEN TO BE A GRACELESS CLOD AND IS IN TROUBLE ON EARTH.

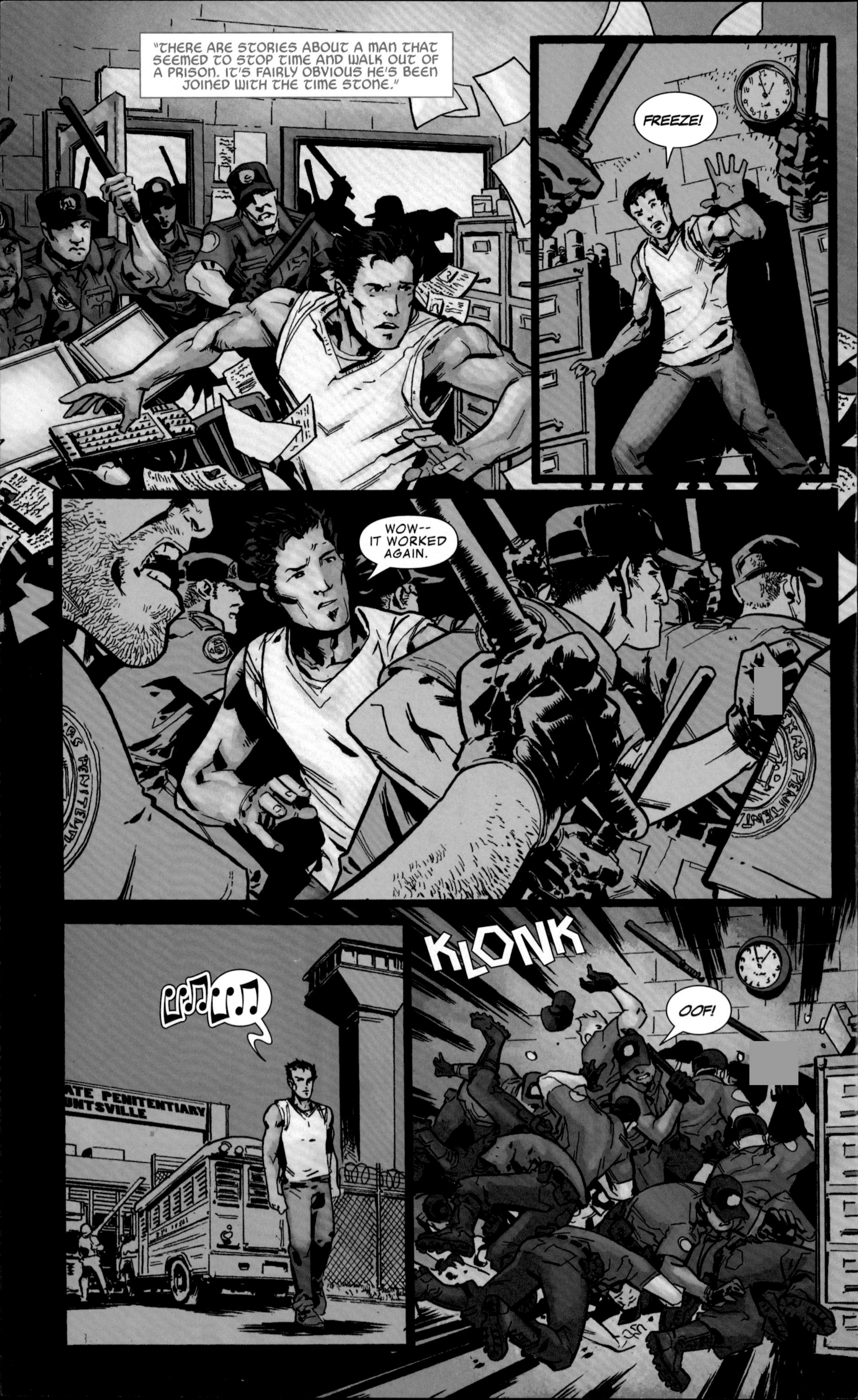
"THERE ARE STORIES ABOUT A MAN THAT SEEMED TO STOP TIME AND WALK OUT OF A PRISON. IT'S FAIRLY OBVIOUS HE'S BEEN JOINED WITH THE TIME STONE."
FREEZE!
WOW-- IT WORKED AGAIN.
ATE PENITENTIARY
UNTSVILLE
KLONK
OOF!

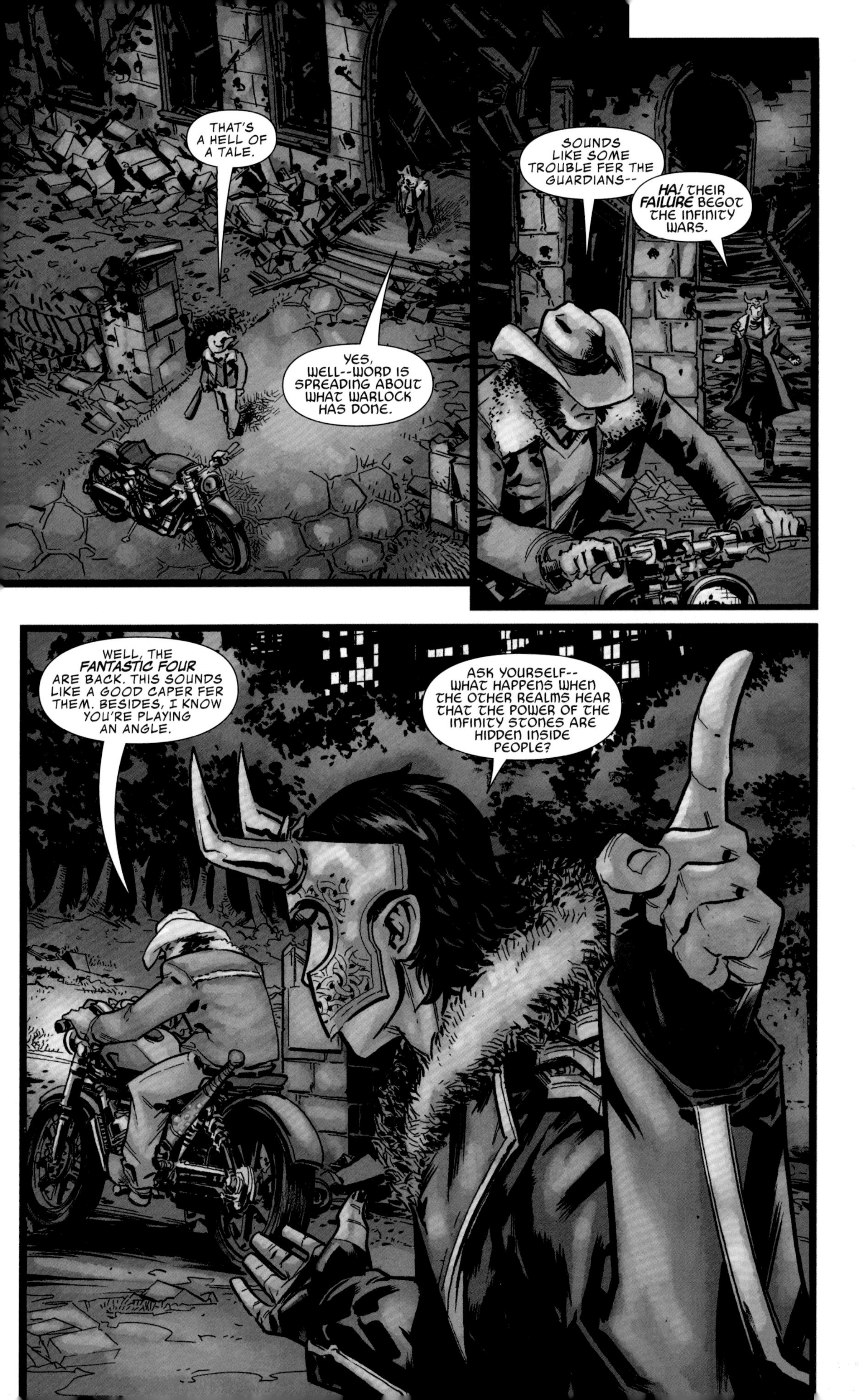
THAT'S A HELL OF A TALE.
YES, WELL--WORD IS SPREADING ABOUT WHAT WARLOCK HAS DONE.
SOUNDS LIKE SOME TROUBLE FER THE GUARDIANS--
HA! THEIR FAILURE BEGOT THE INFINITY WARS.
WELL, THE FANTASTIC FOUR ARE BACK. THIS SOUNDS LIKE A GOOD CAPER FER THEM. BESIDES, I KNOW YOU'RE PLAYING AN ANGLE.
ASK YOURSELF-- WHAT HAPPENS WHEN THE OTHER REALMS HEAR THAT THE POWER OF THE INFINITY STONES ARE HIDDEN INSIDE PEOPLE?

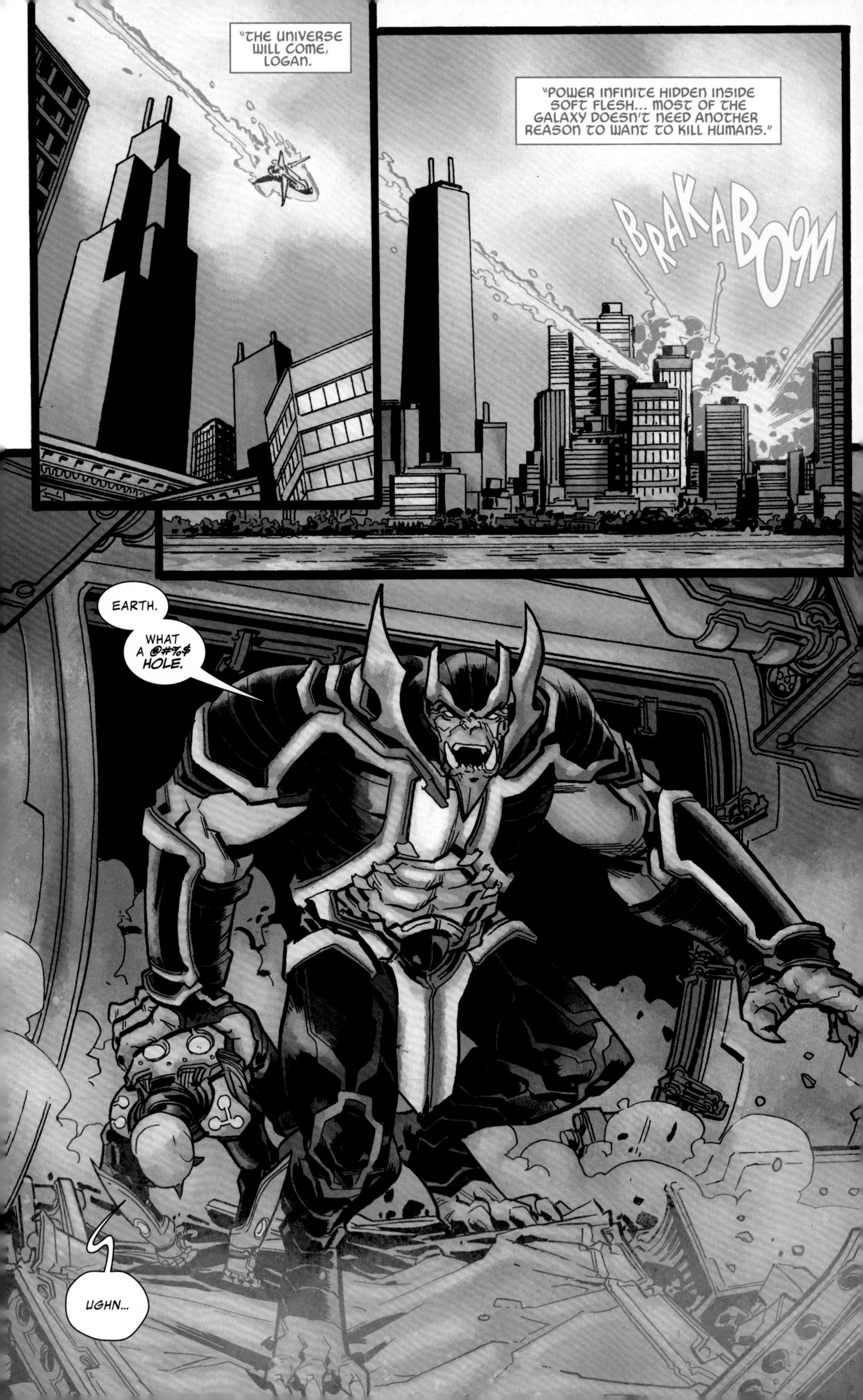
"THE UNIVERSE WILL COME, LOGAN.
"POWER INFINITE HIDDEN INSIDE SOFT FLESH... MOST OF THE GALAXY DOESN'T NEED ANOTHER REASON TO WANT TO KILL HUMANS."
BRAKABOOM
EARTH.
WHAT A @#%$ HOLE.
UGHN...

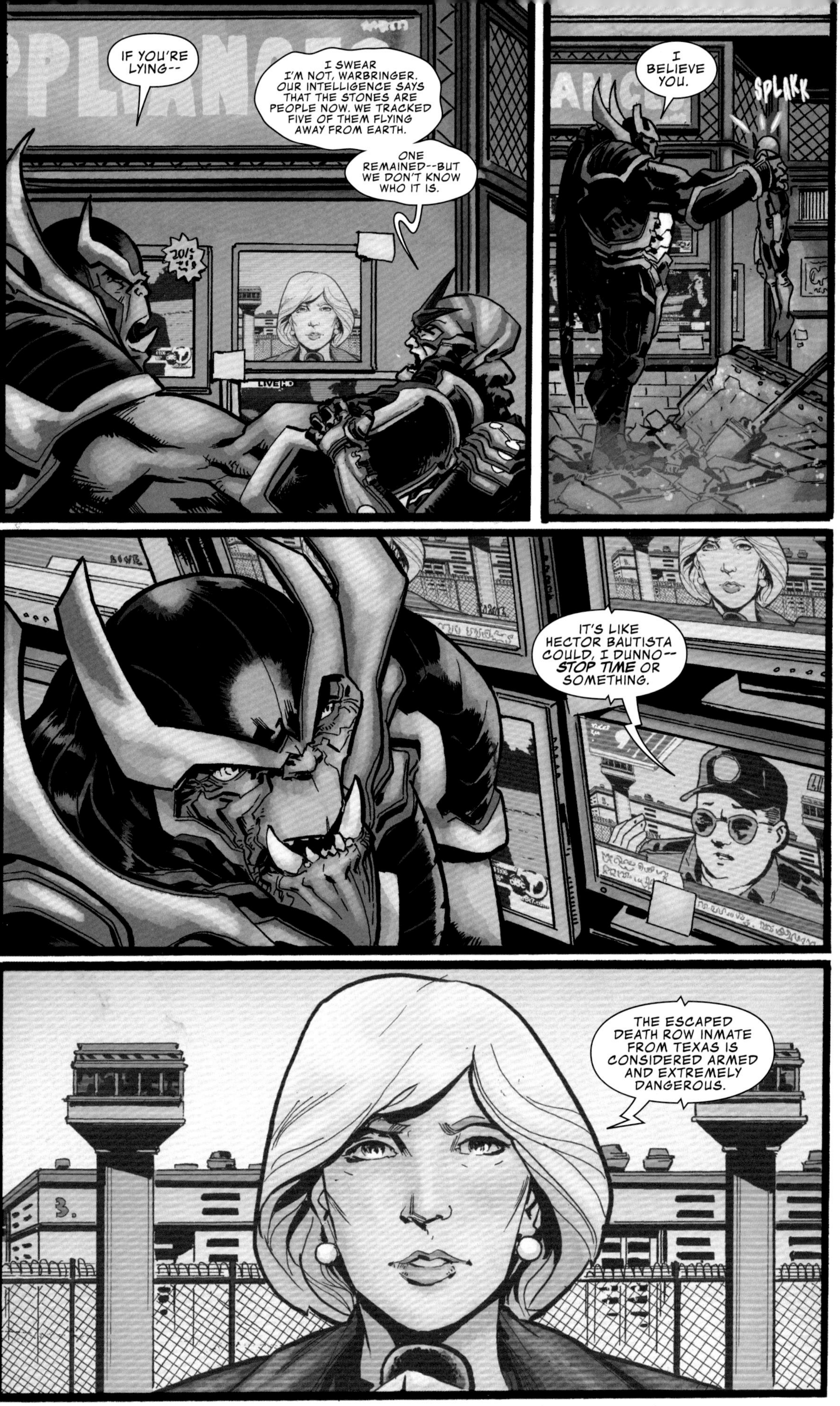
IF YOU'RE LYING--
I SWEAR I'M NOT, WARBRINGER. OUR INTELLIGENCE SAYS THAT THE STONES ARE PEOPLE NOW. WE TRACKED FIVE OF THEM FLYING AWAY FROM EARTH.
ONE REMAINED--BUT WE DON'T KNOW WHO IT IS.
I BELIEVE YOU.
SPLAKK
IT'S LIKE HECTOR BAUTISTA COULD, I DUNNO-- STOP TIME OR SOMETHING.
THE ESCAPED DEATH ROW INMATE FROM TEXAS IS CONSIDERED ARMED AND EXTREMELY DANGEROUS.

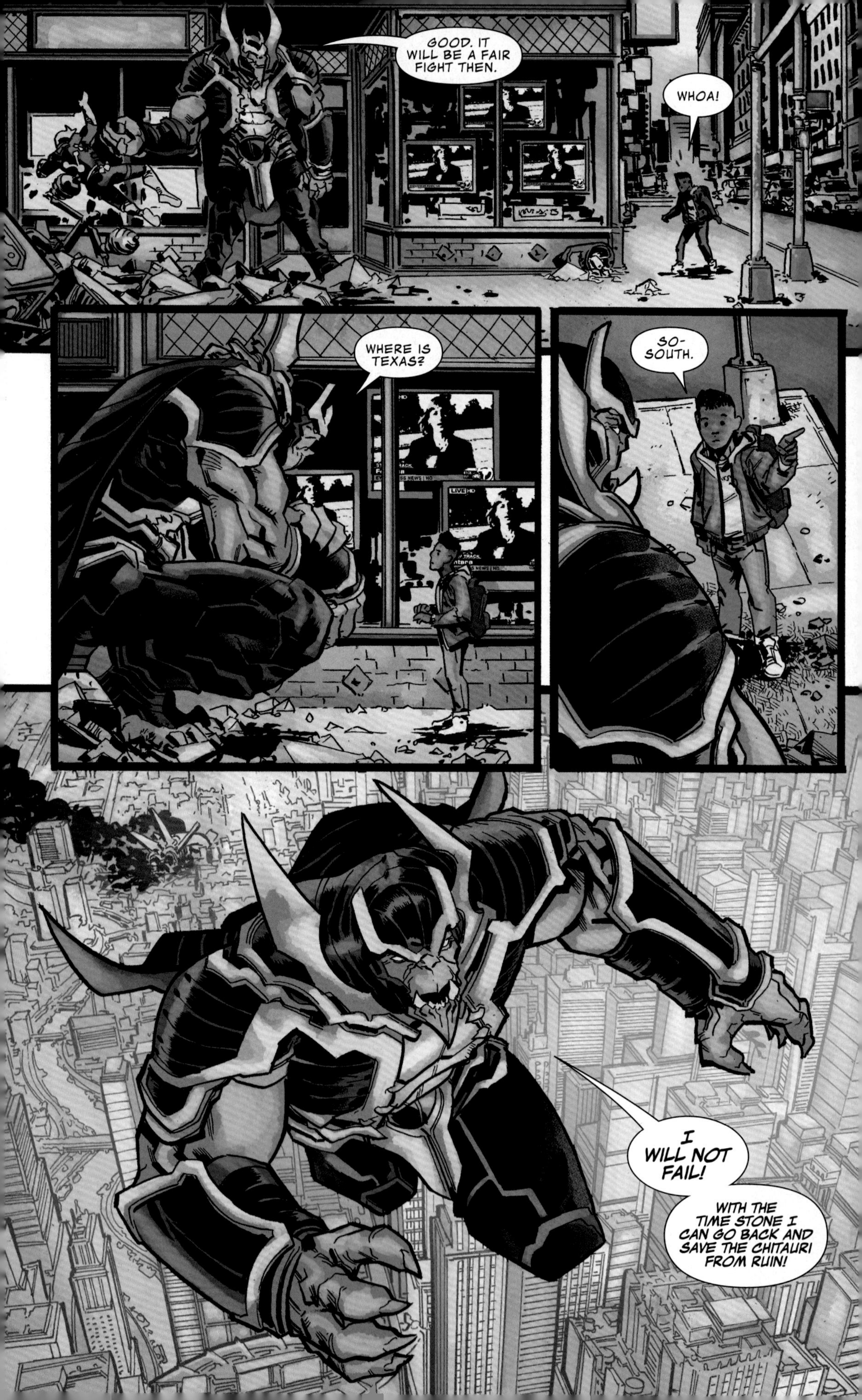
GOOD. IT WILL BE A FAIR FIGHT THEN.
WHOA!
WHERE IS TEXAS?
SO-SOUTH.
I WILL NOT FAIL!
WITH THE TIME STONE I CAN GO BACK AND SAVE THE CHITAURI FROM RUIN!

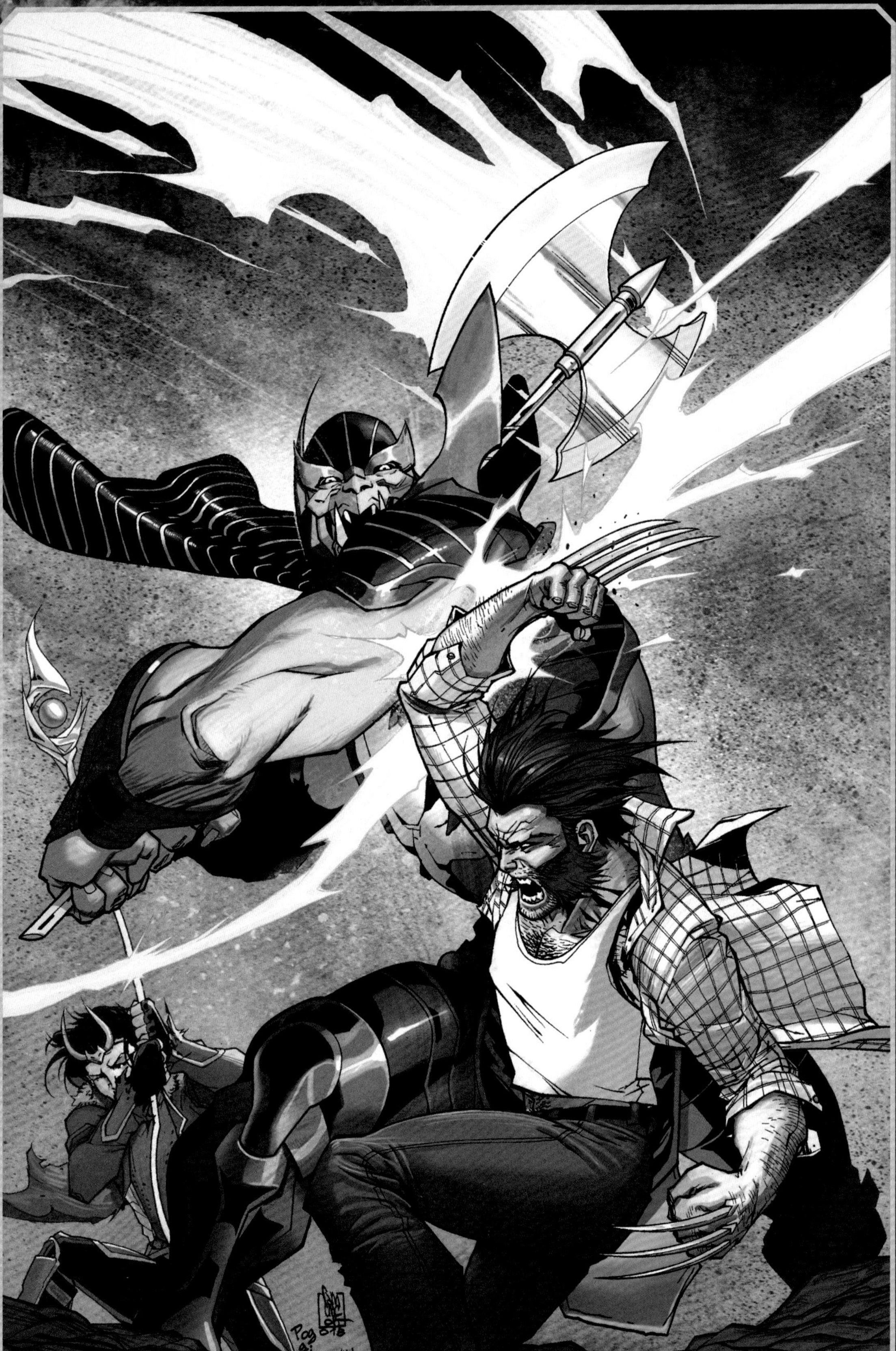

TWO

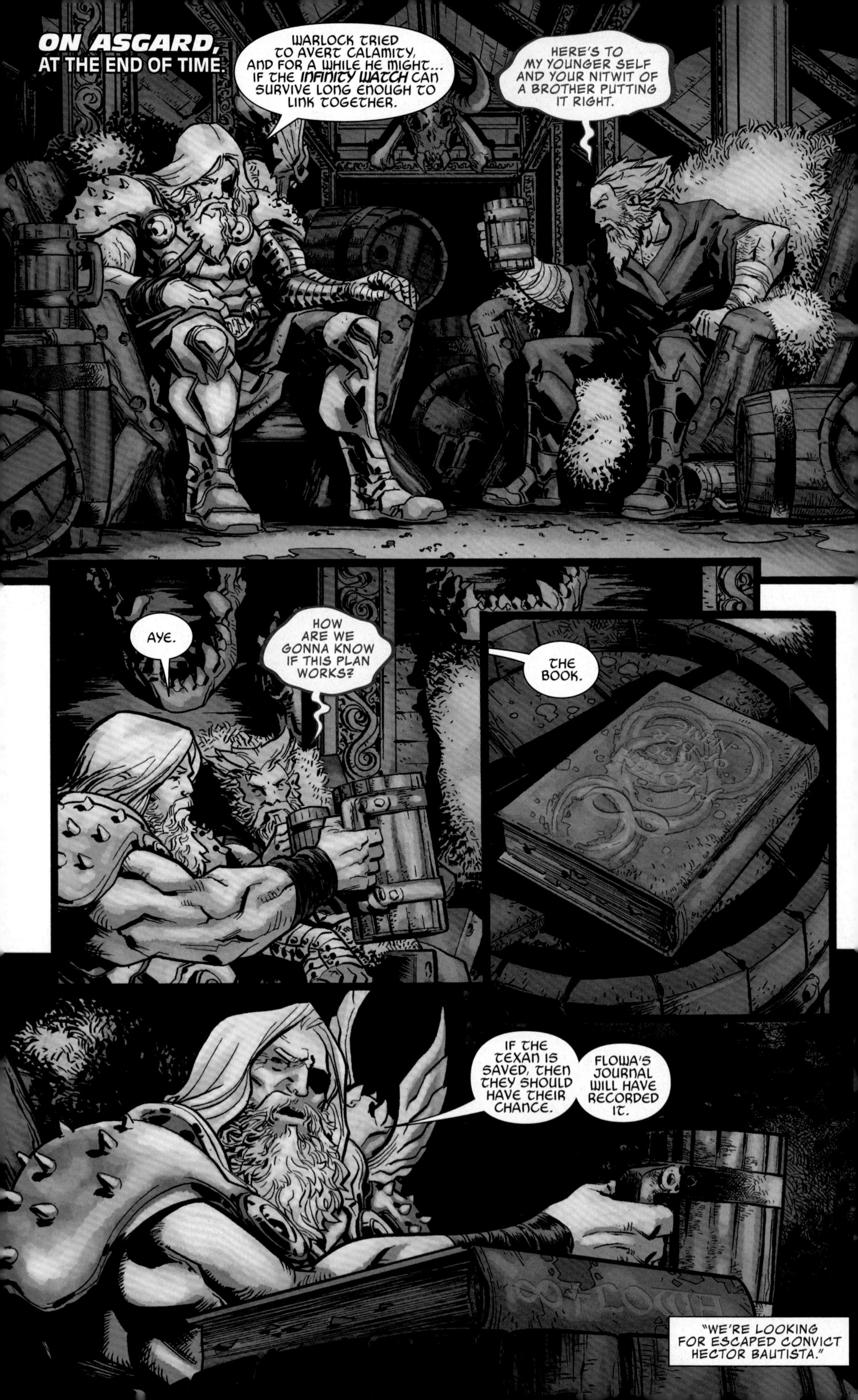
ON ASGARD, AT THE END OF TIME.
WARLOCK TRIED TO AVERT CALAMITY, AND FOR A WHILE HE MIGHT... IF THE INFINITY WATCH CAN SURVIVE LONG ENOUGH TO LINK TOGETHER.
HERE'S TO MY YOUNGER SELF AND YOUR NITWIT OF A BROTHER PUTTING IT RIGHT.
AYE.
HOW ARE WE GONNA KNOW IF THIS PLAN WORKS?
THE BOOK.
IF THE TEXAN IS SAVED, THEN THEY SHOULD HAVE THEIR CHANCE.
FLOWA'S JOURNAL WILL HAVE RECORDED IT.
"WE'RE LOOKING FOR ESCAPED CONVICT HECTOR BAUTISTA."

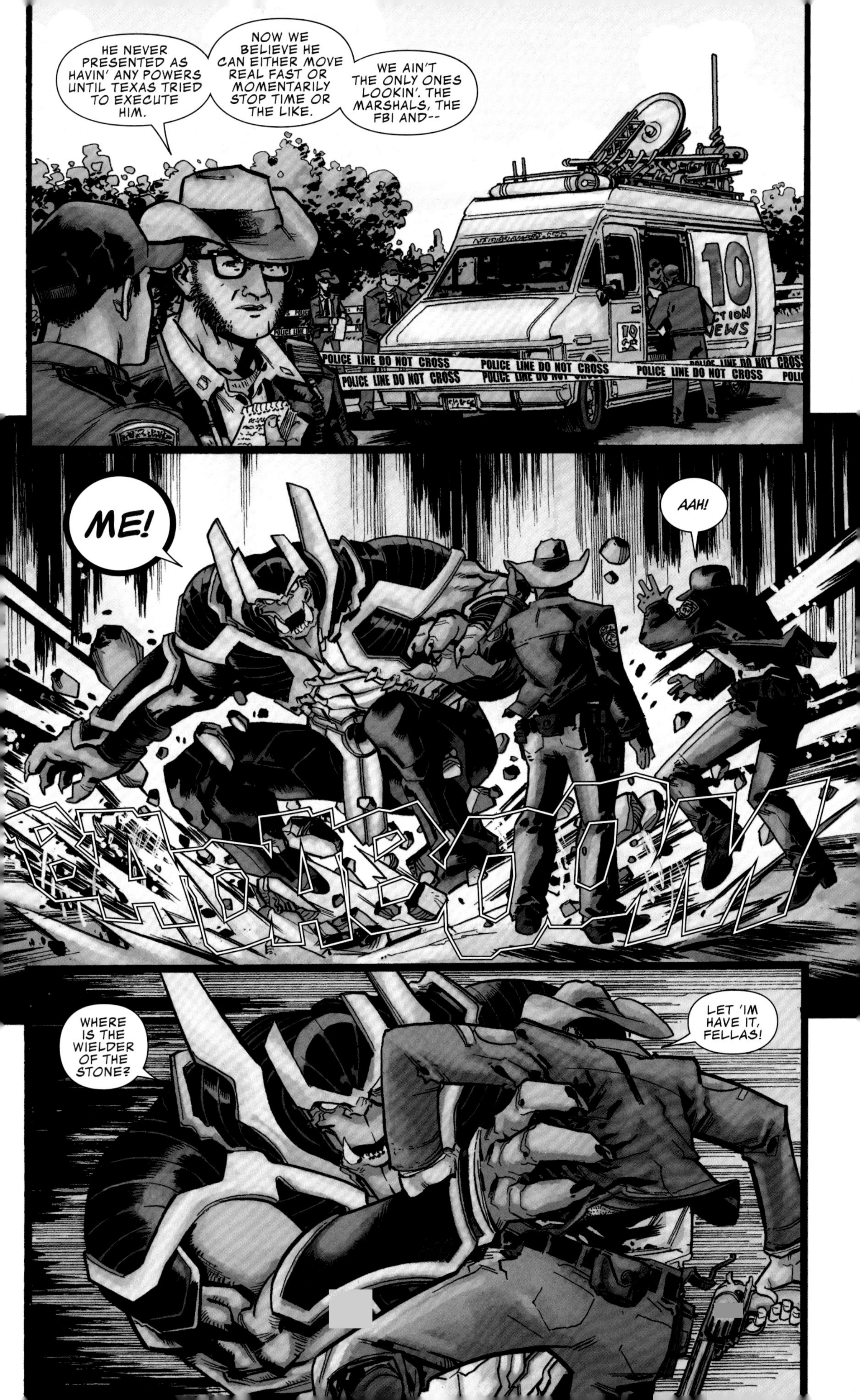
HE NEVER PRESENTED AS HAVIN' ANY POWERS UNTIL TEXAS TRIED TO EXECUTE HIM.
NOW WE BELIEVE HE CAN EITHER MOVE REAL FAST OR MOMENTARILY STOP TIME OR THE LIKE.
WE AIN'T THE ONLY ONES LOOKIN'. THE MARSHALS, THE FBI AND--
10 ACTION NEWS
POLICE LINE DO NOT CROSS
ME!
AAH!
WHERE IS THE WIELDER OF THE STONE?
LET 'IM HAVE IT, FELLAS!

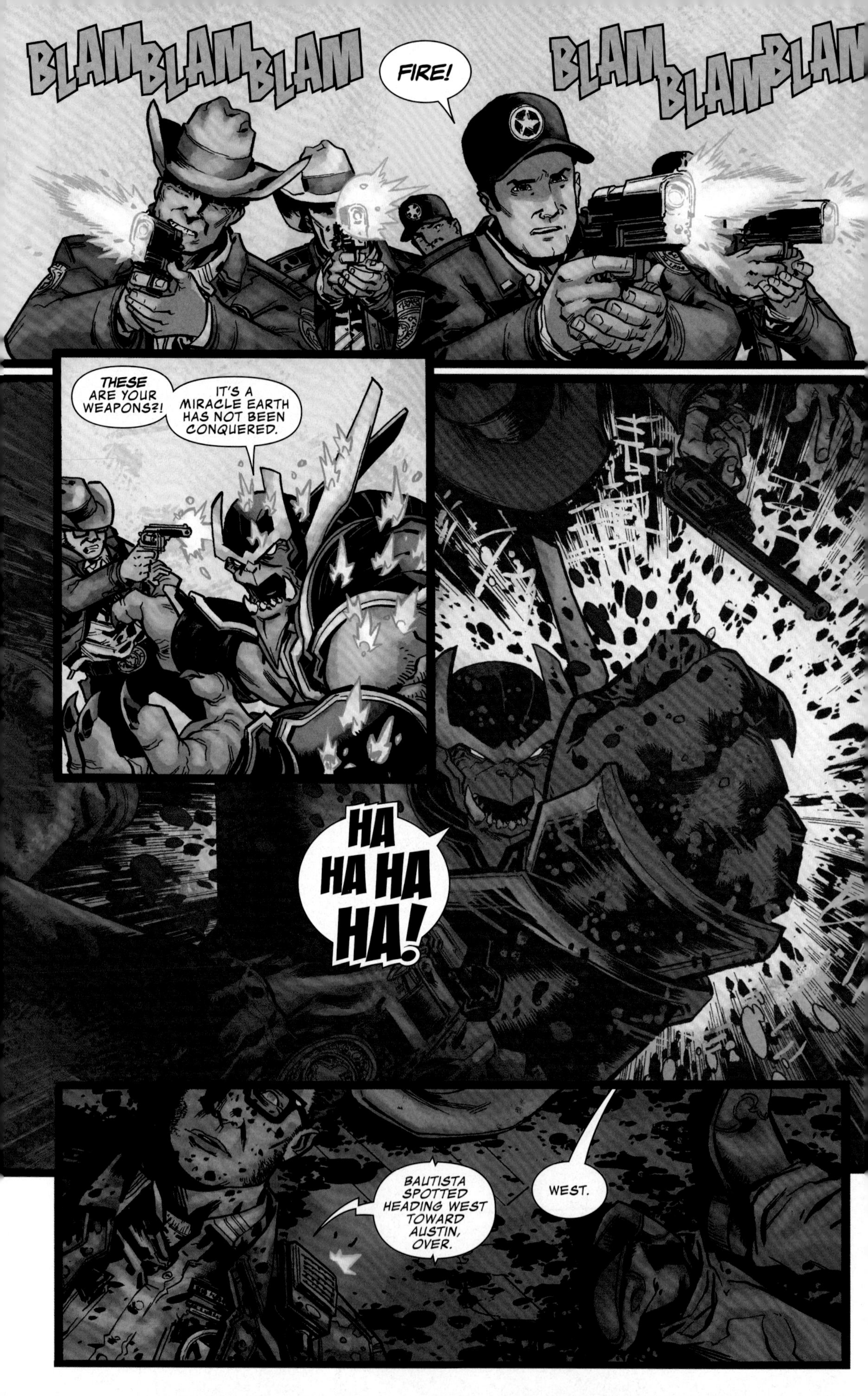
BLAM BLAM BLAM
FIRE!
BLAM BLAM BLAM
THESE ARE YOUR WEAPONS?!
IT'S A MIRACLE EARTH HAS NOT BEEN CONQUERED.
HA HA HA HA!
BAUTISTA SPOTTED HEADING WEST TOWARD AUSTIN, OVER.
WEST.

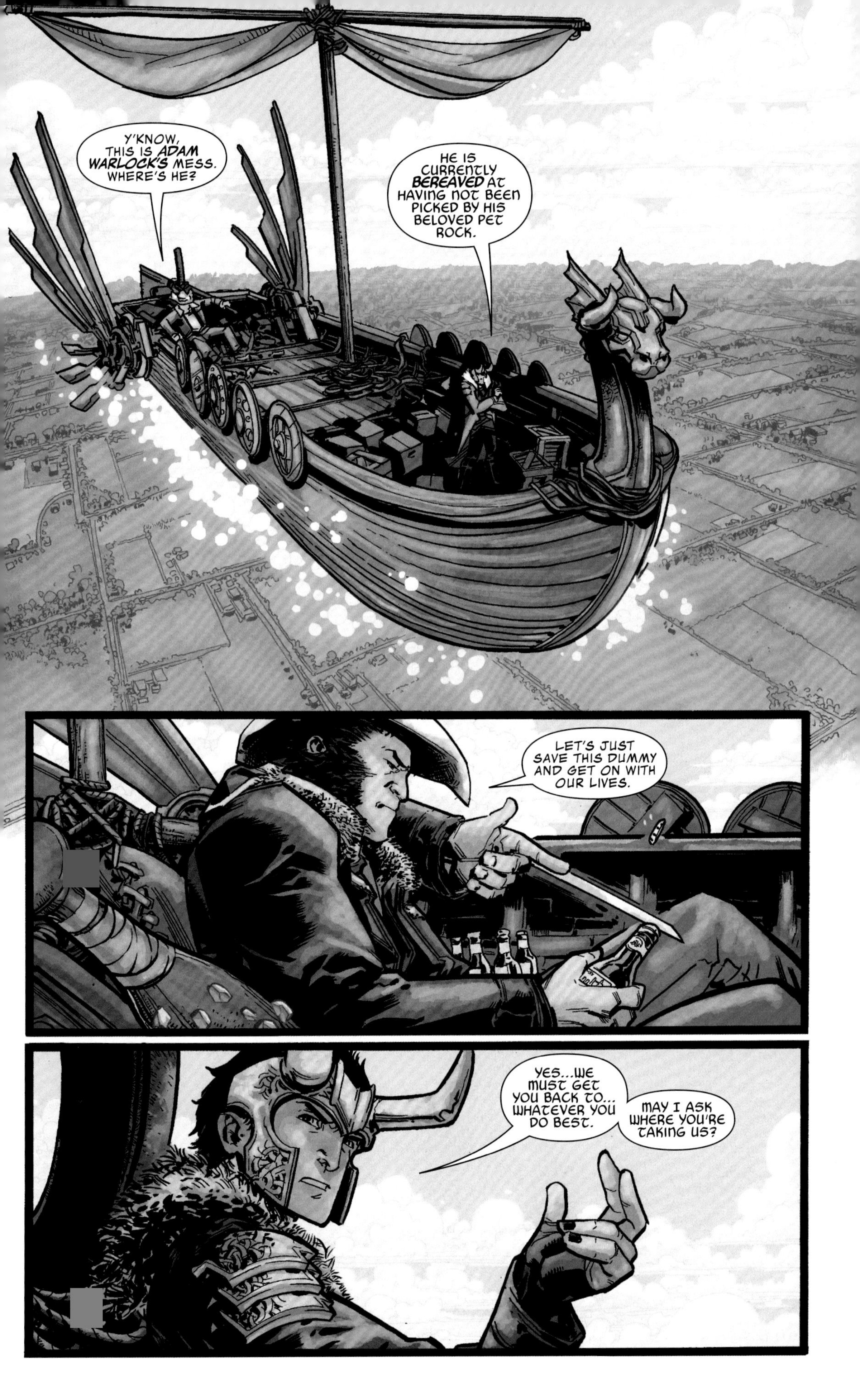
Y'KNOW, THIS IS ADAM WARLOCK'S MESS. WHERE'S HE?
HE IS CURRENTLY BEREAVED AT HAVING NOT BEEN PICKED BY HIS BELOVED PET ROCK.
LET'S JUST SAVE THIS DUMMY AND GET ON WITH OUR LIVES.
YES...WE MUST GET YOU BACK TO... WHATEVER YOU DO BEST.
MAY I ASK WHERE YOU'RE TAKING US?

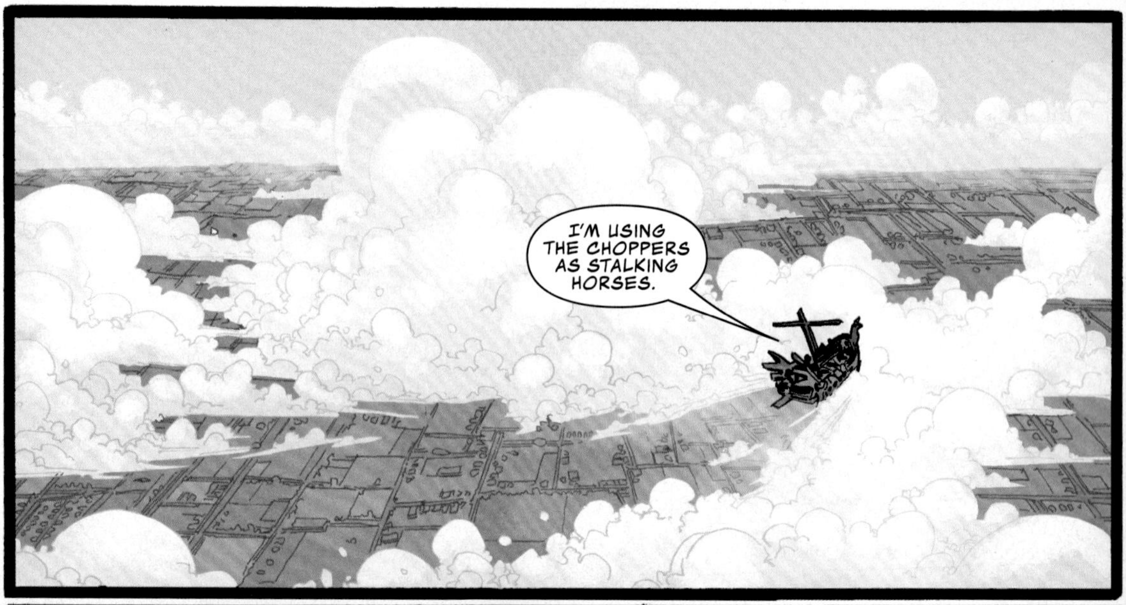
I'M USING THE CHOPPERS AS STALKING HORSES.

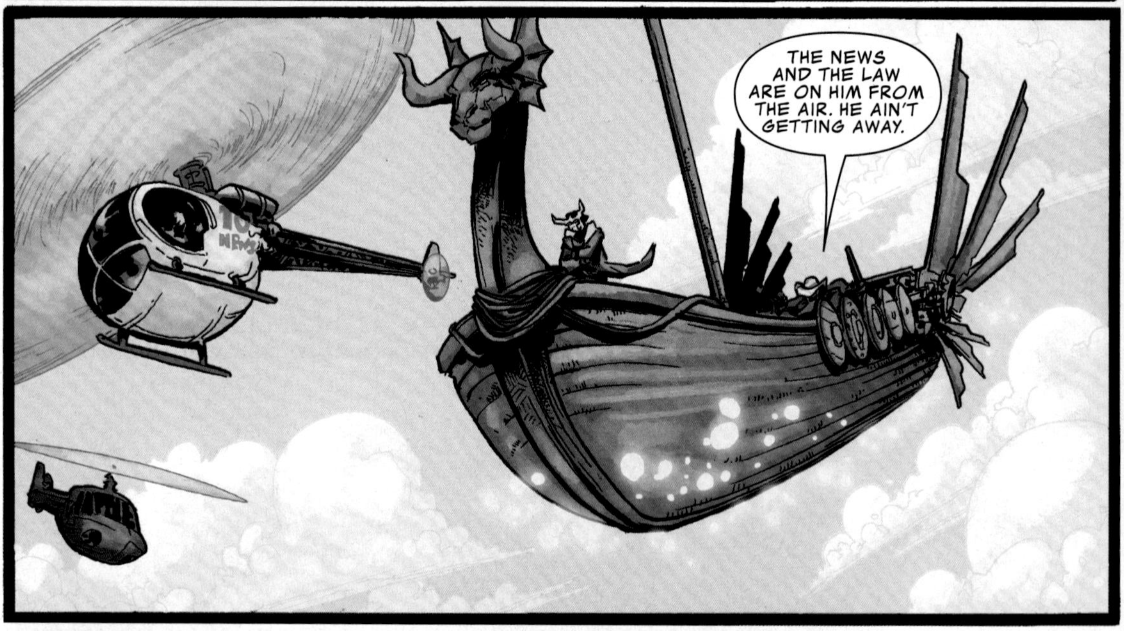
THE NEWS AND THE LAW ARE ON HIM FROM THE AIR. HE AIN'T GETTING AWAY.

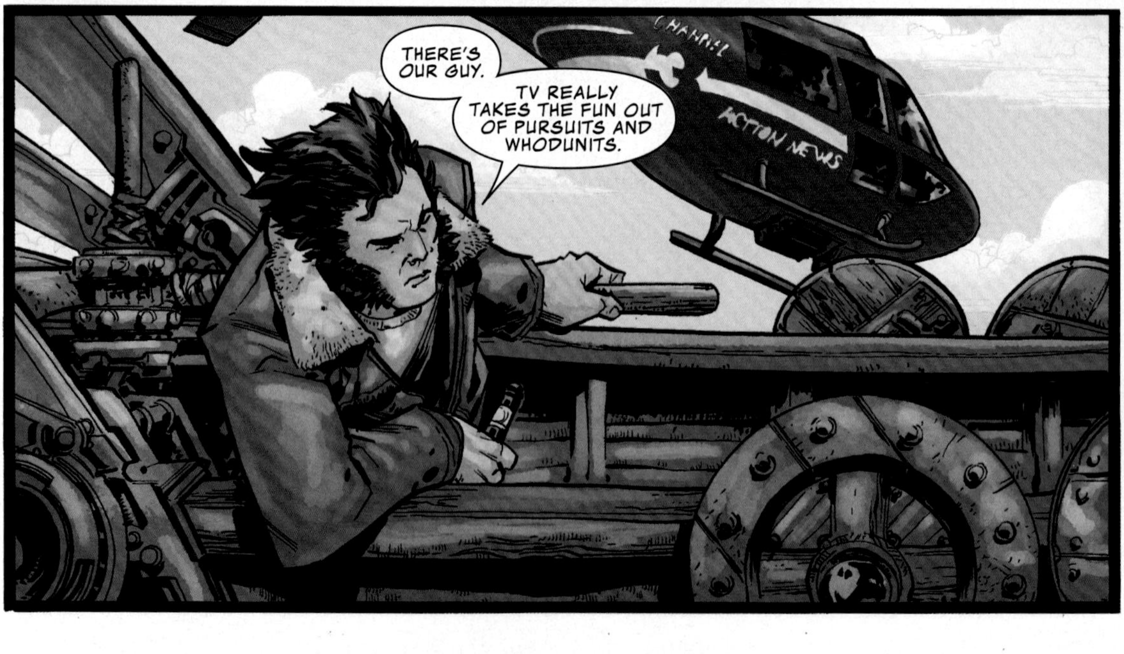
THERE'S OUR GUY.
TV REALLY TAKES THE FUN OUT OF PURSUITS AND WHODUNITS.
ACTION NEWS

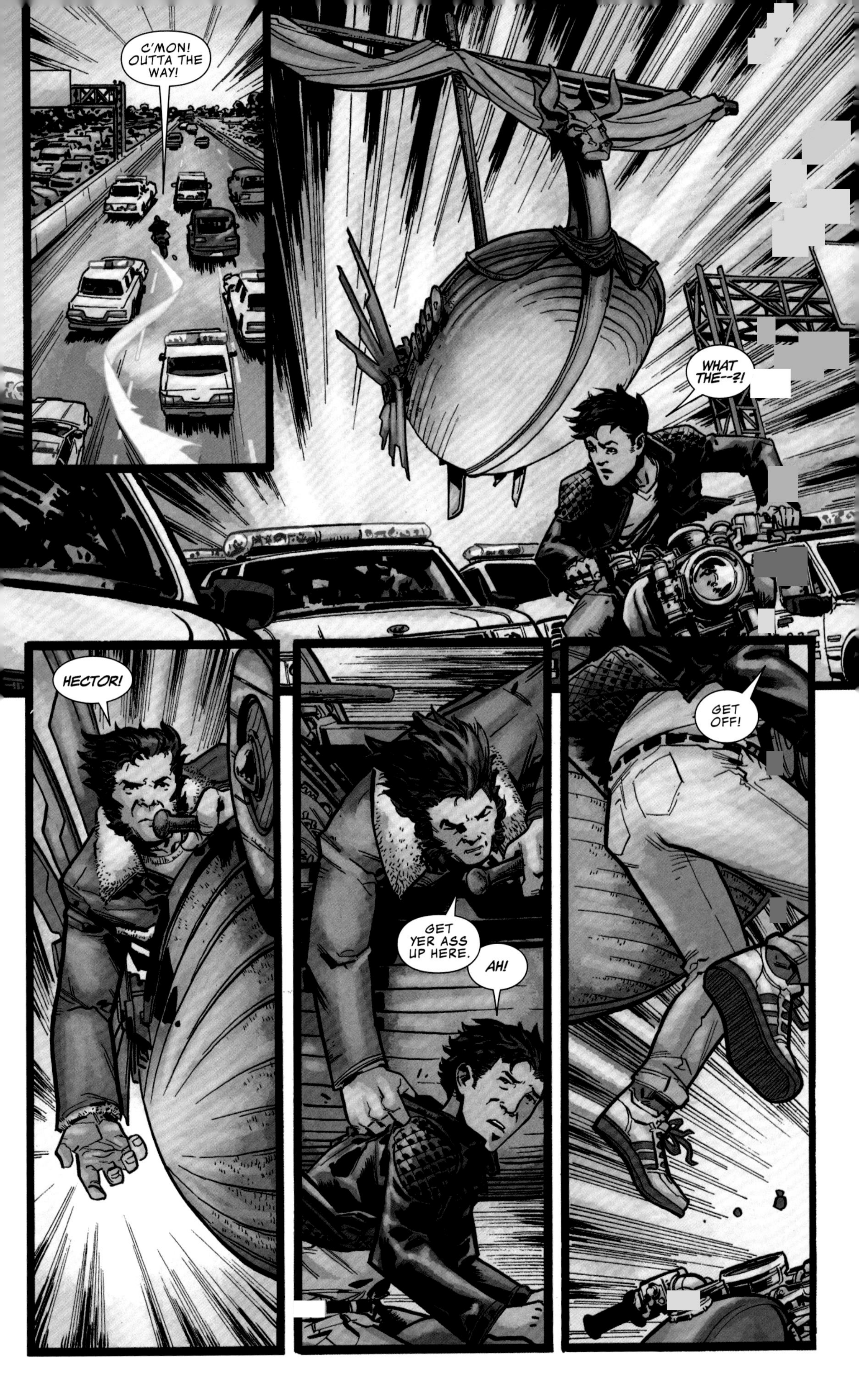
C'MON! OUTTA THE WAY!
WHAT THE--?!
HECTOR!
GET YER ASS UP HERE.
AH!
GET OFF!

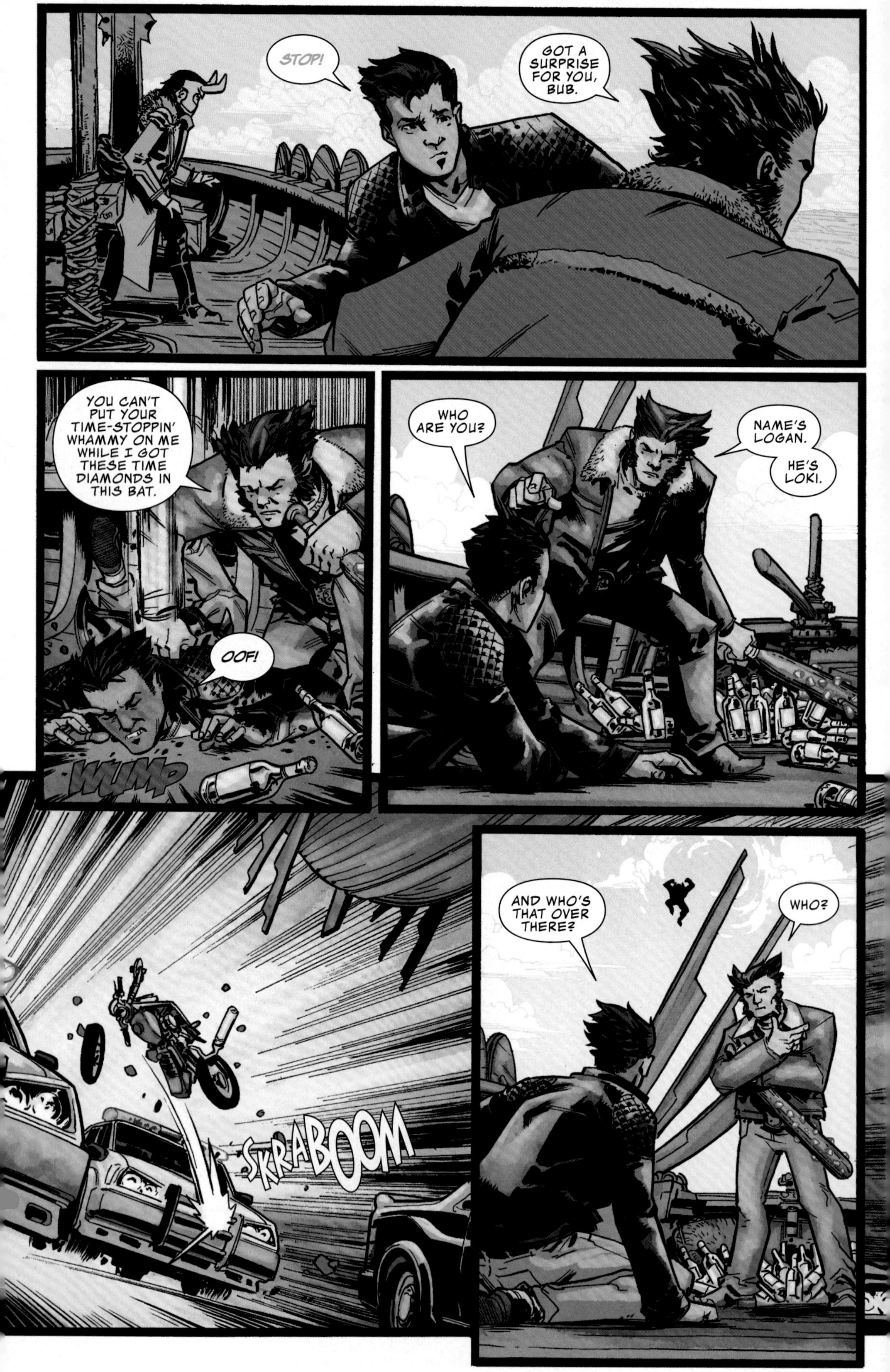
STOP!
GOT A SURPRISE FOR YOU, BUB.
YOU CAN'T PUT YOUR TIME-STOPPIN' WHAMMY ON ME WHILE I GOT THESE TIME DIAMONDS IN THIS BAT.
OOF!
WUMP
WHO ARE YOU?
NAME'S LOGAN.
HE'S LOKI.
SKRABOOM
AND WHO'S THAT OVER THERE?
WHO?

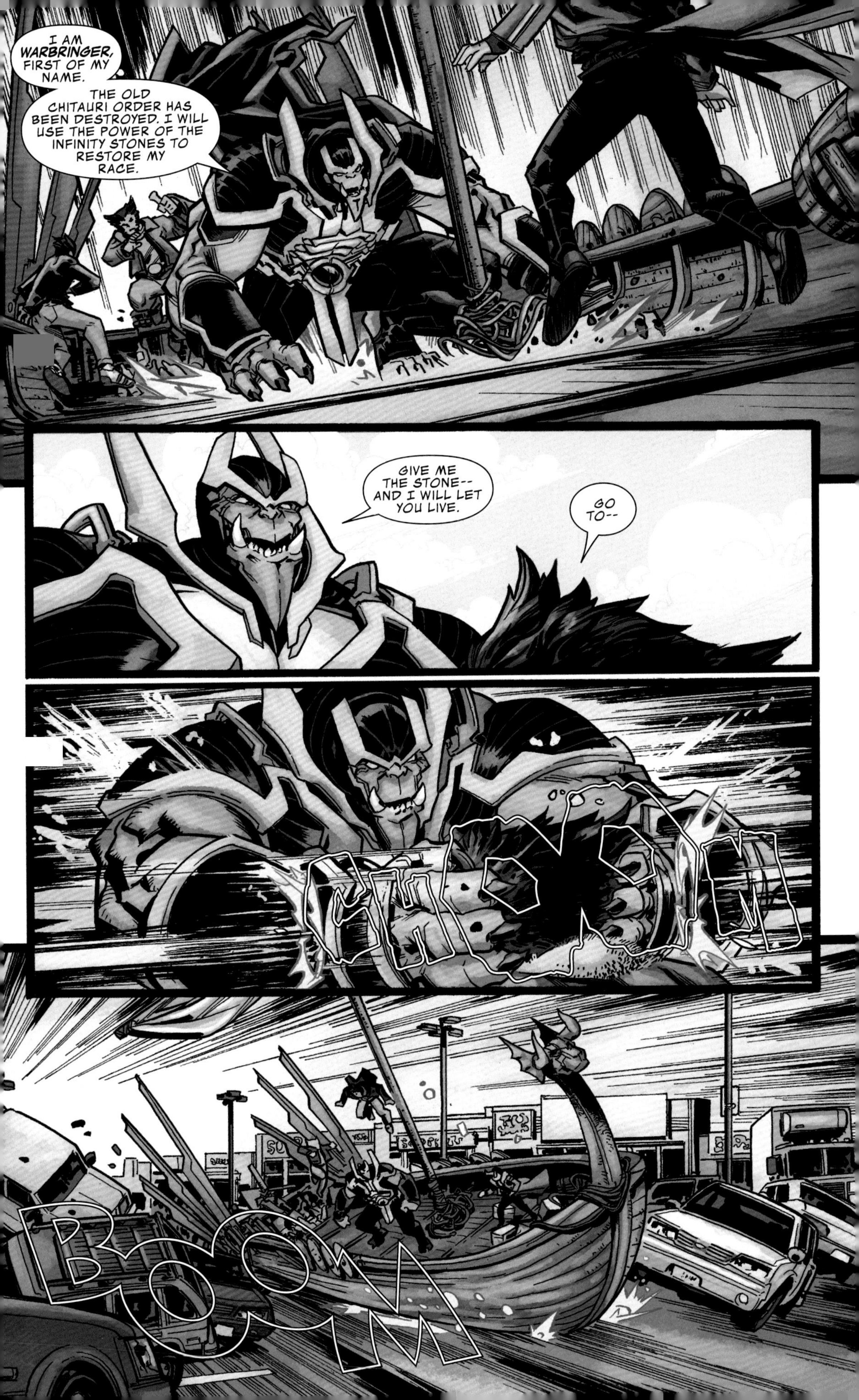
I AM WARBRINGER, FIRST OF MY NAME.
THE OLD CHITAURI ORDER HAS BEEN DESTROYED. I WILL USE THE POWER OF THE INFINITY STONES TO RESTORE MY RACE.
GIVE ME THE STONE-- AND I WILL LET YOU LIVE.
GO TO--
BOOM

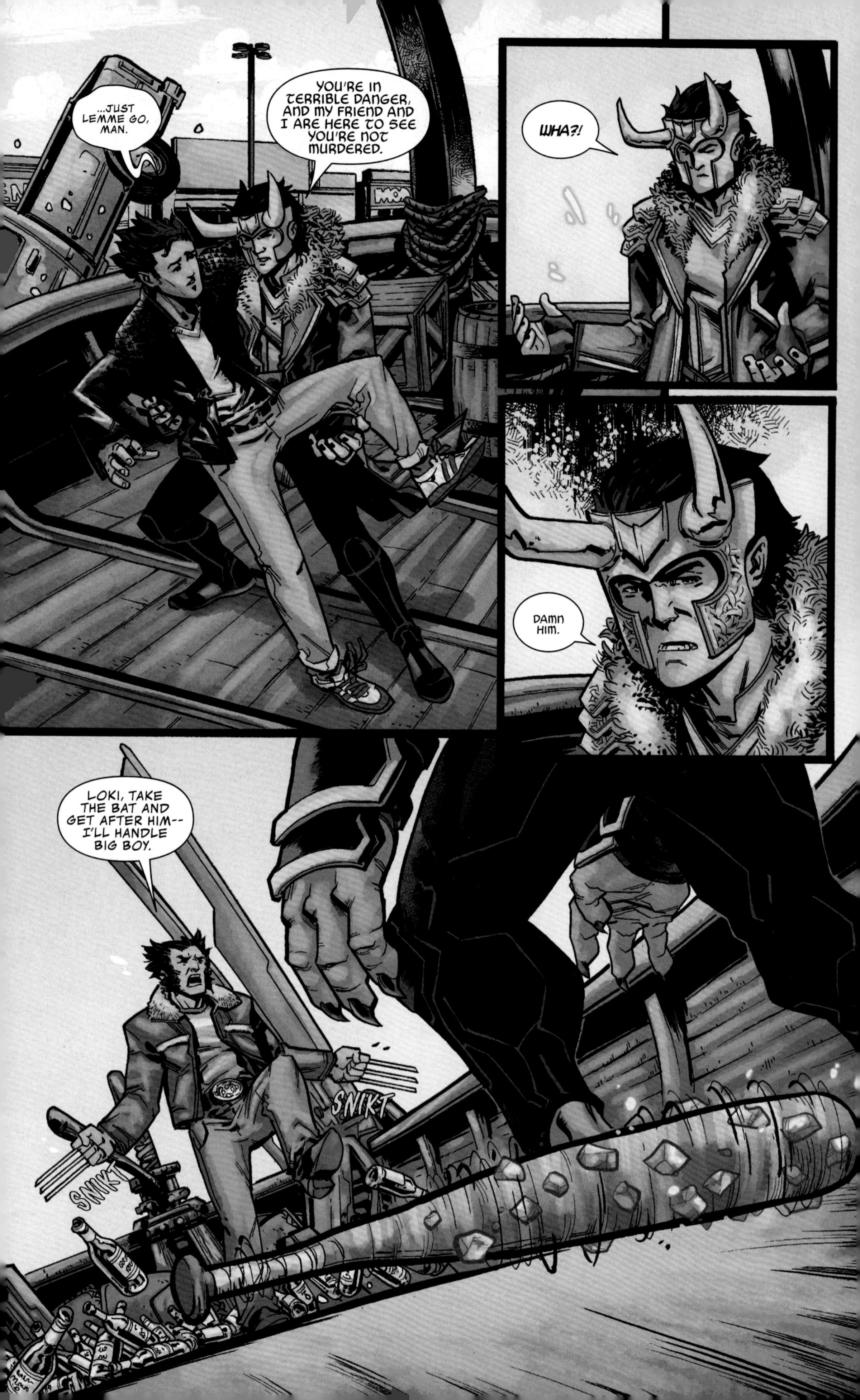
...JUST LEMME GO, MAN.
YOU'RE IN TERRIBLE DANGER, AND MY FRIEND AND I ARE HERE TO SEE YOU'RE NOT MURDERED.
WHA?!
DAMN HIM.
LOKI, TAKE THE BAT AND GET AFTER HIM-- I'LL HANDLE BIG BOY.
SNIKT
SNIKT

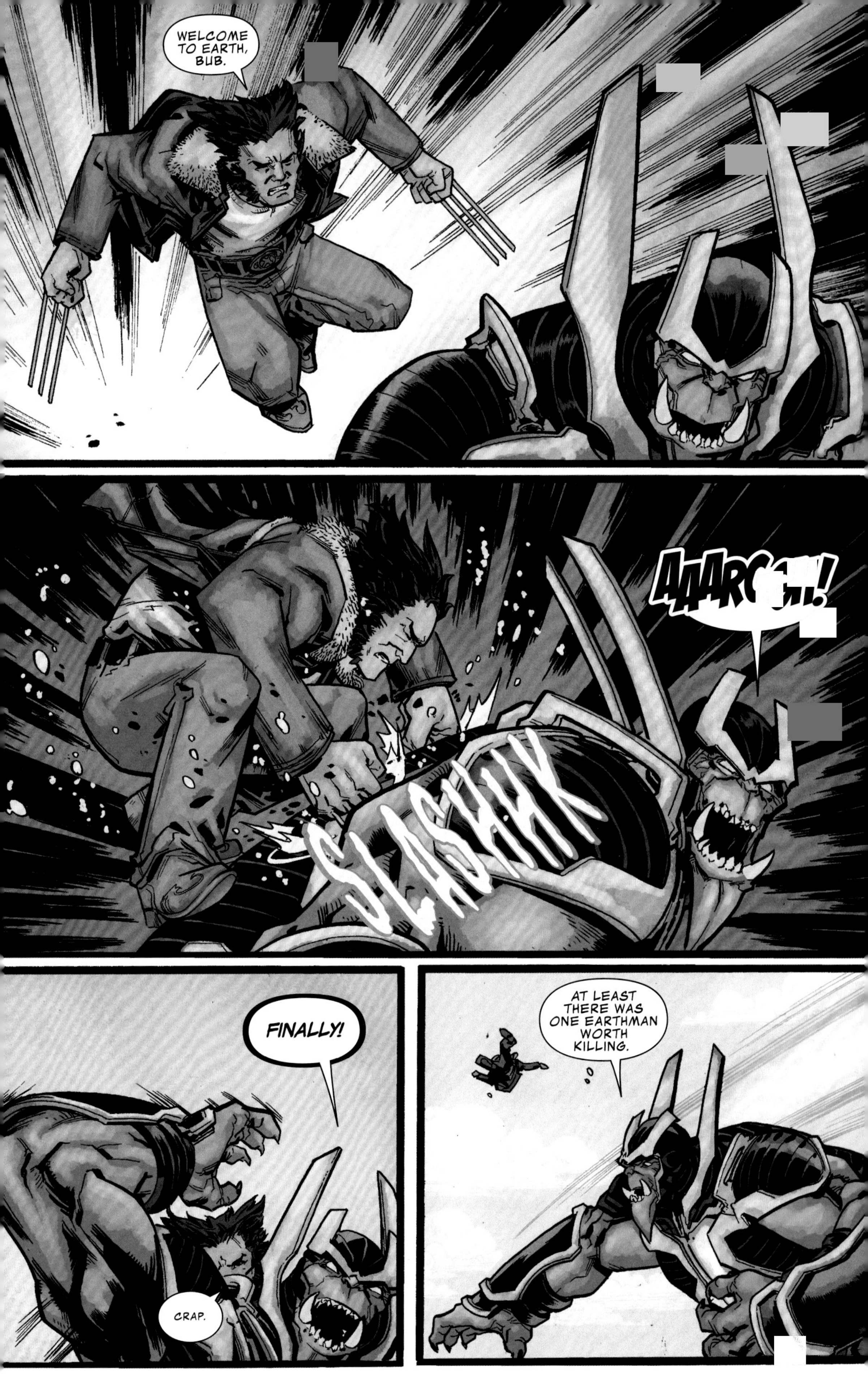

WELCOME TO EARTH, BUB.
SLASHHK
FINALLY!
CRAP.
AT LEAST THERE WAS ONE EARTHMAN WORTH KILLING.

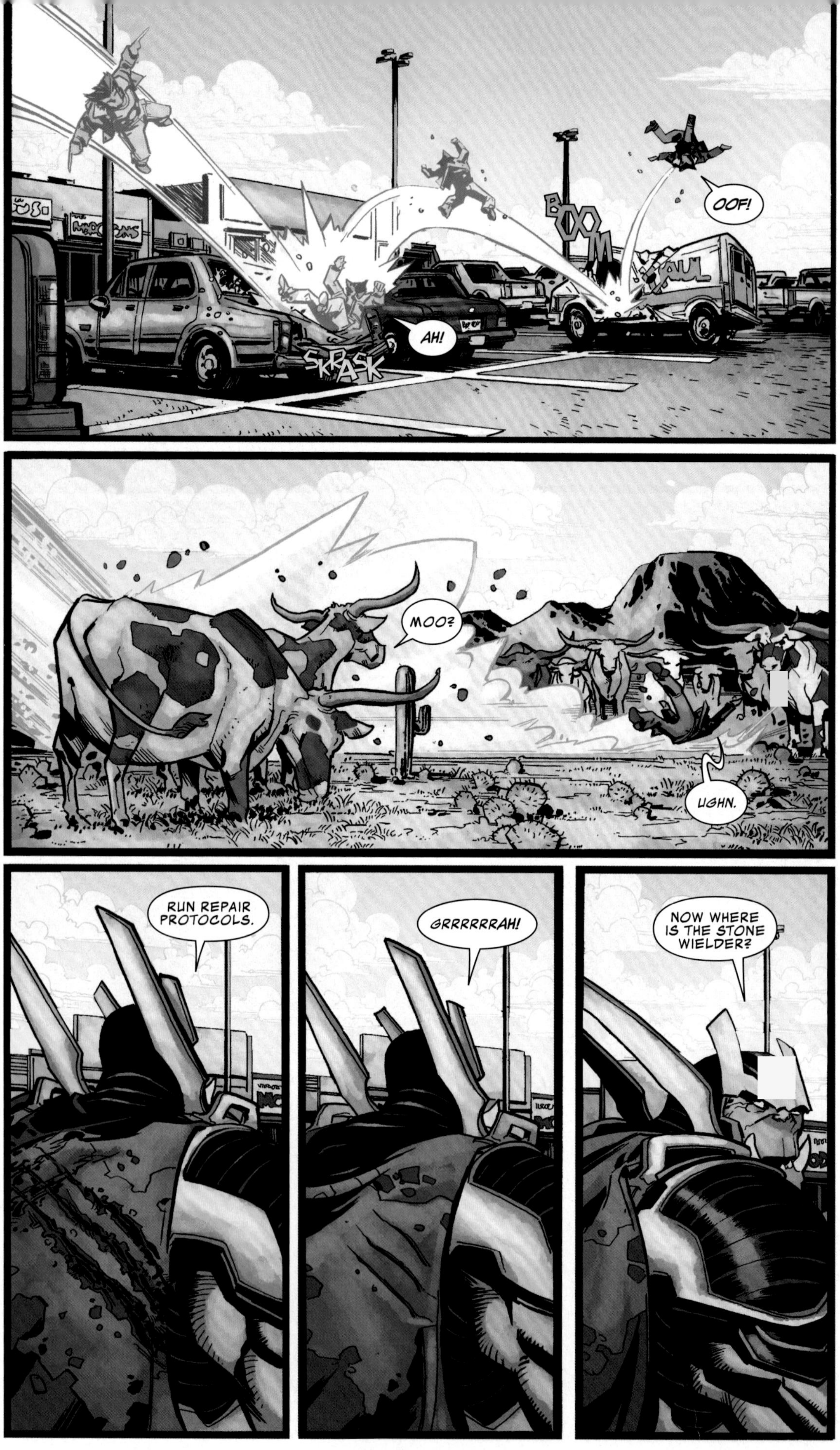
BOOM
OOF!
SKRASK
AH!
MOO?
UGHN.
RUN REPAIR PROTOCOLS.
GRRRRRRAH!
NOW WHERE IS THE STONE WIELDER?

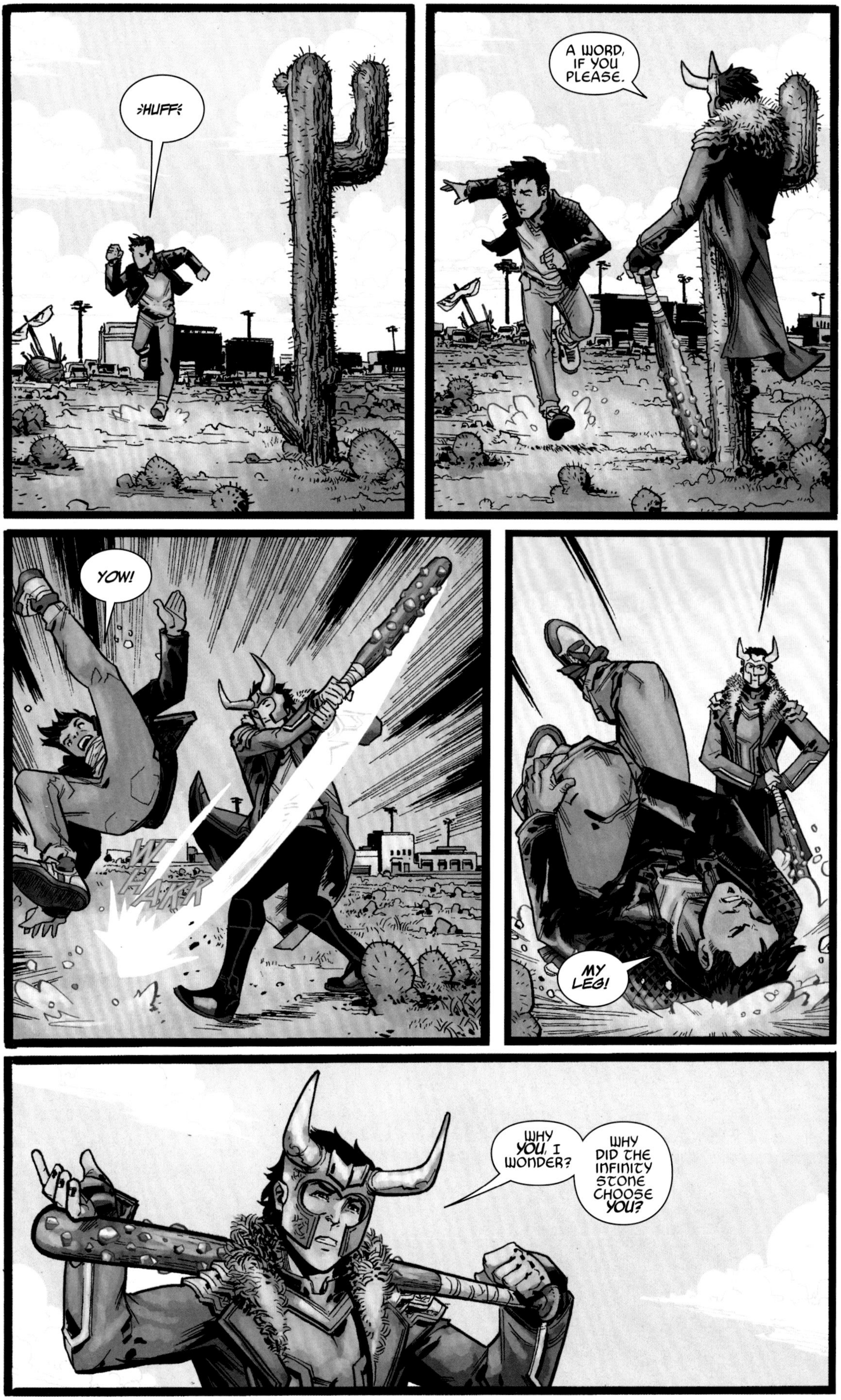

HUFF
A WORD, IF YOU PLEASE.
YOW!
WHAKK
MY LEG!
WHY YOU, I WONDER?
WHY DID THE INFINITY STONE CHOOSE YOU?

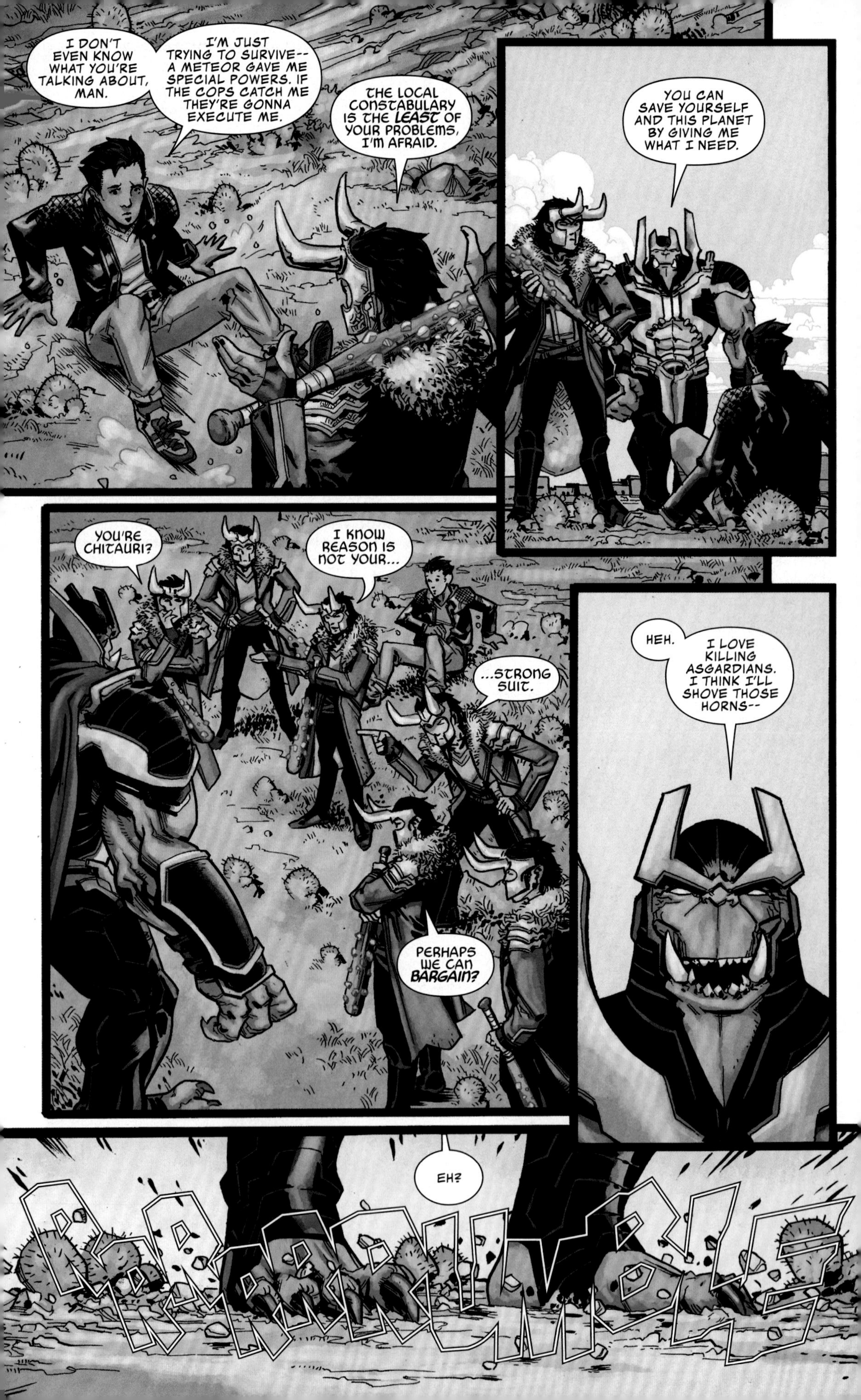
I DON'T EVEN KNOW WHAT YOU'RE TALKING ABOUT, MAN.
I'M JUST TRYING TO SURVIVE-- A METEOR GAVE ME SPECIAL POWERS. IF THE COPS CATCH ME THEY'RE GONNA EXECUTE ME.
THE LOCAL CONSTABULARY IS THE LEAST OF YOUR PROBLEMS, I'M AFRAID.
YOU CAN SAVE YOURSELF AND THIS PLANET BY GIVING ME WHAT I NEED.
YOU'RE CHITAURI?
I KNOW REASON IS NOT YOUR...
...STRONG SUIT.
PERHAPS WE CAN BARGAIN?
HEH.
I LOVE KILLING ASGARDIANS. I THINK I'LL SHOVE THOSE HORNS--
EH?

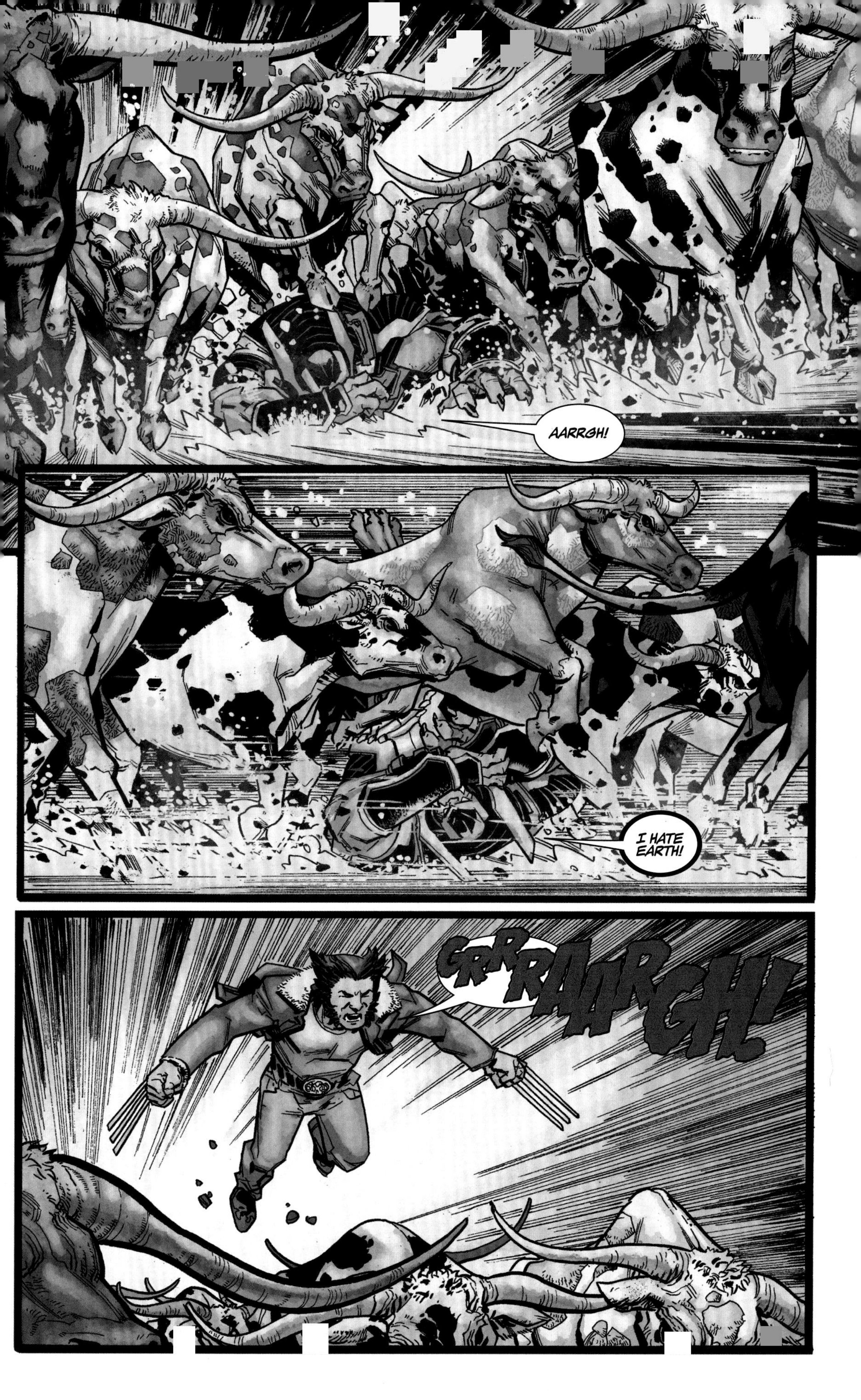
AARRGH!
I HATE EARTH!
GRRRAARGH!

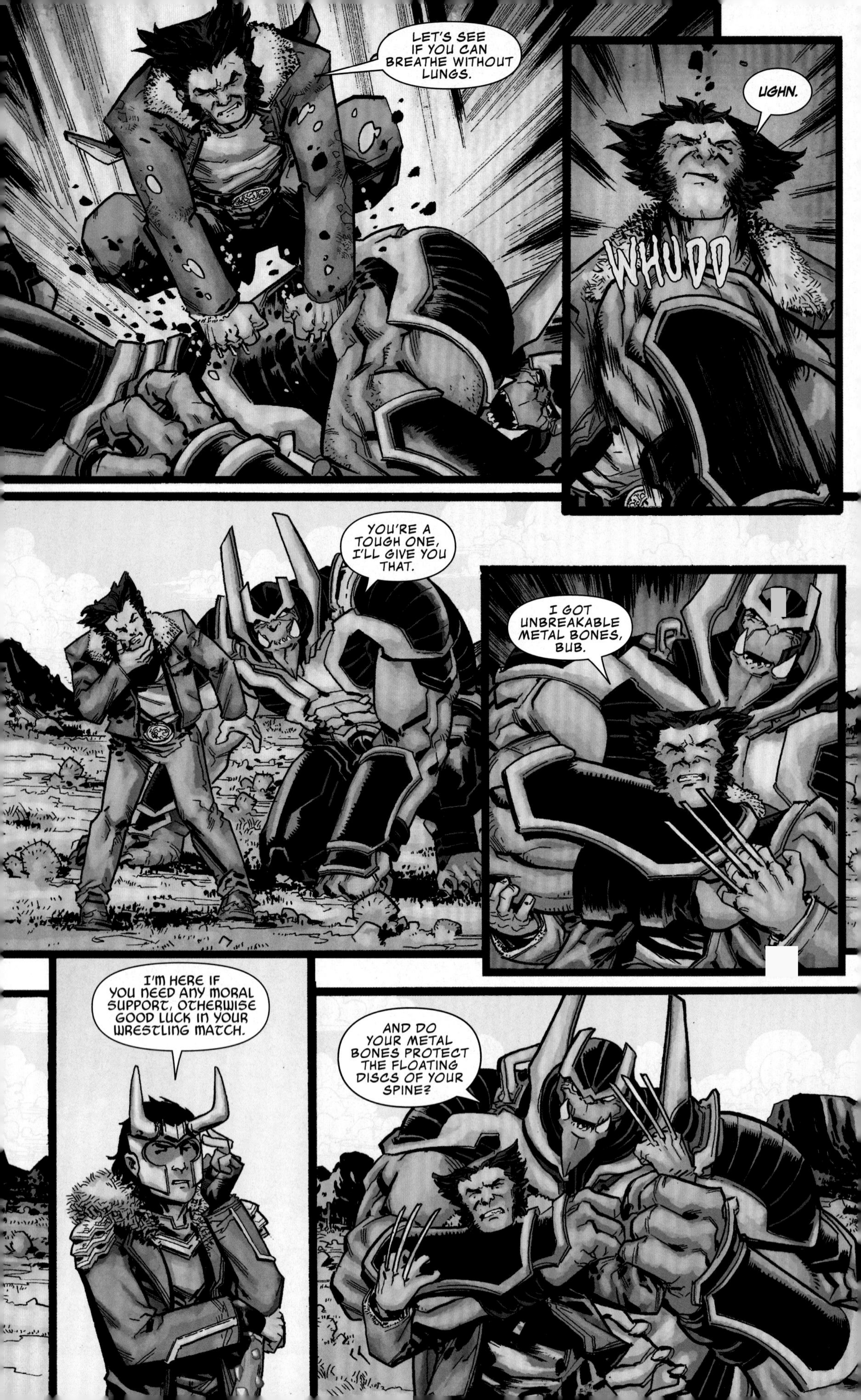
LET'S SEE IF YOU CAN BREATHE WITHOUT LUNGS.
UGHN.
WHUDD
YOU'RE A TOUGH ONE, I'LL GIVE YOU THAT.
I GOT UNBREAKABLE METAL BONES, BUB.
I'M HERE IF YOU NEED ANY MORAL SUPPORT, OTHERWISE GOOD LUCK IN YOUR WRESTLING MATCH.
AND DO YOUR METAL BONES PROTECT THE FLOATING DISCS OF YOUR SPINE?

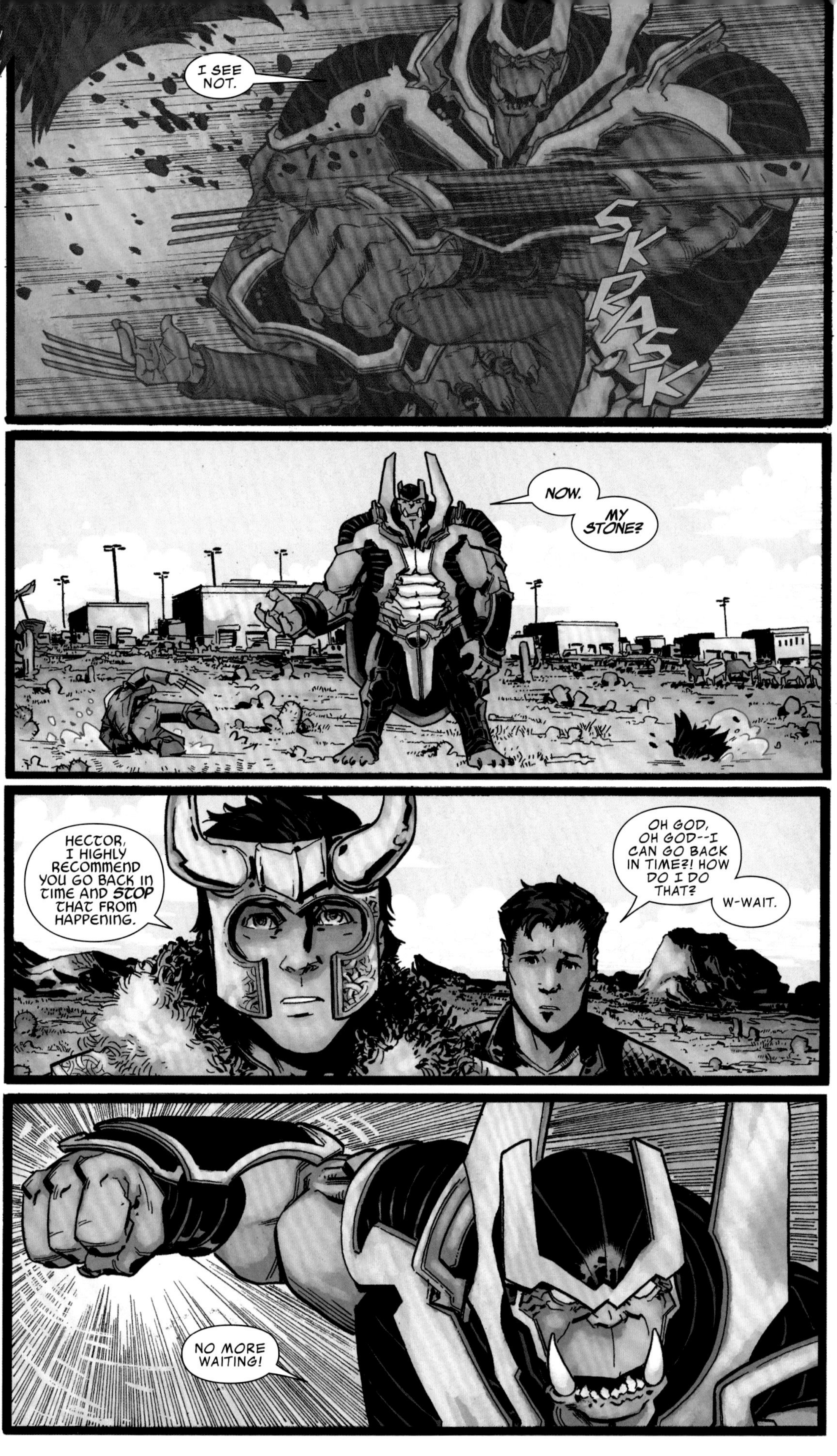
I SEE NOT.
SKRASK
NOW.
MY STONE?
HECTOR, I HIGHLY RECOMMEND YOU GO BACK IN TIME AND STOP THAT FROM HAPPENING.
OH GOD, OH GOD--I CAN GO BACK IN TIME?! HOW DO I DO THAT?
W-WAIT.
NO MORE WAITING!

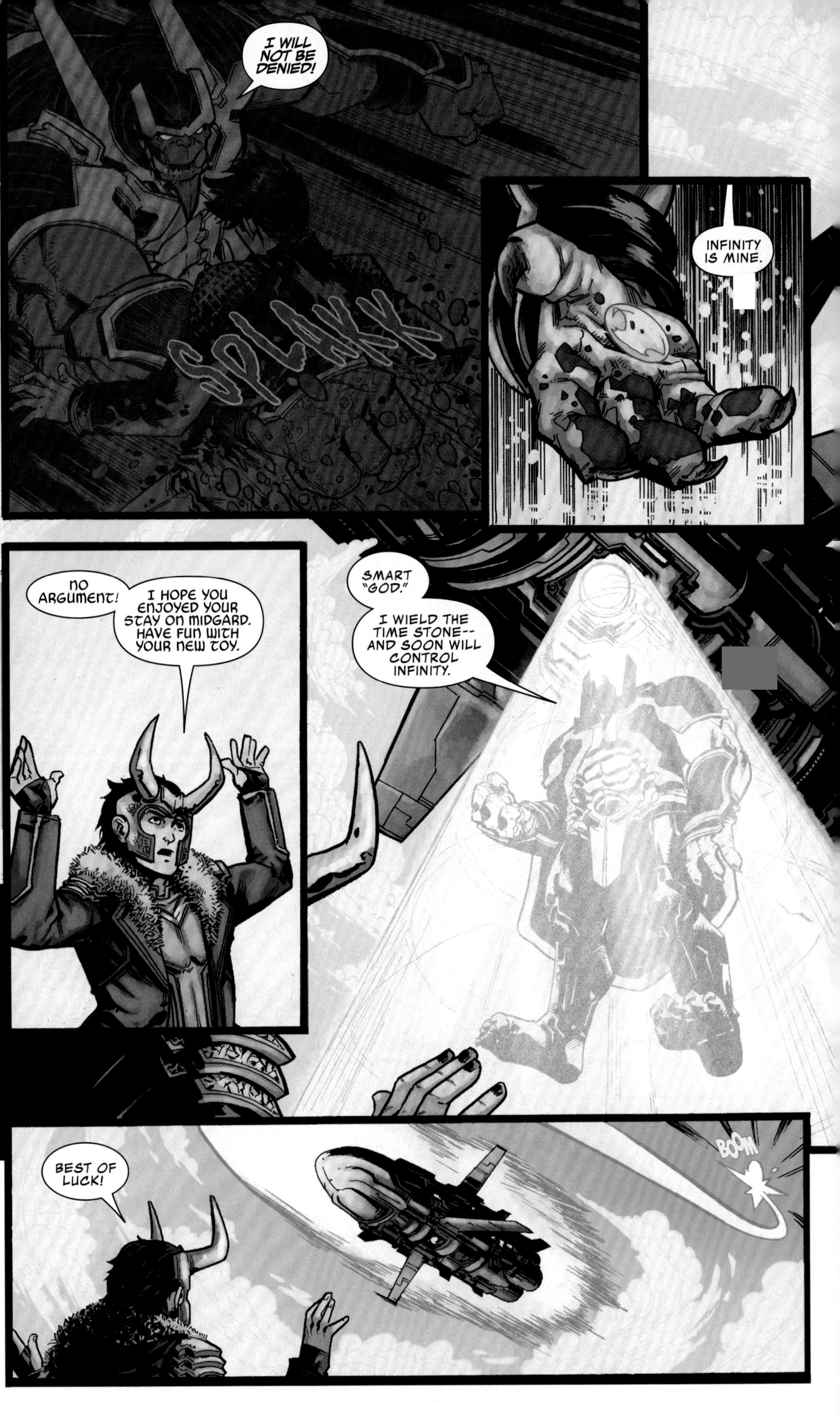
I WILL NOT BE DENIED!
SPLAKK
INFINITY IS MINE.
NO ARGUMENT!
I HOPE YOU ENJOYED YOUR STAY ON MIDGARD. HAVE FUN WITH YOUR NEW TOY.
SMART "GOD."
I WIELD THE TIME STONE-- AND SOON WILL CONTROL INFINITY.
BEST OF LUCK!
BOOM

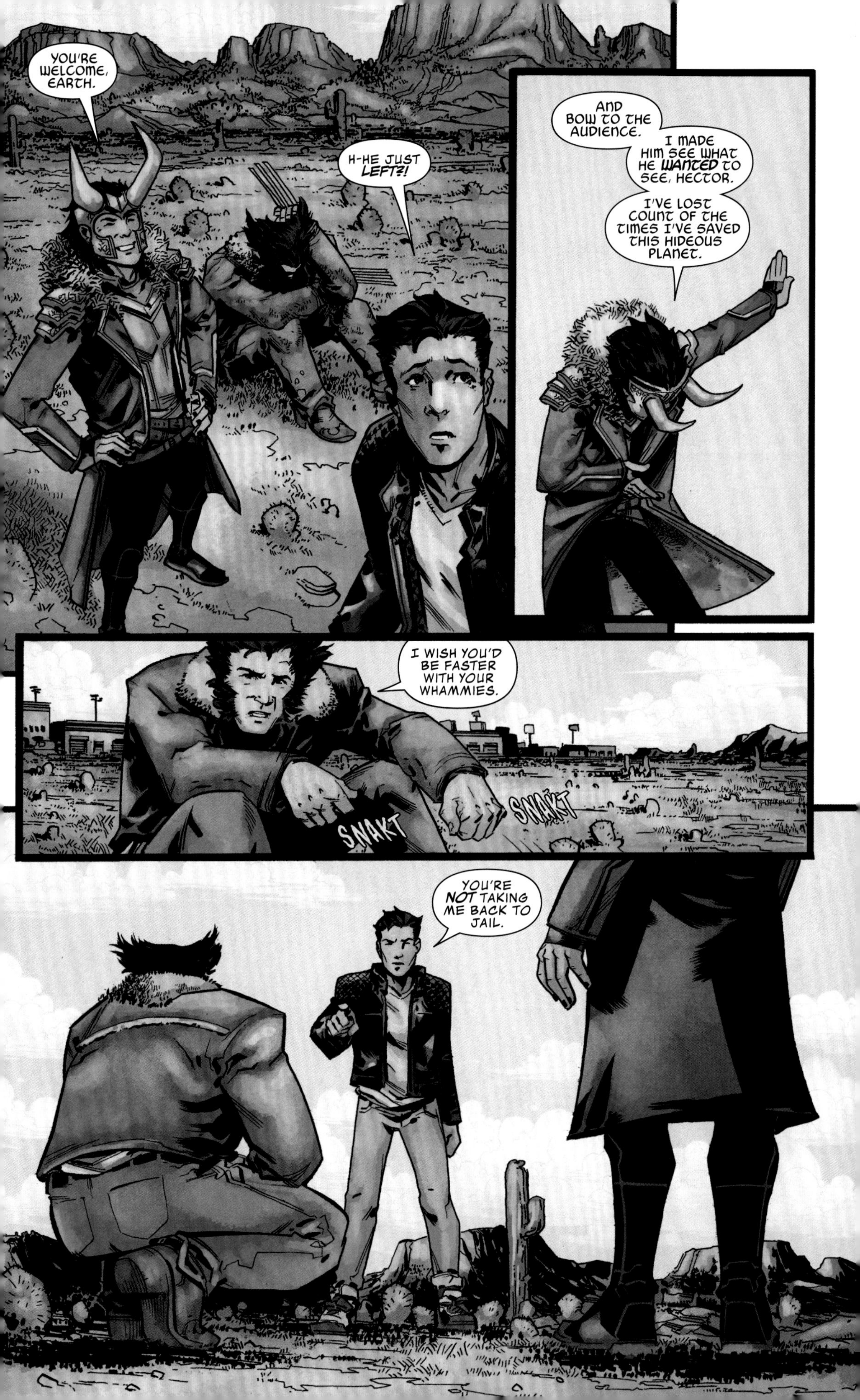
YOU'RE WELCOME, EARTH.
H-HE JUST LEFT?!
AND BOW TO THE AUDIENCE.
I MADE HIM SEE WHAT HE WANTED TO SEE, HECTOR.
I'VE LOST COUNT OF THE TIMES I'VE SAVED THIS HIDEOUS PLANET.
I WISH YOU'D BE FASTER WITH YOUR WHAMMIES.
SNAKT
SNAKT
YOU'RE NOT TAKING ME BACK TO JAIL.

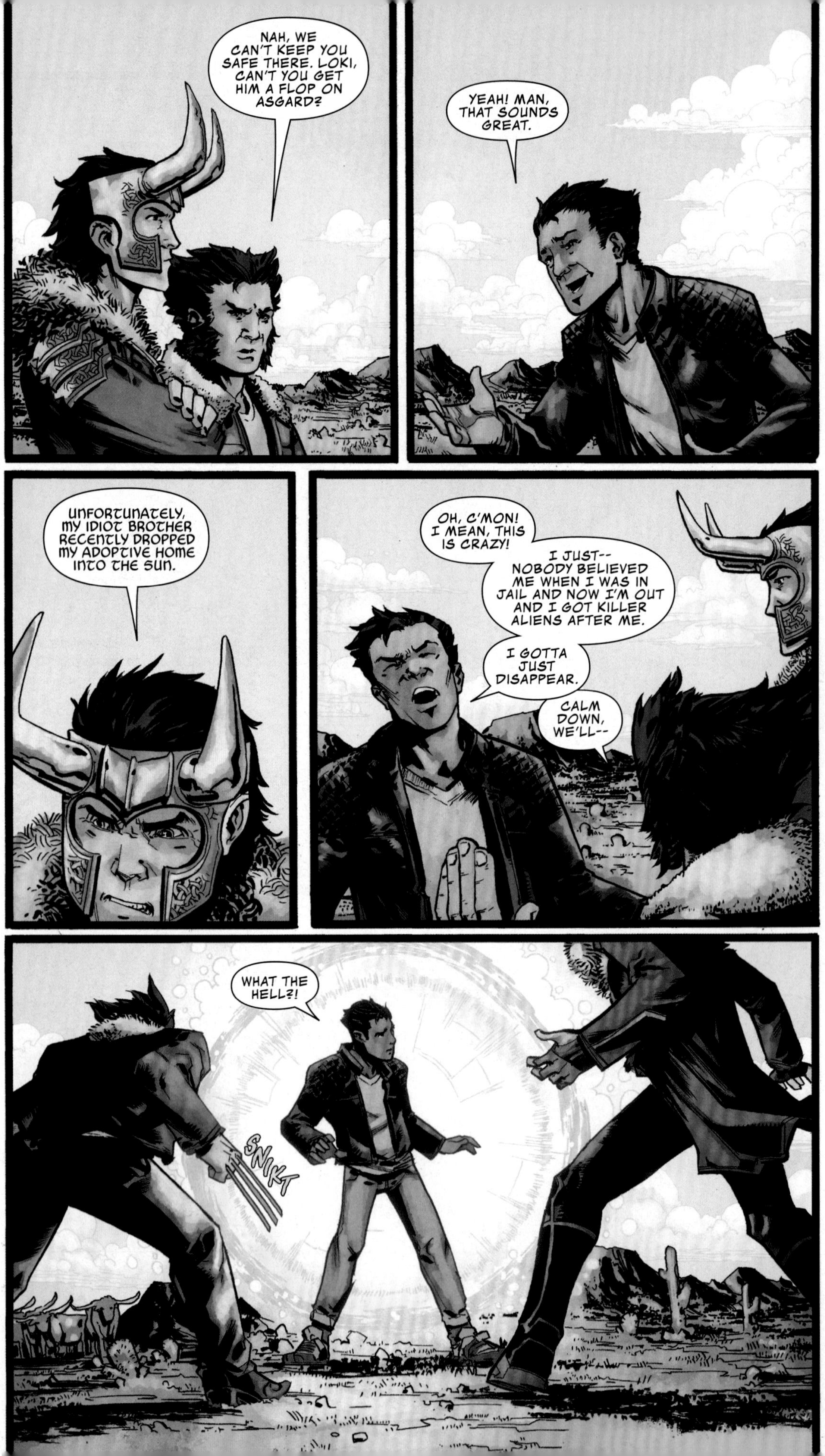
NAH, WE CAN'T KEEP YOU SAFE THERE. LOKI, CAN'T YOU GET HIM A FLOP ON ASGARD?
YEAH! MAN, THAT SOUNDS GREAT.
UNFORTUNATELY, MY IDIOT BROTHER RECENTLY DROPPED MY ADOPTIVE HOME INTO THE SUN.
OH, C'MON! I MEAN, THIS IS CRAZY!
I JUST-- NOBODY BELIEVED ME WHEN I WAS IN JAIL AND NOW I'M OUT AND I GOT KILLER ALIENS AFTER ME.
I GOTTA JUST DISAPPEAR.
CALM DOWN, WE'LL--
WHAT THE HELL?!
SNIKT

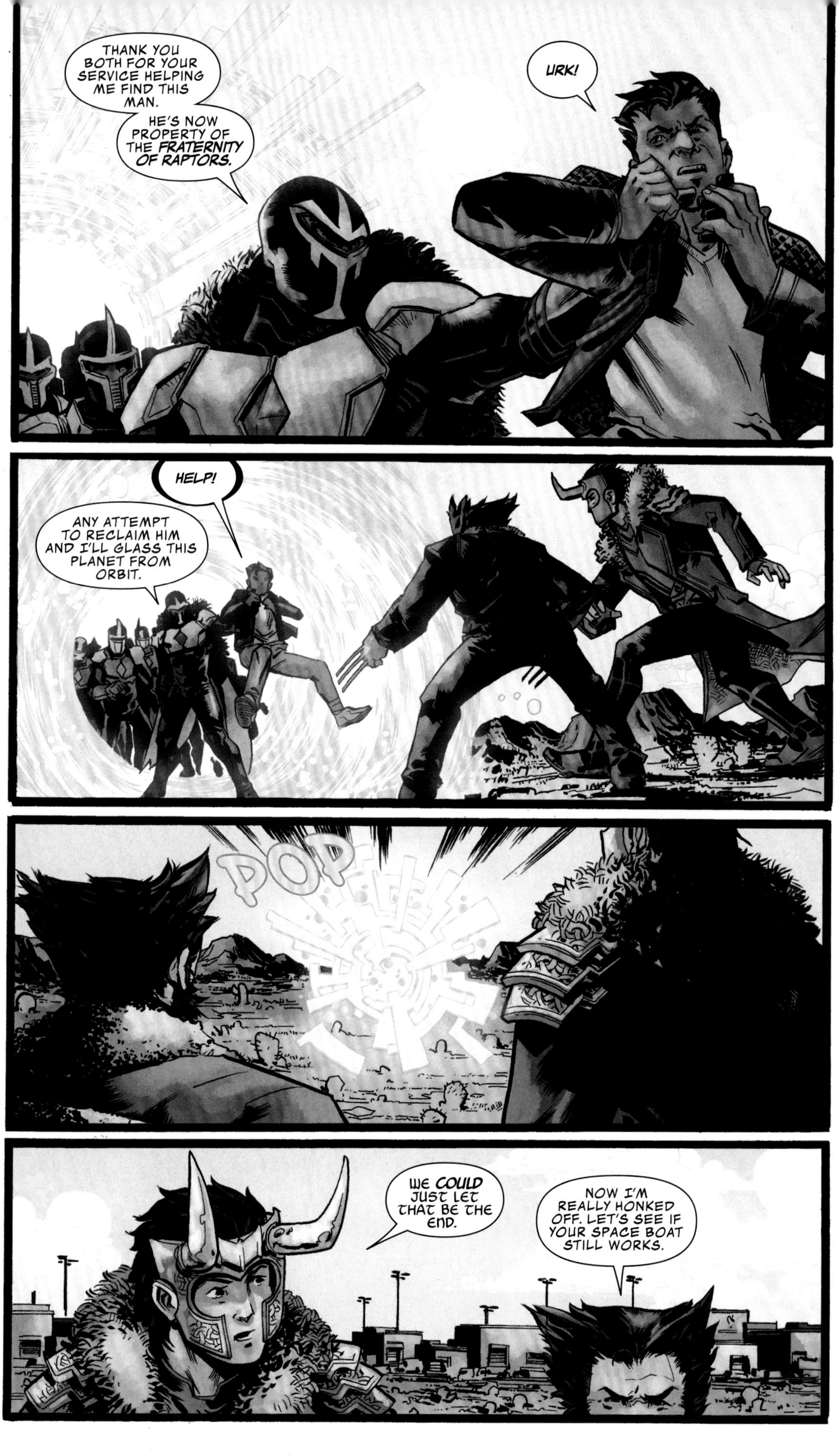
THANK YOU BOTH FOR YOUR SERVICE HELPING ME FIND THIS MAN.
HE'S NOW PROPERTY OF THE FRATERNITY OF RAPTORS.
URK!
HELP!
ANY ATTEMPT TO RECLAIM HIM AND I'LL GLASS THIS PLANET FROM ORBIT.
POP
WE COULD JUST LET THAT BE THE END.
NOW I'M REALLY HONKED OFF. LET'S SEE IF YOUR SPACE BOAT STILL WORKS.

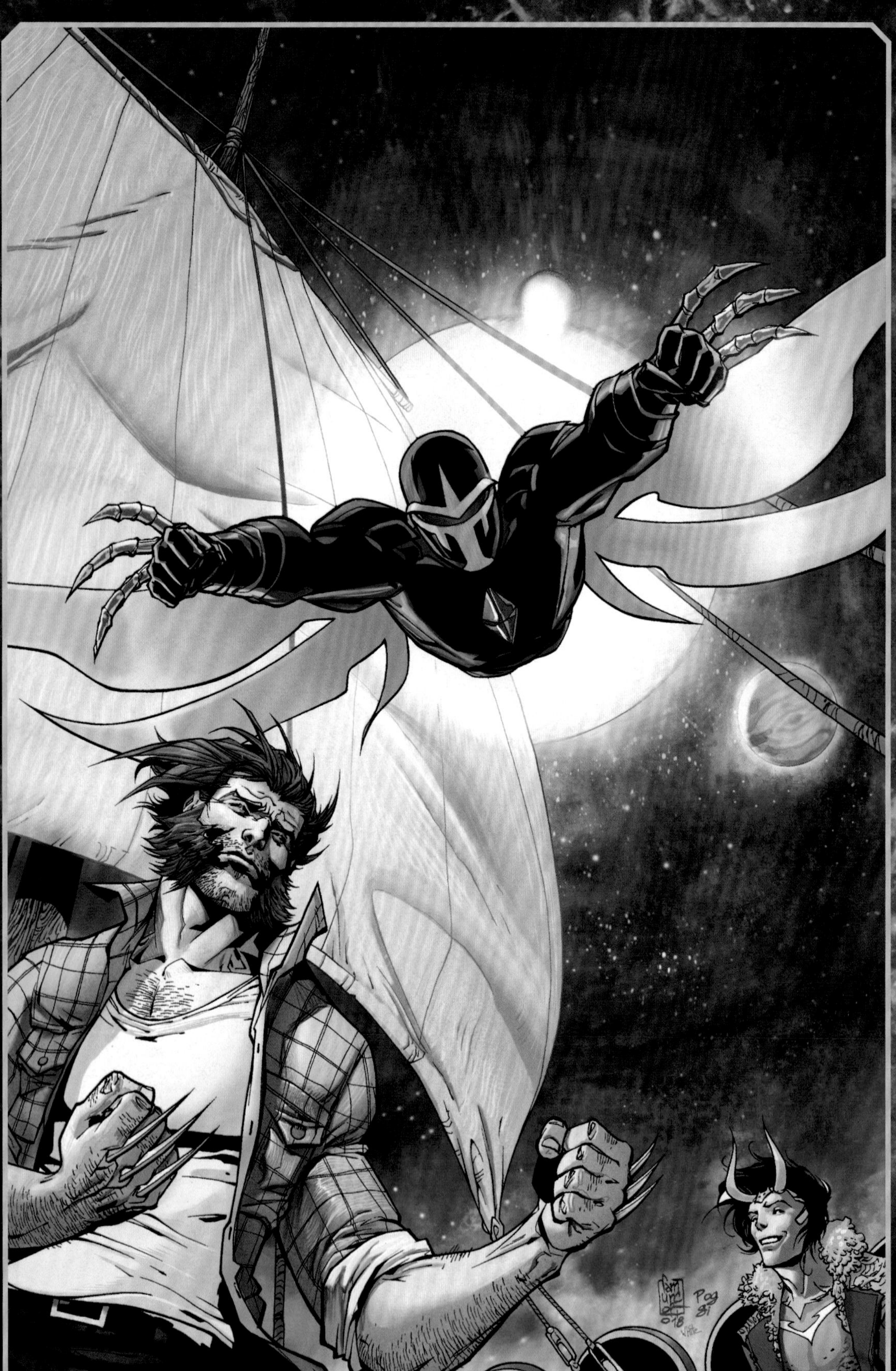

THREE

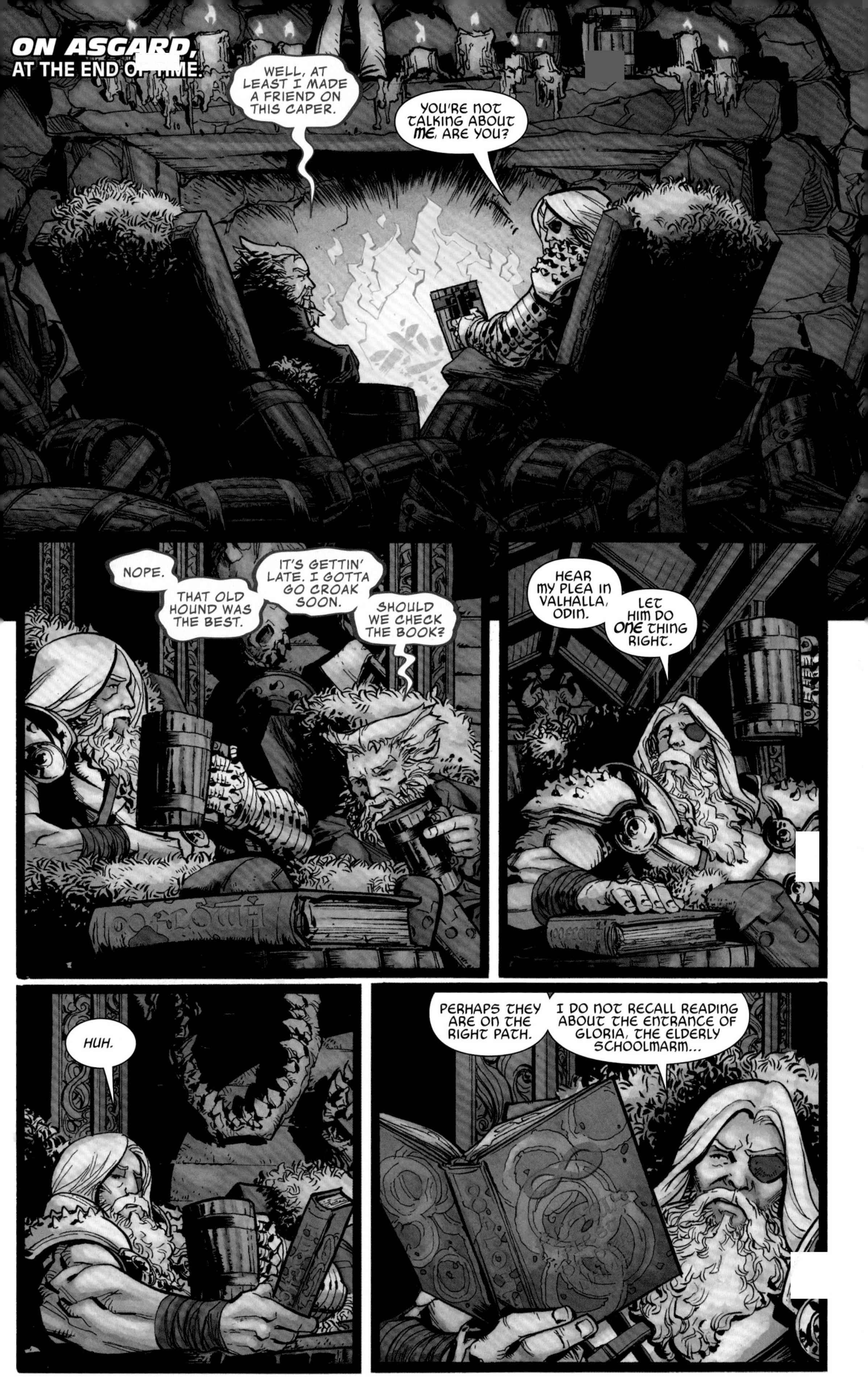

ON ASGARD,
AT THE END OF TIME.
WELL, AT LEAST I MADE A FRIEND ON THIS CAPER.
YOU'RE NOT TALKING ABOUT ME, ARE YOU?
NOPE.
THAT OLD HOUND WAS THE BEST.
IT'S GETTIN' LATE. I GOTTA GO CROAK SOON.
SHOULD WE CHECK THE BOOK?
HEAR MY PLEA IN VALHALLA, ODIN.
LET HIM DO ONE THING RIGHT.
HUH.
PERHAPS THEY ARE ON THE RIGHT PATH.
I DO NOT RECALL READING ABOUT THE ENTRANCE OF GLORIA, THE ELDERLY SCHOOLMARM...

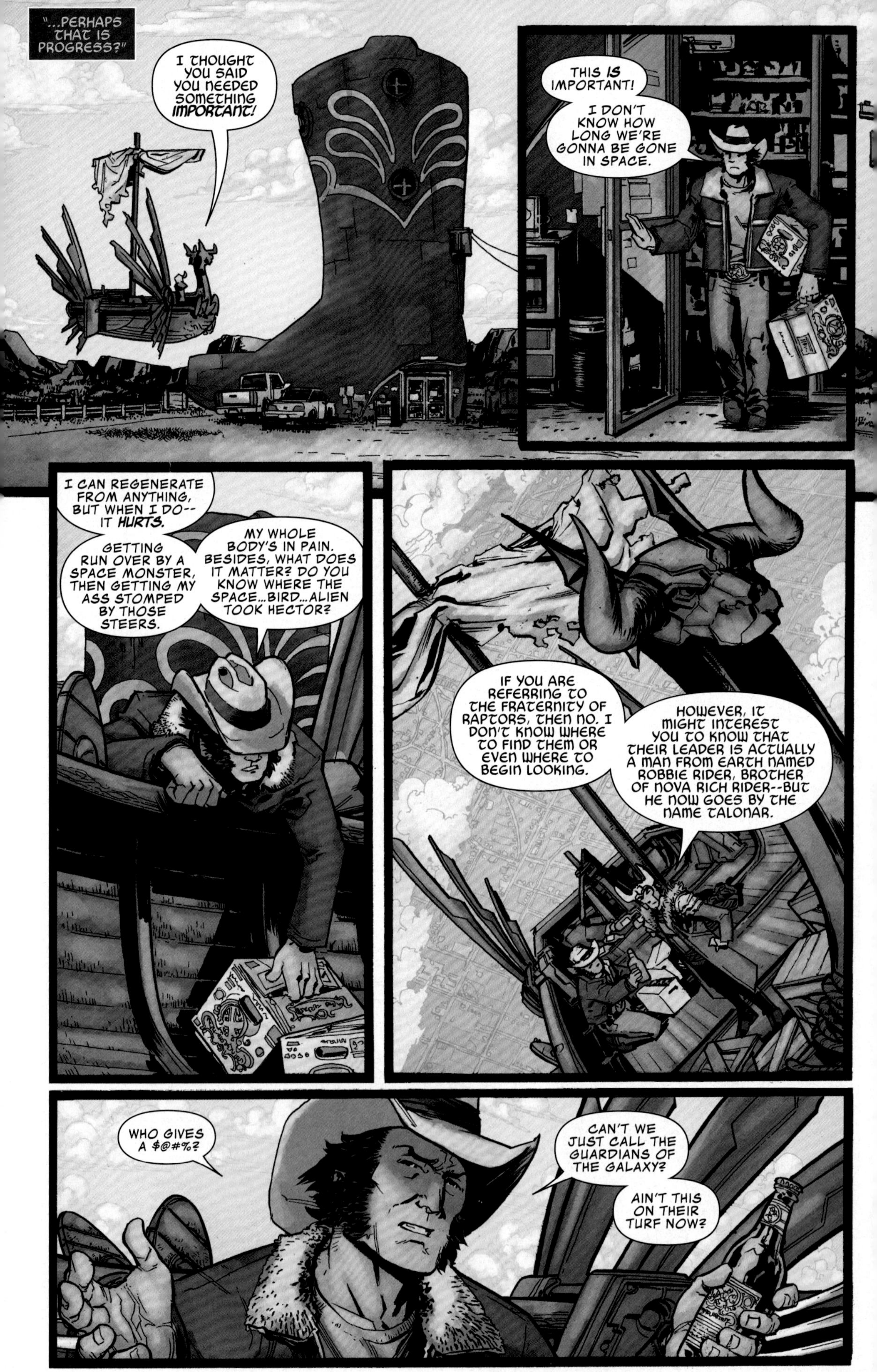
"...PERHAPS THAT IS PROGRESS?"
I THOUGHT YOU SAID YOU NEEDED SOMETHING IMPORTANT!
THIS IS IMPORTANT!
I DON'T KNOW HOW LONG WE'RE GONNA BE GONE IN SPACE.
I CAN REGENERATE FROM ANYTHING, BUT WHEN I DO-- IT HURTS.
GETTING RUN OVER BY A SPACE MONSTER, THEN GETTING MY ASS STOMPED BY THOSE STEERS.
MY WHOLE BODY'S IN PAIN. BESIDES, WHAT DOES IT MATTER? DO YOU KNOW WHERE THE SPACE...BIRD...ALIEN TOOK HECTOR?
IF YOU ARE REFERRING TO THE FRATERNITY OF RAPTORS, THEN NO. I DON'T KNOW WHERE TO FIND THEM OR EVEN WHERE TO BEGIN LOOKING.
HOWEVER, IT MIGHT INTEREST YOU TO KNOW THAT THEIR LEADER IS ACTUALLY A MAN FROM EARTH NAMED ROBBIE RIDER, BROTHER OF NOVA RICH RIDER--BUT HE NOW GOES BY THE NAME TALONAR.
WHO GIVES A $@#%?
CAN'T WE JUST CALL THE GUARDIANS OF THE GALAXY?
AIN'T THIS ON THEIR TURF NOW?

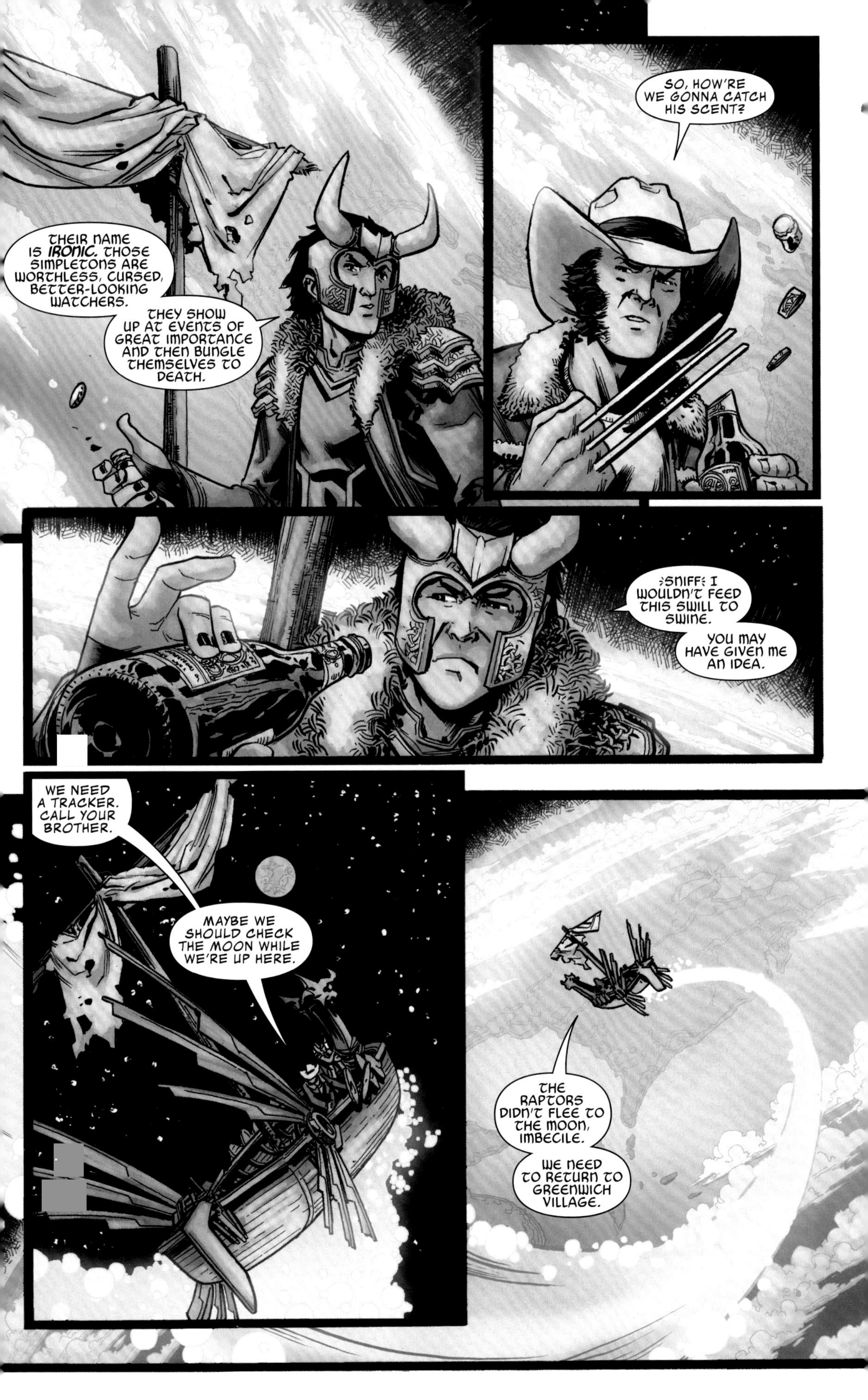
THEIR NAME IS IRONIC. THOSE SIMPLETONS ARE WORTHLESS, CURSED, BETTER-LOOKING WATCHERS.
THEY SHOW UP AT EVENTS OF GREAT IMPORTANCE AND THEN BUNGLE THEMSELVES TO DEATH.
SO, HOW'RE WE GONNA CATCH HIS SCENT?
SNIFF I WOULDN'T FEED THIS SWILL TO SWINE.
YOU MAY HAVE GIVEN ME AN IDEA.
WE NEED A TRACKER. CALL YOUR BROTHER.
MAYBE WE SHOULD CHECK THE MOON WHILE WE'RE UP HERE.
THE RAPTORS DIDN'T FLEE TO THE MOON, IMBECILE.
WE NEED TO RETURN TO GREENWICH VILLAGE.

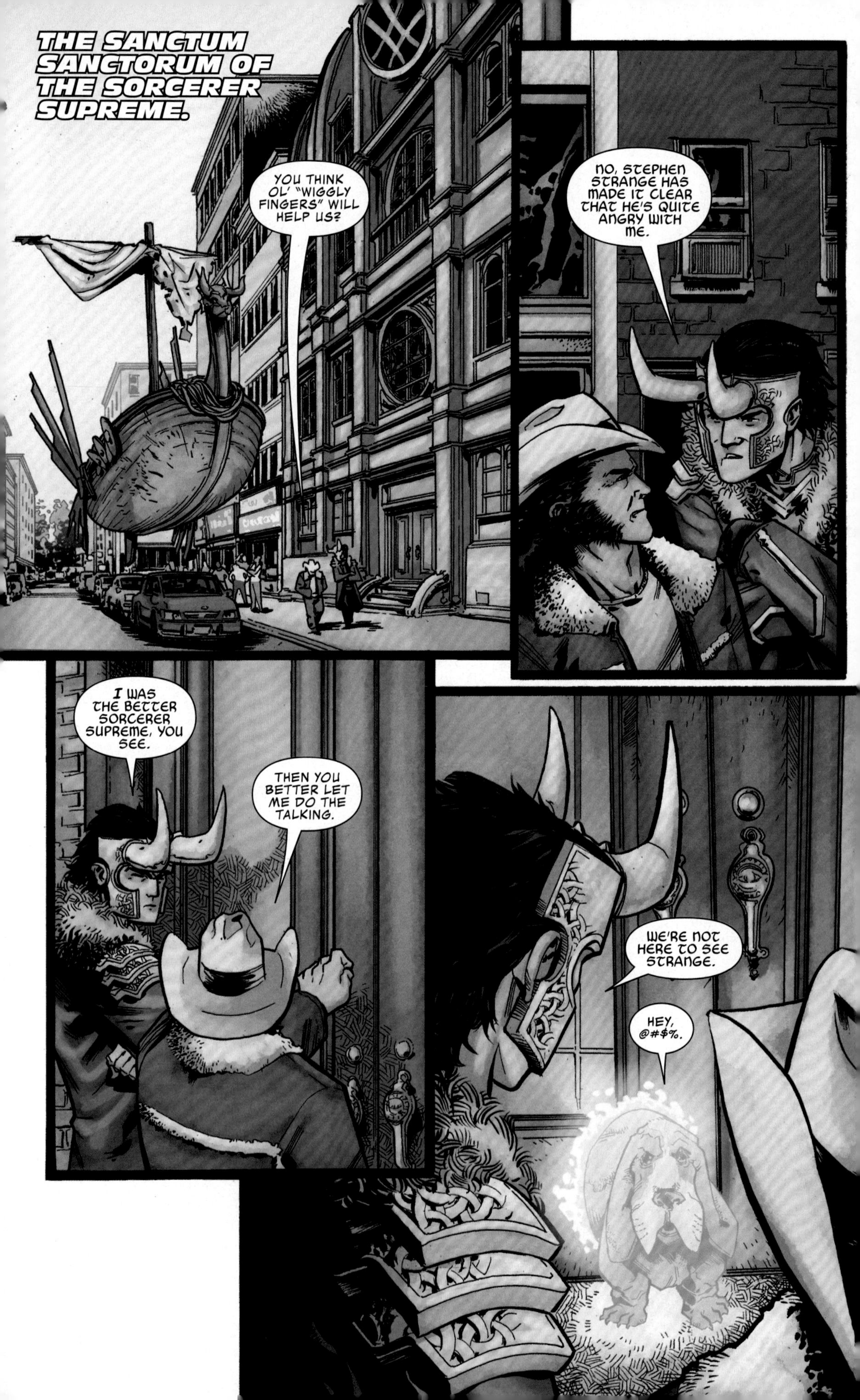
THE SANCTUM SANCTORUM OF THE SORCERER SUPREME.
YOU THINK OL' "WIGGLY FINGERS" WILL HELP US?
NO, STEPHEN STRANGE HAS MADE IT CLEAR THAT HE'S QUITE ANGRY WITH ME.
I WAS THE BETTER SORCERER SUPREME, YOU SEE.
THEN YOU BETTER LET ME DO THE TALKING.
WE'RE NOT HERE TO SEE STRANGE.
HEY, @#$%.

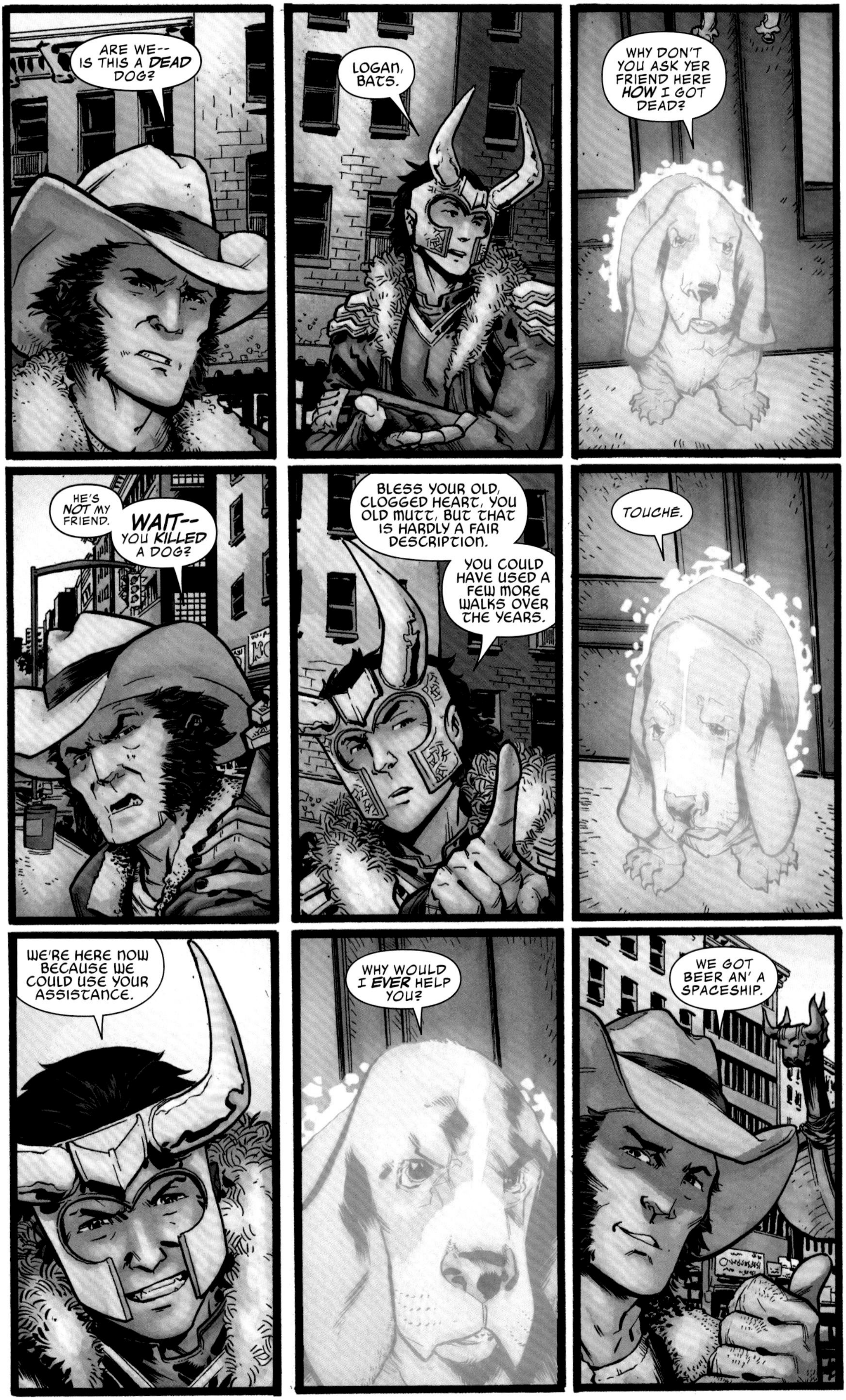

ARE WE-- IS THIS A DEAD DOG?
LOGAN, BATS.
WHY DON'T YOU ASK YER FRIEND HERE HOW I GOT DEAD?
HE'S NOT MY FRIEND.
WAIT-- YOU KILLED A DOG?
BLESS YOUR OLD, CLOGGED HEART, YOU OLD MUTT, BUT THAT IS HARDLY A FAIR DESCRIPTION.
YOU COULD HAVE USED A FEW MORE WALKS OVER THE YEARS.
TOUCHÉ.
WE'RE HERE NOW BECAUSE WE COULD USE YOUR ASSISTANCE.
WHY WOULD I EVER HELP YOU?
WE GOT BEER AN' A SPACESHIP.

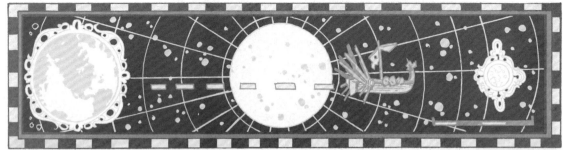

AROOOOOO!

THAT'S NOT REALLY SANITARY.

IF YOU DON'T DRINK IT, I WILL.

FINE.

LAP LAP LAP LAP LAP

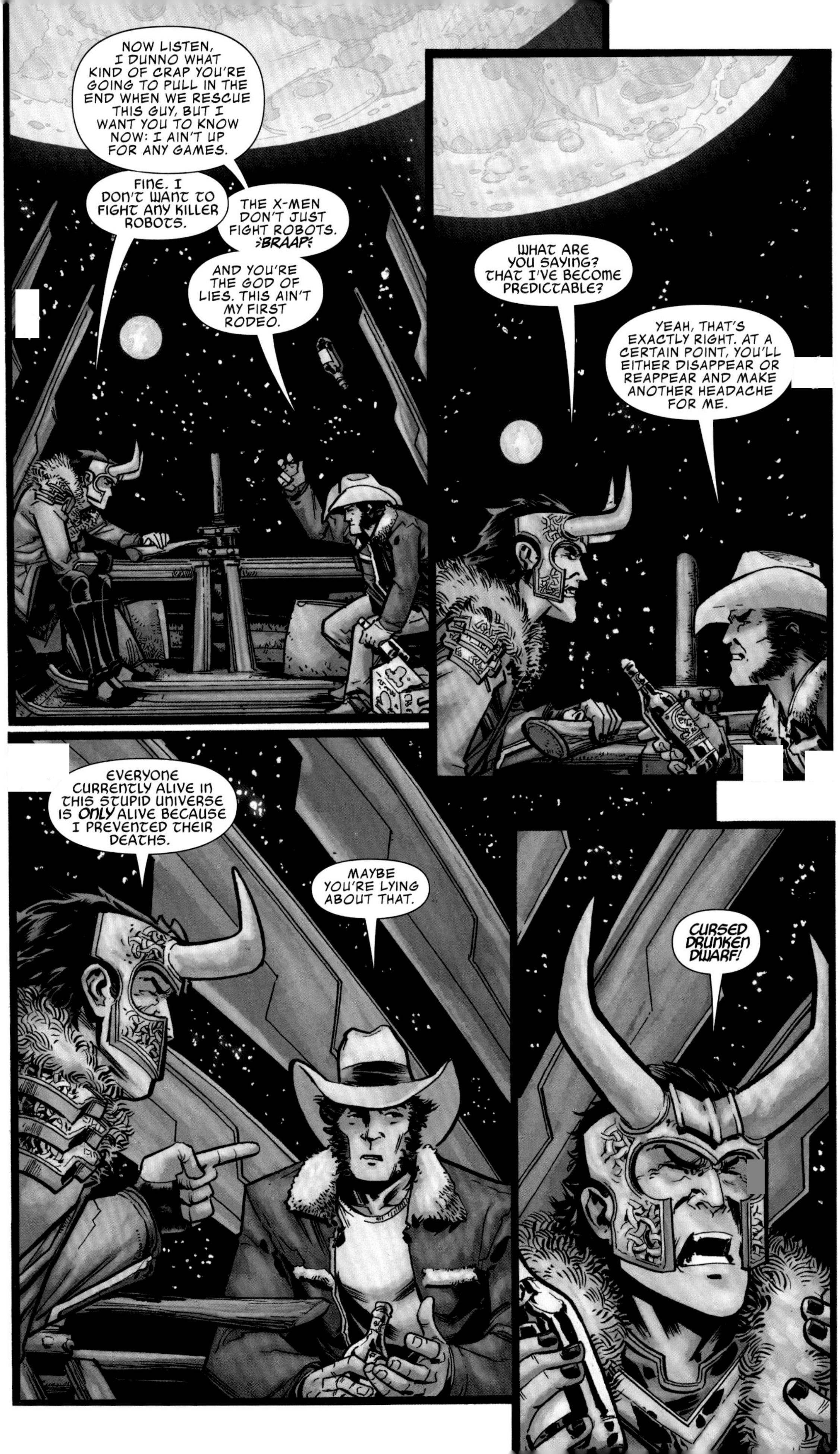
NOW LISTEN, I DUNNO WHAT KIND OF CRAP YOU'RE GOING TO PULL IN THE END WHEN WE RESCUE THIS GUY, BUT I WANT YOU TO KNOW NOW: I AIN'T UP FOR ANY GAMES.
FINE. I DON'T WANT TO FIGHT ANY KILLER ROBOTS.
THE X-MEN DON'T JUST FIGHT ROBOTS. BRAAP
AND YOU'RE THE GOD OF LIES. THIS AIN'T MY FIRST RODEO.
WHAT ARE YOU SAYING? THAT I'VE BECOME PREDICTABLE?
YEAH, THAT'S EXACTLY RIGHT. AT A CERTAIN POINT, YOU'LL EITHER DISAPPEAR OR REAPPEAR AND MAKE ANOTHER HEADACHE FOR ME.
EVERYONE CURRENTLY ALIVE IN THIS STUPID UNIVERSE IS ONLY ALIVE BECAUSE I PREVENTED THEIR DEATHS.
MAYBE YOU'RE LYING ABOUT THAT.
CURSED DRUNKEN DWARF!

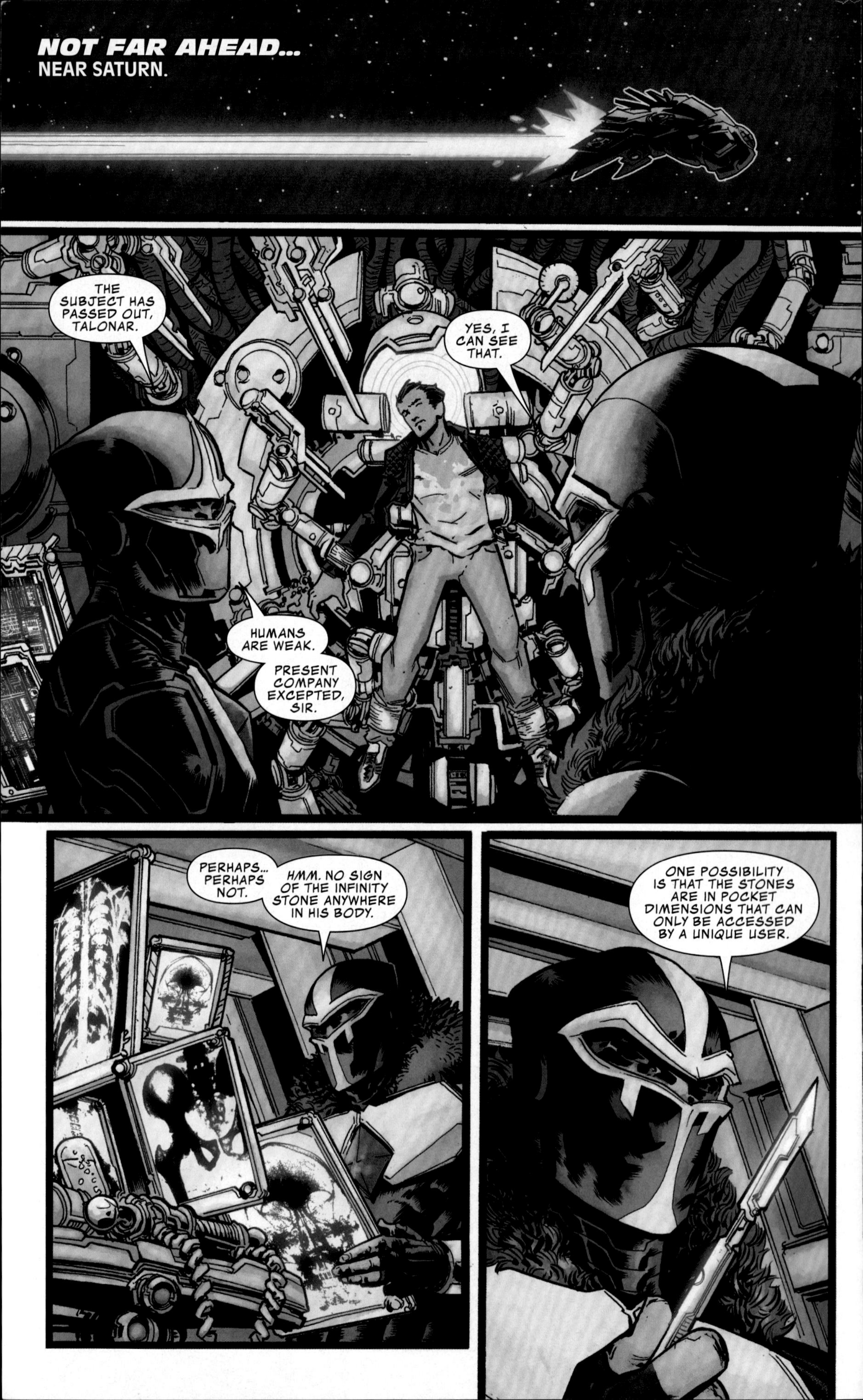
NOT FAR AHEAD...
NEAR SATURN.
THE SUBJECT HAS PASSED OUT, TALONAR.
YES, I CAN SEE THAT.
HUMANS ARE WEAK.
PRESENT COMPANY EXCEPTED, SIR.
HMM. NO SIGN OF THE INFINITY STONE ANYWHERE IN HIS BODY.
PERHAPS... PERHAPS NOT.
ONE POSSIBILITY IS THAT THE STONES ARE IN POCKET DIMENSIONS THAT CAN ONLY BE ACCESSED BY A UNIQUE USER.

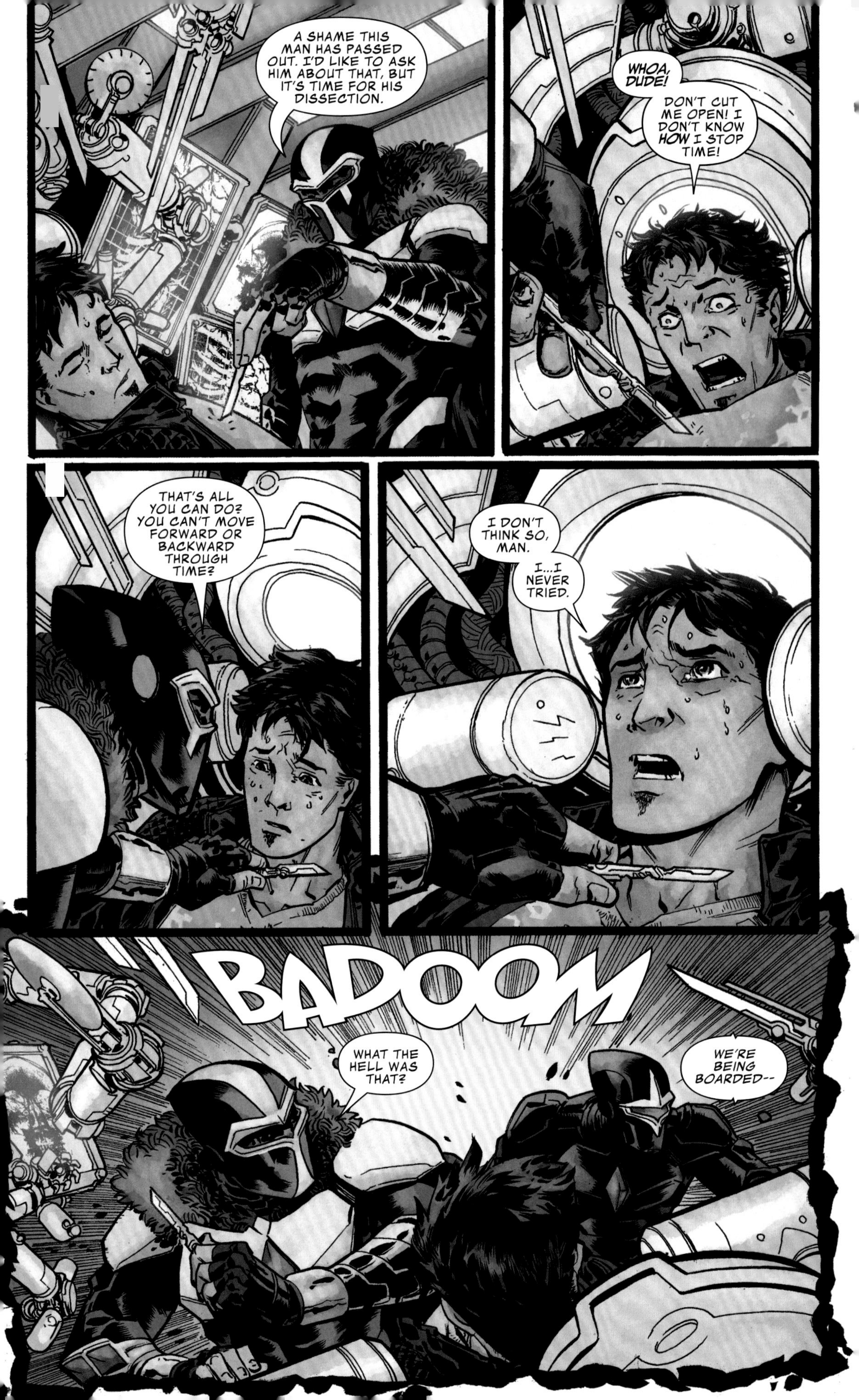
A SHAME THIS MAN HAS PASSED OUT. I'D LIKE TO ASK HIM ABOUT THAT, BUT IT'S TIME FOR HIS DISSECTION.
WHOA, DUDE!
DON'T CUT ME OPEN! I DON'T KNOW HOW I STOP TIME!
THAT'S ALL YOU CAN DO? YOU CAN'T MOVE FORWARD OR BACKWARD THROUGH TIME?
I DON'T THINK SO, MAN.
I...I NEVER TRIED.
BADOOM
WHAT THE HELL WAS THAT?
WE'RE BEING BOARDED--

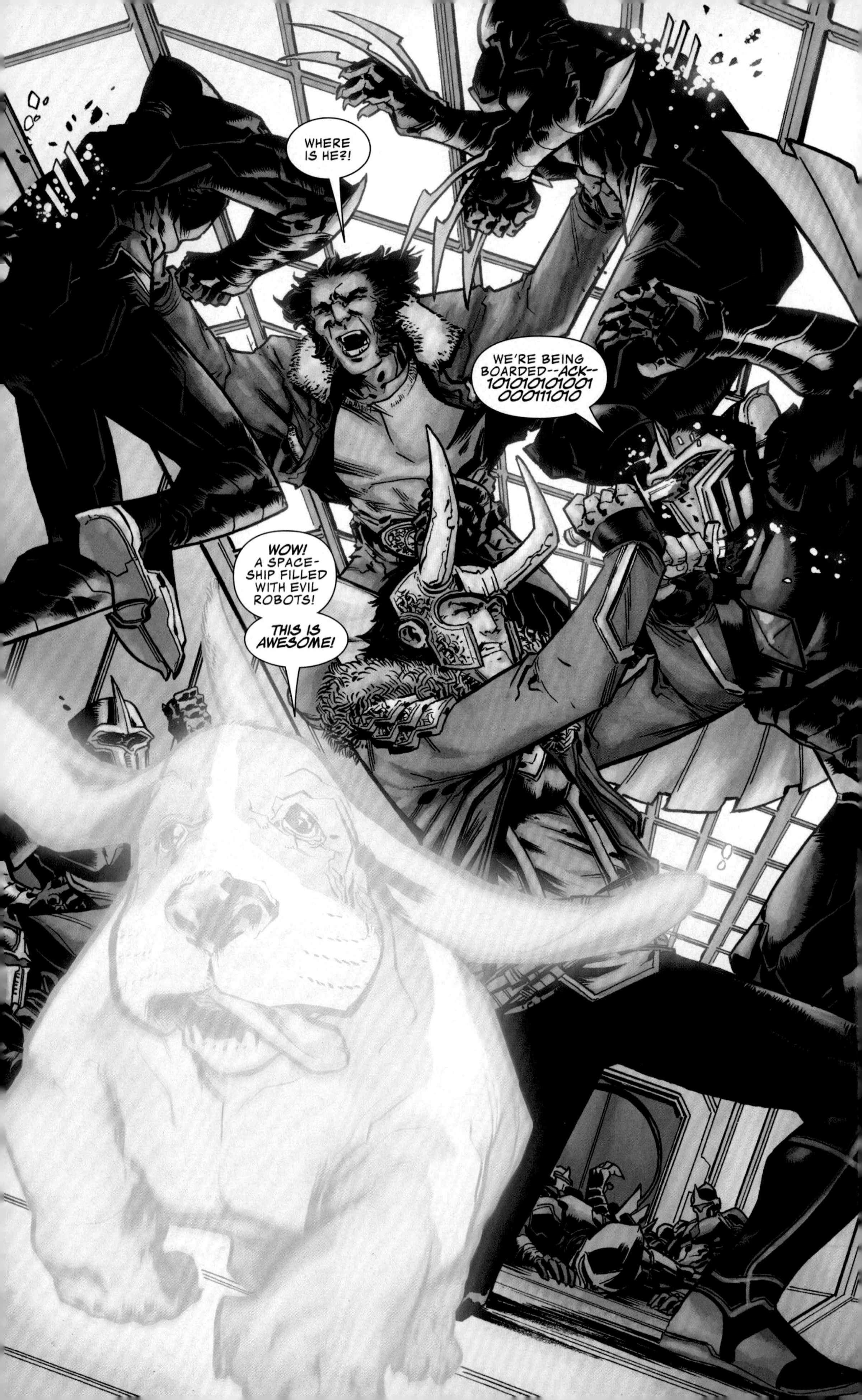
WHERE IS HE?!
WE'RE BEING BOARDED--ACK-- 1010101010101 000111010
WOW! A SPACE-SHIP FILLED WITH EVIL ROBOTS!
THIS IS AWESOME!

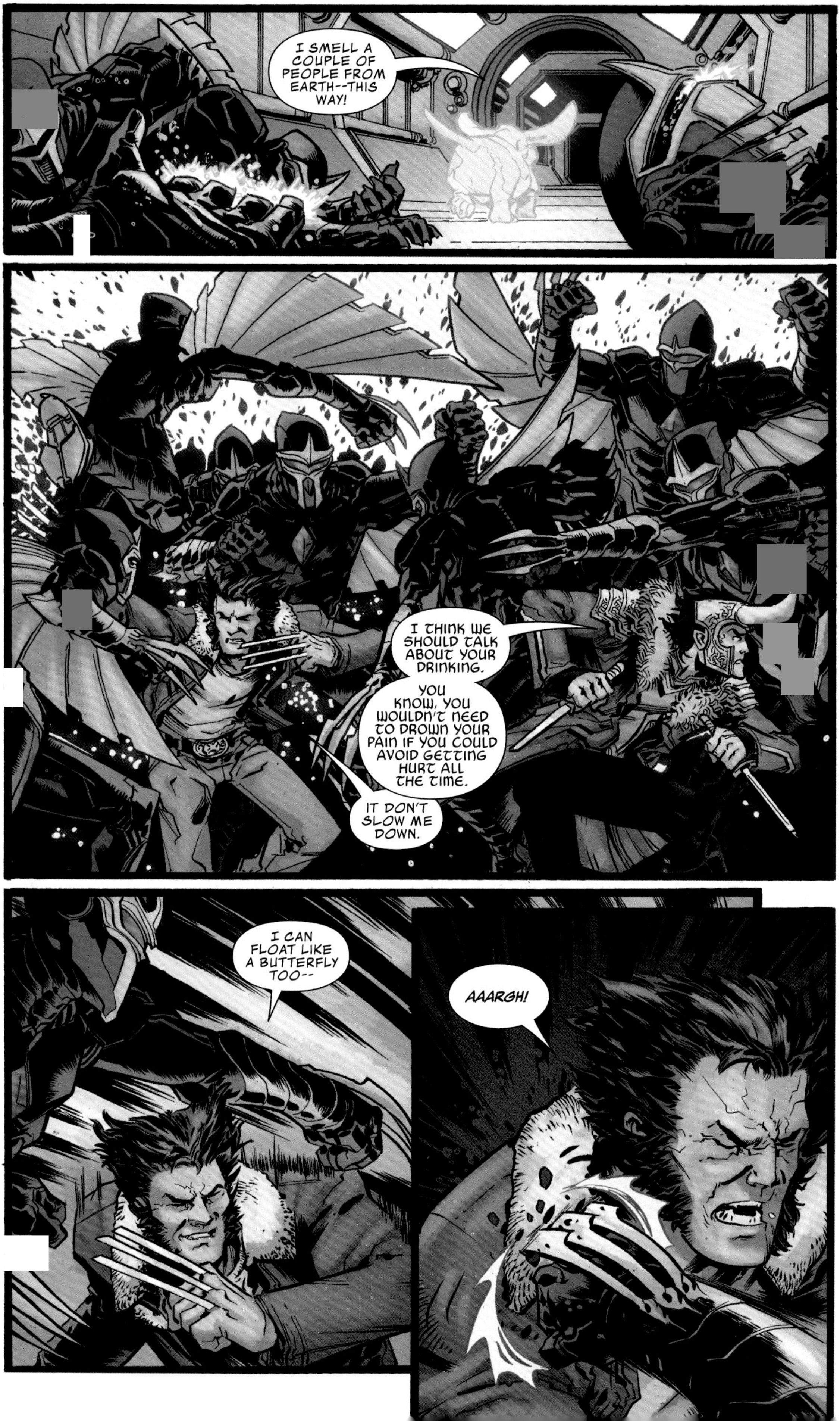
I SMELL A COUPLE OF PEOPLE FROM EARTH--THIS WAY!
I THINK WE SHOULD TALK ABOUT YOUR DRINKING.
YOU KNOW, YOU WOULDN'T NEED TO DROWN YOUR PAIN IF YOU COULD AVOID GETTING HURT ALL THE TIME.
IT DON'T SLOW ME DOWN.
I CAN FLOAT LIKE A BUTTERFLY TOO--
AAARGH!

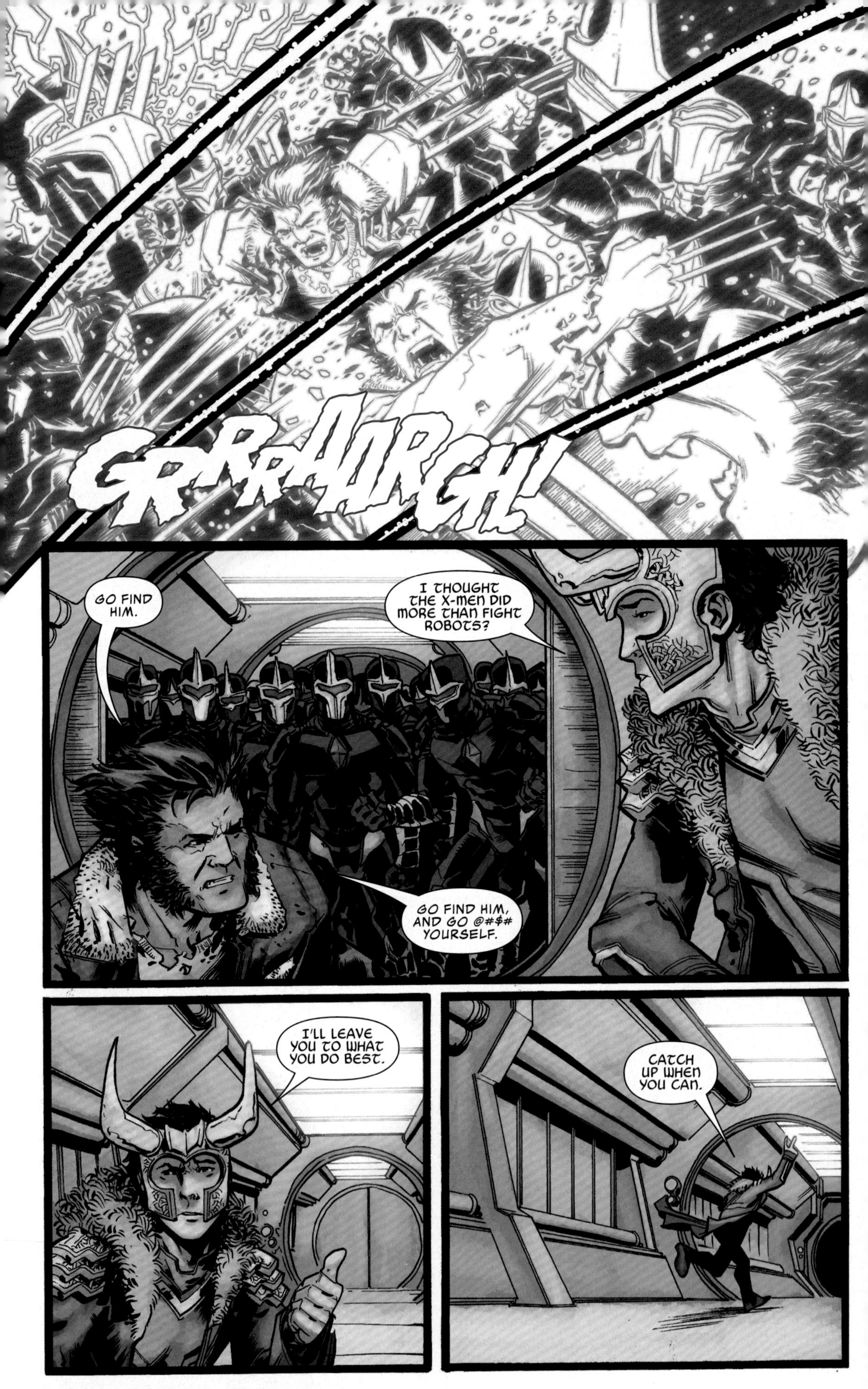
GRRRAAARGH!
GO FIND HIM.
I THOUGHT THE X-MEN DID MORE THAN FIGHT ROBOTS?
GO FIND HIM, AND GO @#$# YOURSELF.
I'LL LEAVE YOU TO WHAT YOU DO BEST.
CATCH UP WHEN YOU CAN.

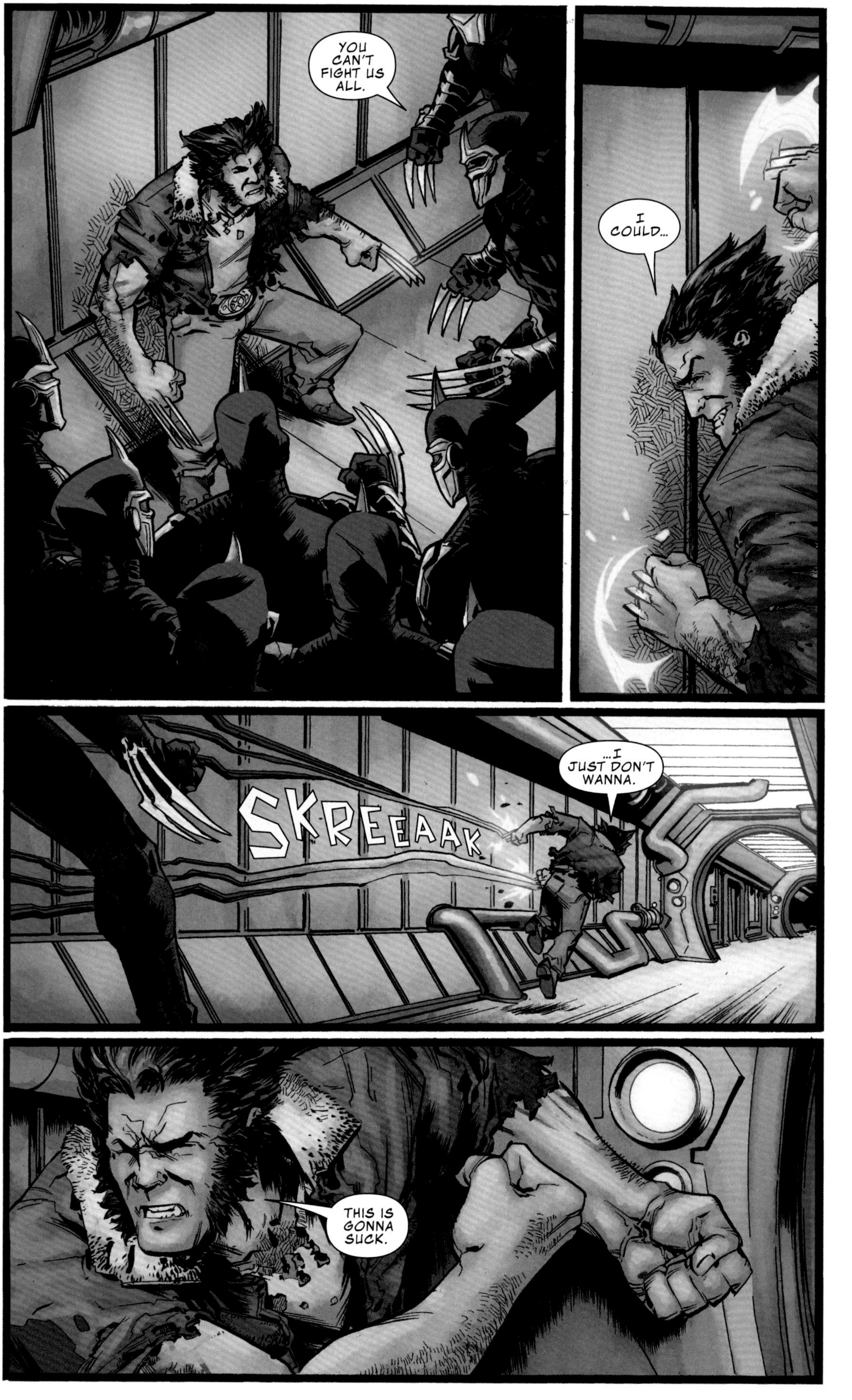
YOU CAN'T FIGHT US ALL.
I COULD...
SKREEAAK
...I JUST DON'T WANNA.
THIS IS GONNA SUCK.

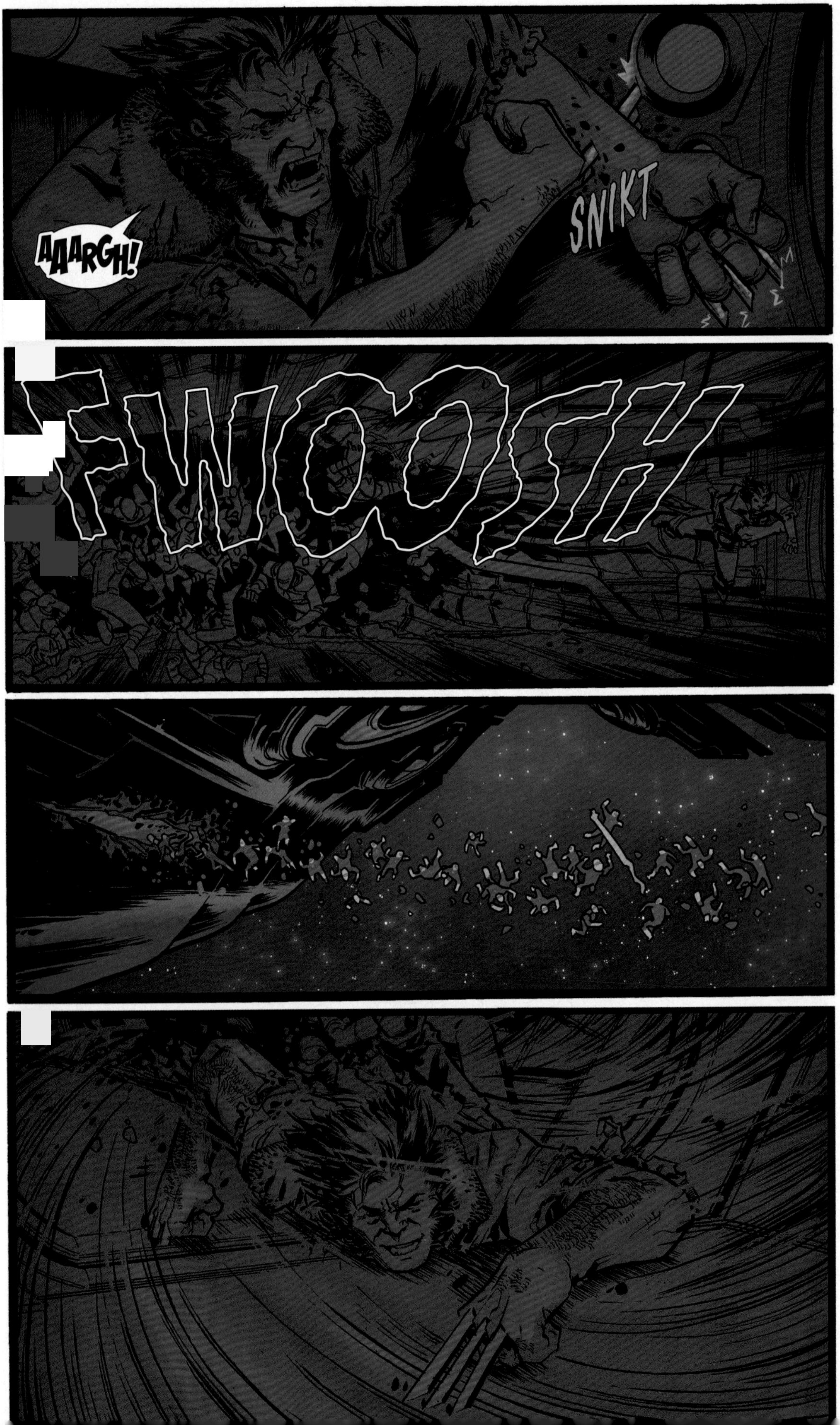
AAARGH!
SNIKT
FWOOSH

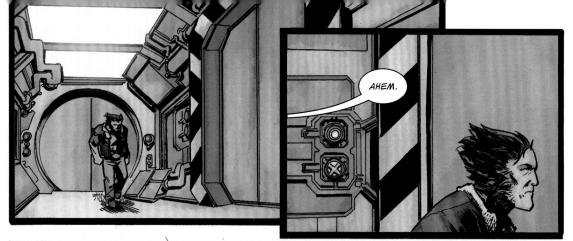

AHEM.

WE CAN SURVIVE THE VACUUM OF SPACE.

AW, C'MON. FINE. WE'LL DO IT--

--THE HARD WAY!

EJECTING THREAT.

MINIMIZE CLOSE QUARTERS COMBAT WITH SUBJECT.

HIS ADAMANTIUM POSES A THREAT TO THE VESSEL.

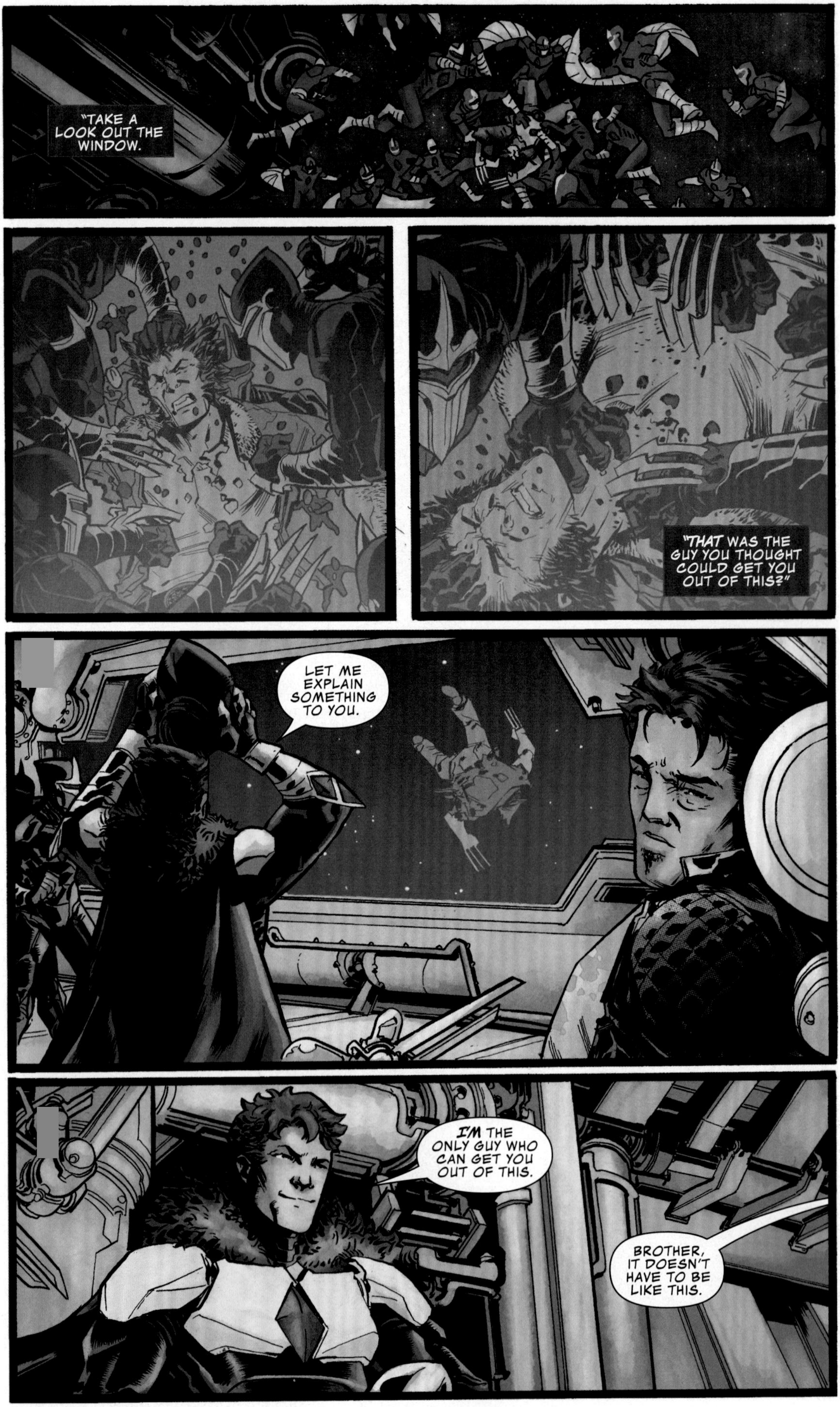
"TAKE A LOOK OUT THE WINDOW.
"THAT WAS THE GUY YOU THOUGHT COULD GET YOU OUT OF THIS?"
LET ME EXPLAIN SOMETHING TO YOU.
I'M THE ONLY GUY WHO CAN GET YOU OUT OF THIS.
BROTHER, IT DOESN'T HAVE TO BE LIKE THIS.

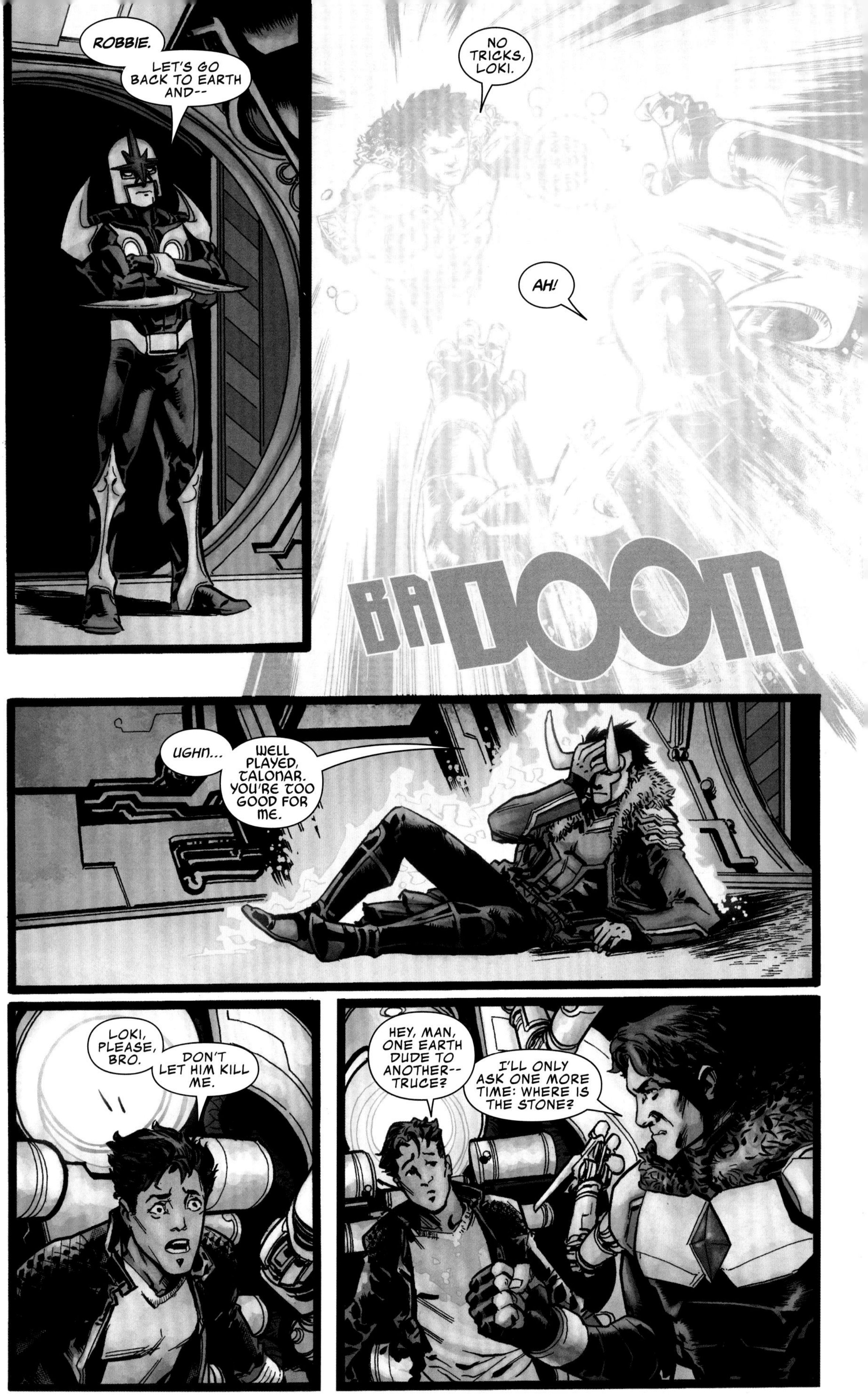
ROBBIE.
LET'S GO BACK TO EARTH AND--
NO TRICKS, LOKI.
AH!
BADOOM
UGHN...
WELL PLAYED, TALONAR. YOU'RE TOO GOOD FOR ME.
LOKI, PLEASE, BRO.
DON'T LET HIM KILL ME.
HEY, MAN, ONE EARTH DUDE TO ANOTHER-- TRUCE?
I'LL ONLY ASK ONE MORE TIME: WHERE IS THE STONE?

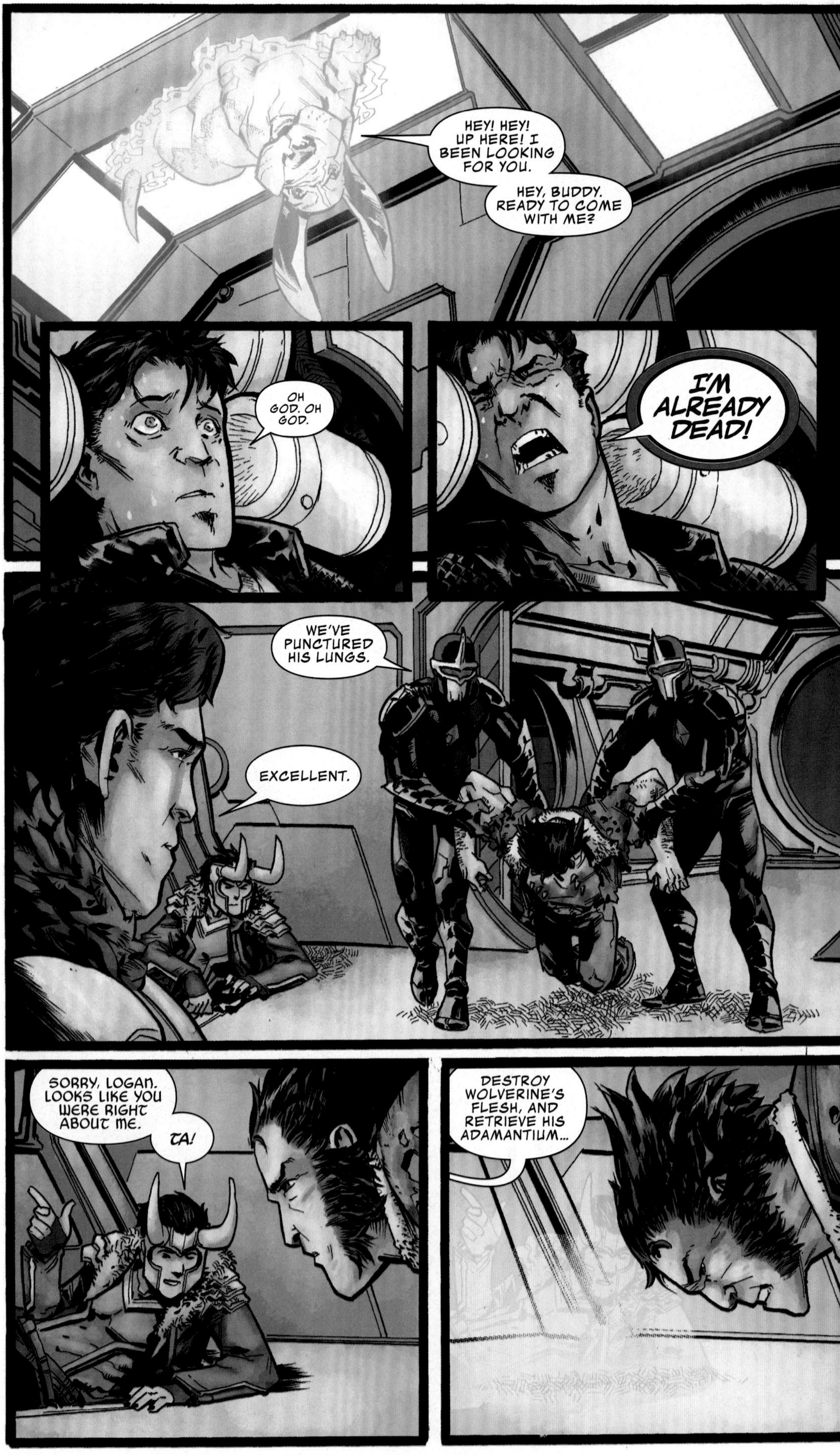
HEY! HEY! UP HERE! I BEEN LOOKING FOR YOU.
HEY, BUDDY. READY TO COME WITH ME?
OH GOD. OH GOD.
I'M ALREADY DEAD!
WE'VE PUNCTURED HIS LUNGS.
EXCELLENT.
SORRY, LOGAN. LOOKS LIKE YOU WERE RIGHT ABOUT ME.
TA!
DESTROY WOLVERINE'S FLESH, AND RETRIEVE HIS ADAMANTIUM...

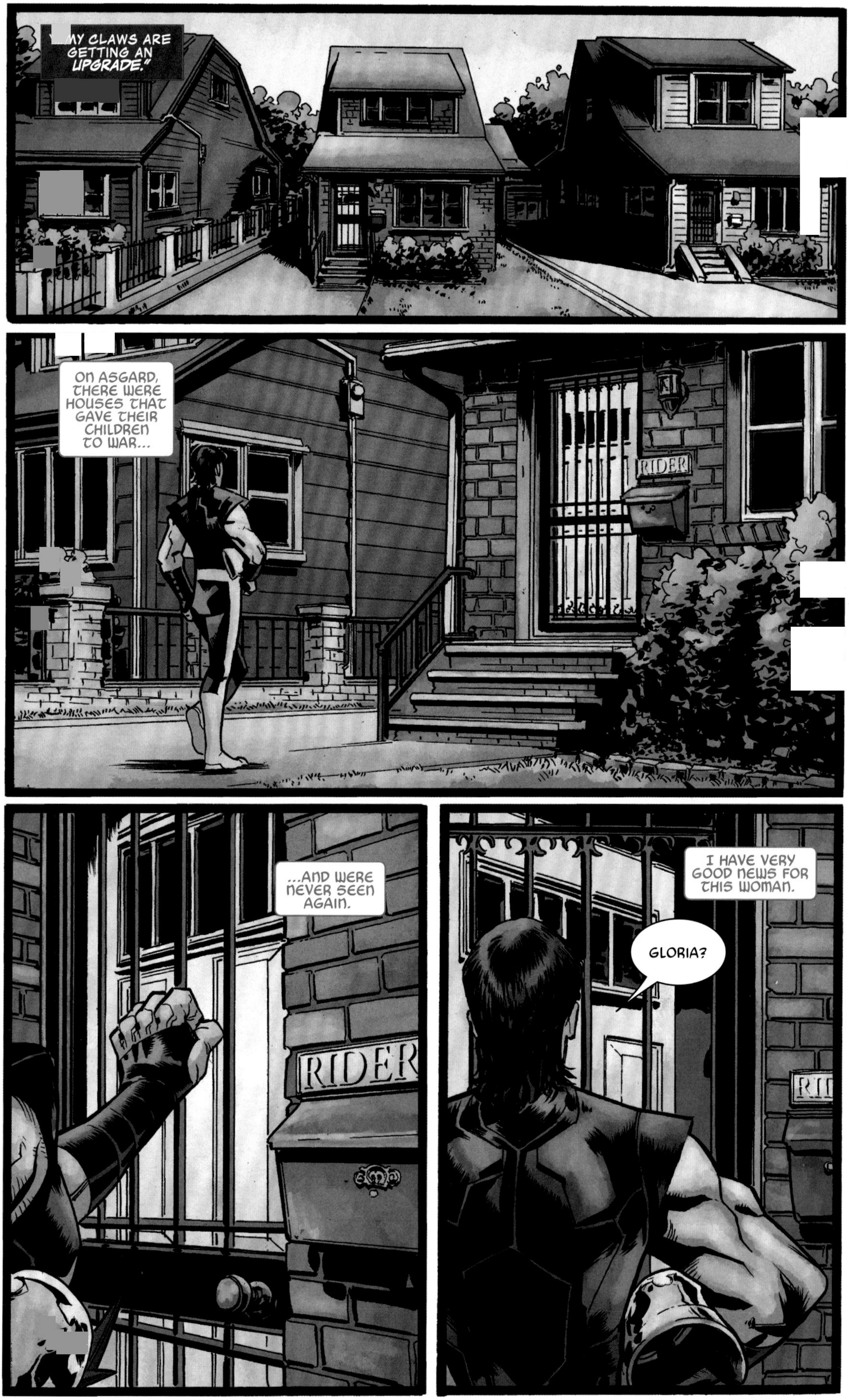
MY CLAWS ARE GETTING AN UPGRADE."
ON ASGARD, THERE WERE HOUSES THAT GAVE THEIR CHILDREN TO WAR...
RIDER
...AND WERE NEVER SEEN AGAIN.
RIDER
I HAVE VERY GOOD NEWS FOR THIS WOMAN.
GLORIA?

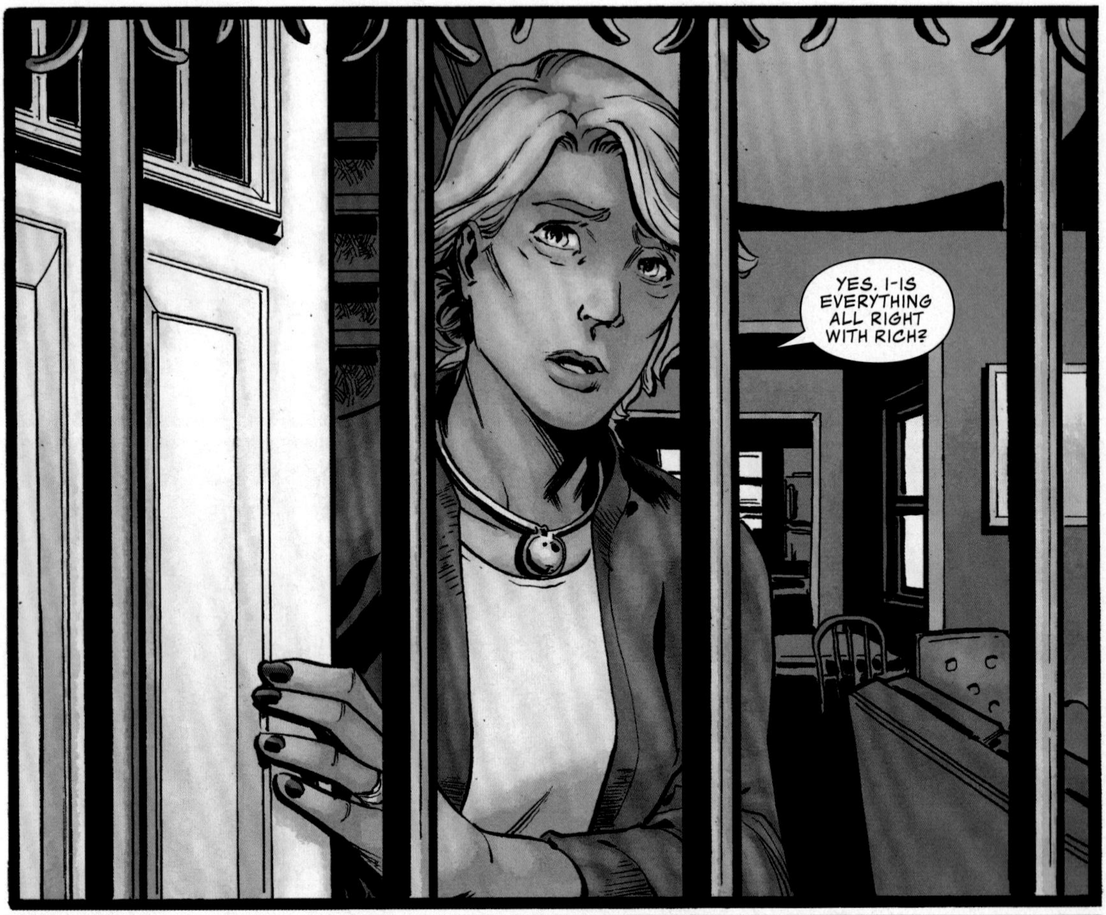
YES. I-IS EVERYTHING ALL RIGHT WITH RICH?

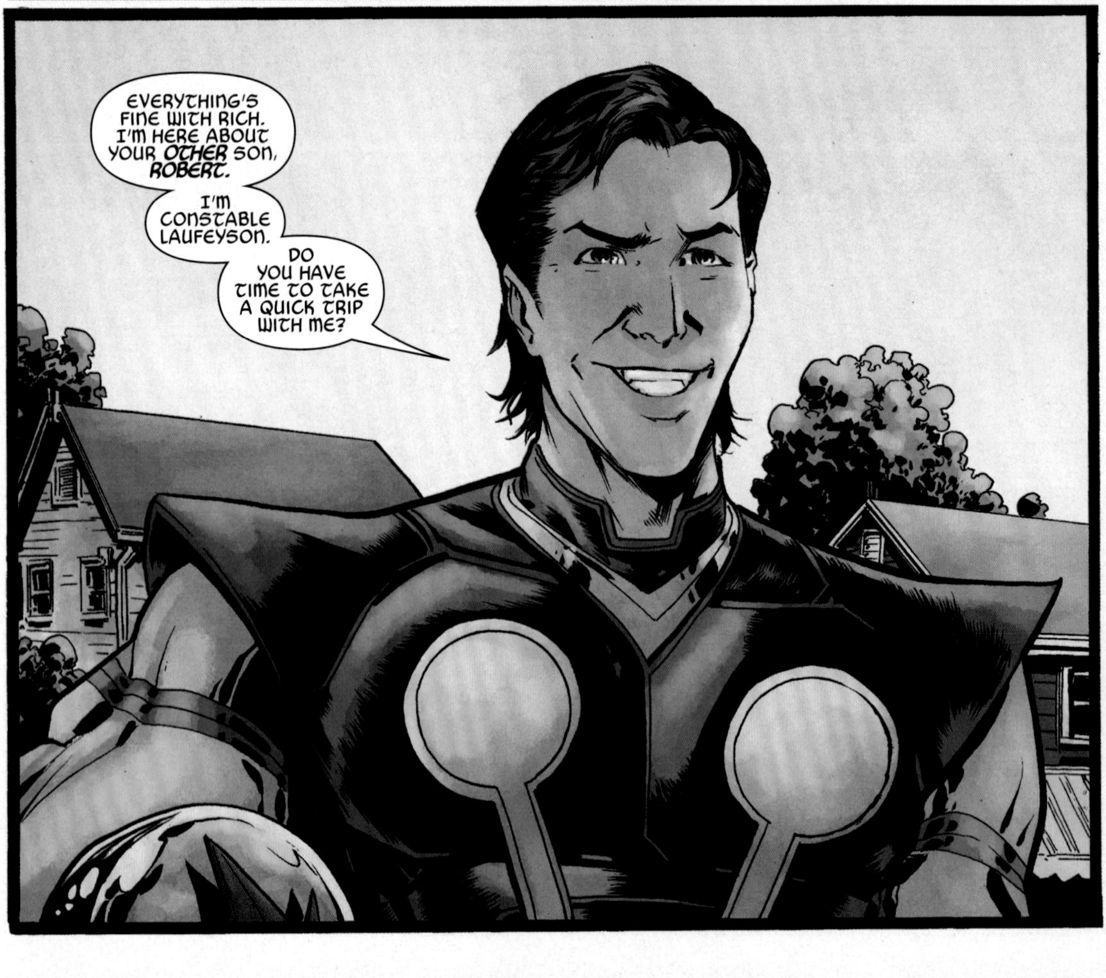
EVERYTHING'S FINE WITH RICH. I'M HERE ABOUT YOUR OTHER SON, ROBERT.
I'M CONSTABLE LAUFEYSON.
DO YOU HAVE TIME TO TAKE A QUICK TRIP WITH ME?

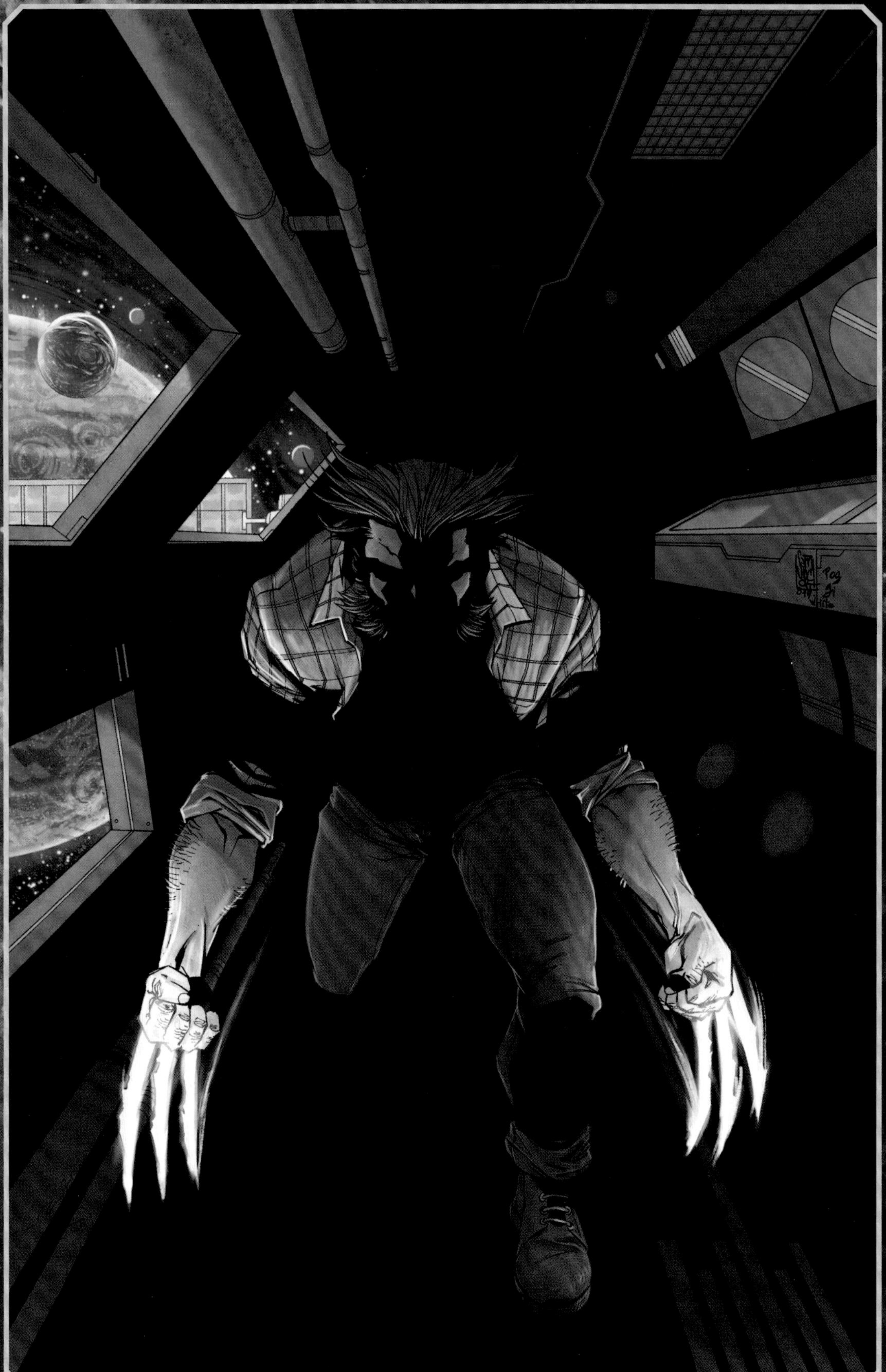

FOUR

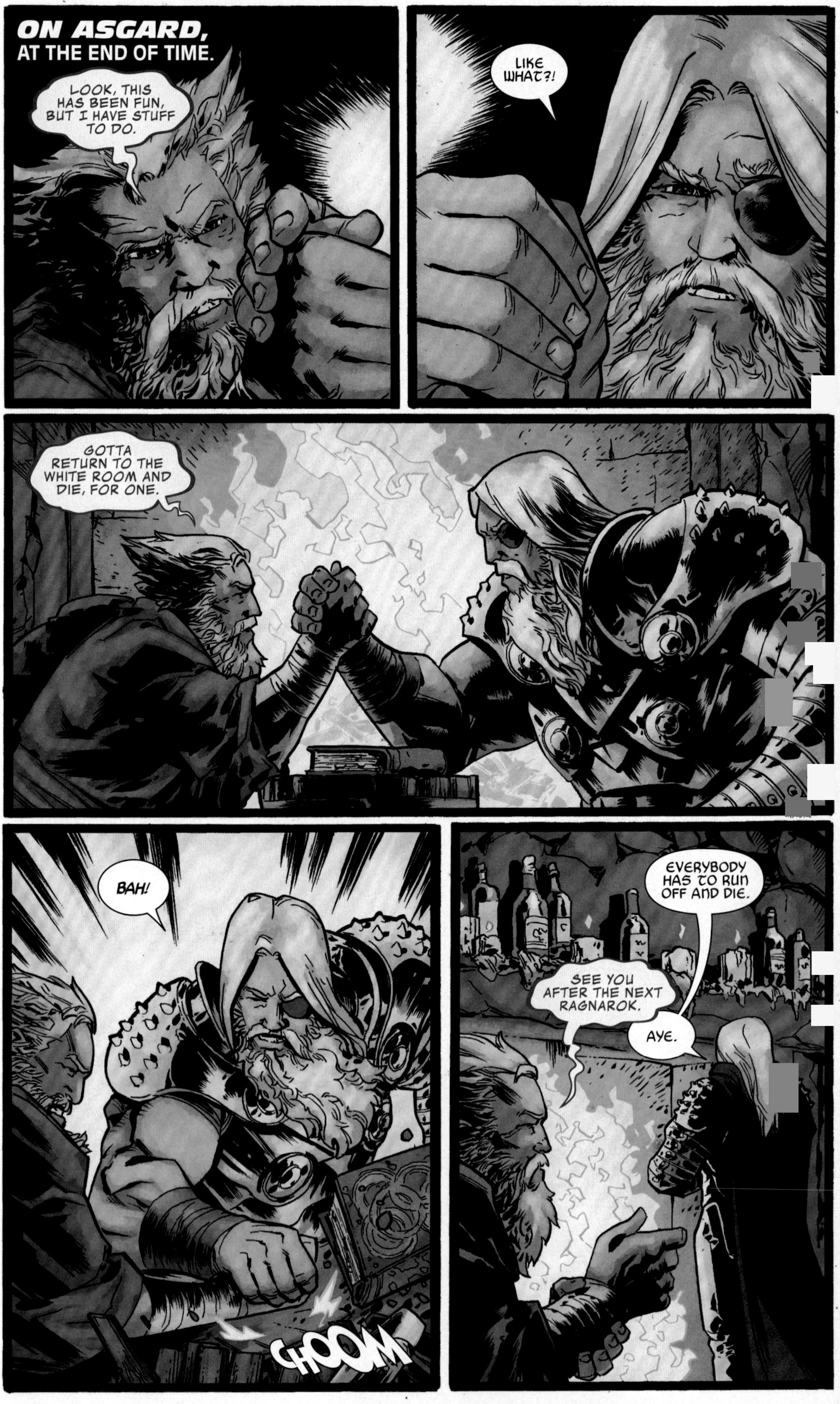
ON ASGARD,
AT THE END OF TIME.
LOOK, THIS HAS BEEN FUN, BUT I HAVE STUFF TO DO.
LIKE WHAT?!
GOTTA RETURN TO THE WHITE ROOM AND DIE, FOR ONE.
BAH!
CHOOM
EVERYBODY HAS TO RUN OFF AND DIE.
SEE YOU AFTER THE NEXT RAGNAROK.
AYE.

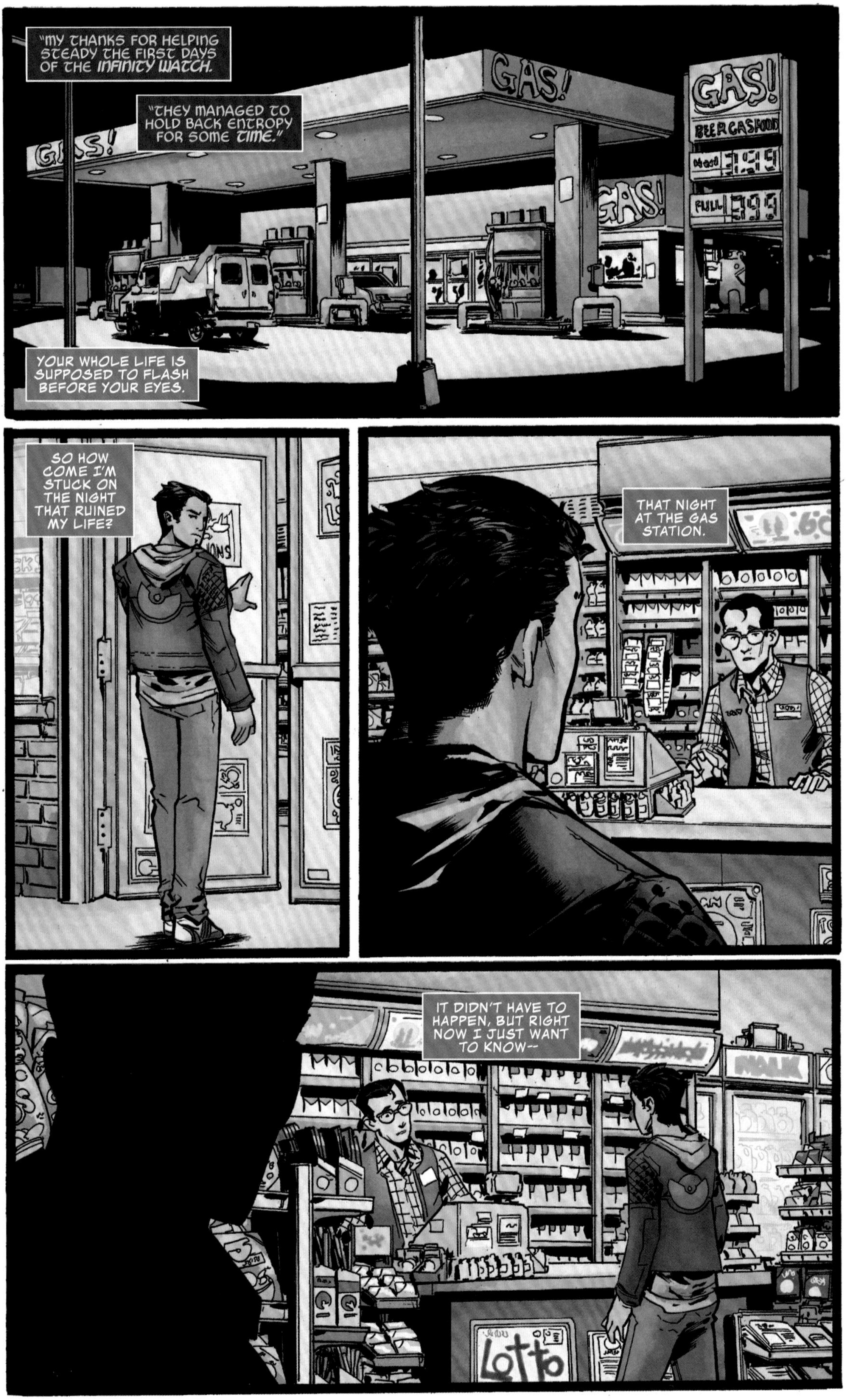
"MY THANKS FOR HELPING STEADY THE FIRST DAYS OF THE INFINITY WATCH.
"THEY MANAGED TO HOLD BACK ENTROPY FOR SOME TIME."
GAS!
GAS!
BEER GAS FOOD
GAS!
YOUR WHOLE LIFE IS SUPPOSED TO FLASH BEFORE YOUR EYES.
SO HOW COME I'M STUCK ON THE NIGHT THAT RUINED MY LIFE?
THAT NIGHT AT THE GAS STATION.
IT DIDN'T HAVE TO HAPPEN, BUT RIGHT NOW I JUST WANT TO KNOW--
MILK
Lotto

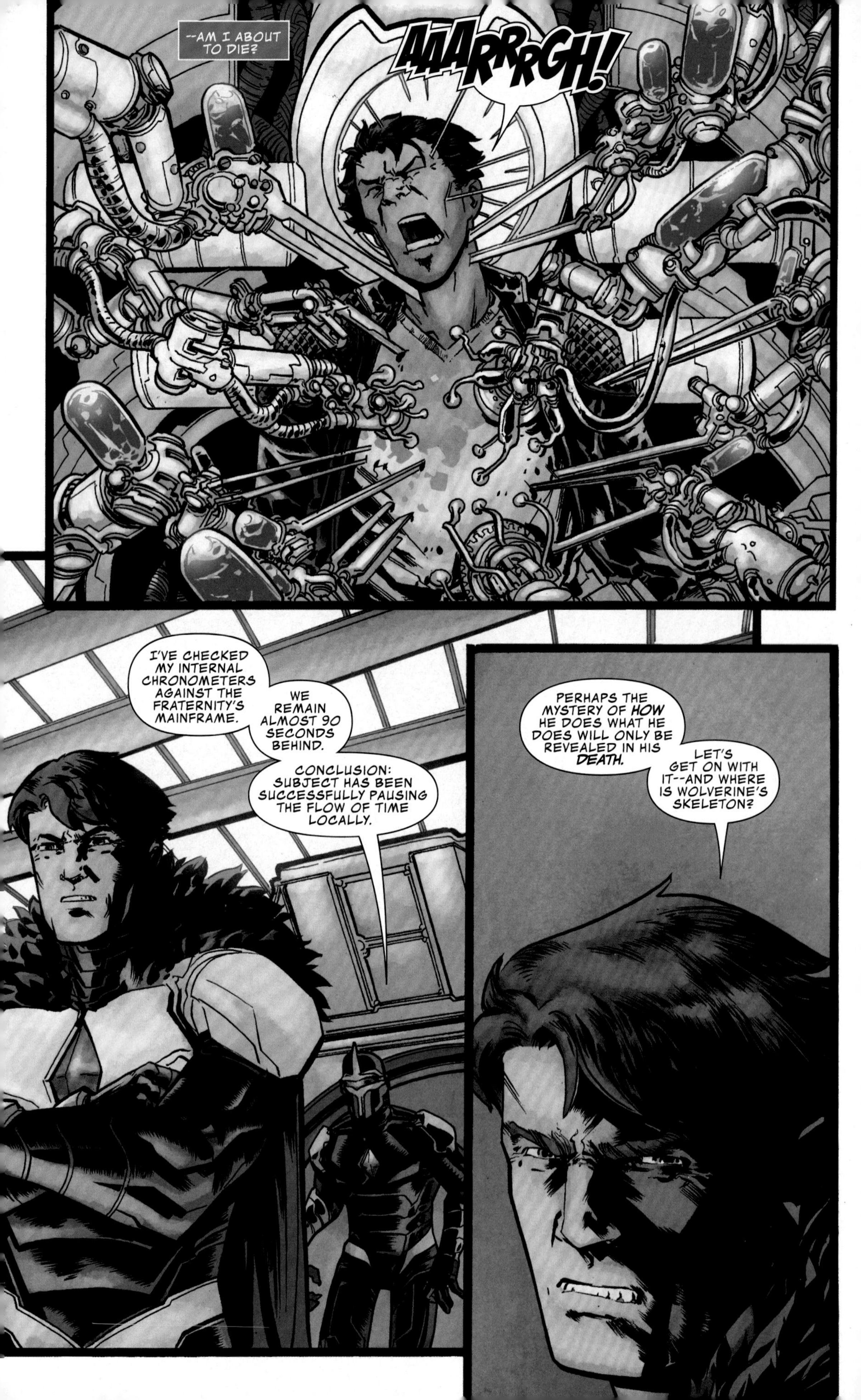
--AM I ABOUT TO DIE?
AAARRRGH!
I'VE CHECKED MY INTERNAL CHRONOMETERS AGAINST THE FRATERNITY'S MAINFRAME.
WE REMAIN ALMOST 90 SECONDS BEHIND.
CONCLUSION: SUBJECT HAS BEEN SUCCESSFULLY PAUSING THE FLOW OF TIME LOCALLY.
PERHAPS THE MYSTERY OF HOW HE DOES WHAT HE DOES WILL ONLY BE REVEALED IN HIS DEATH.
LET'S GET ON WITH IT--AND WHERE IS WOLVERINE'S SKELETON?

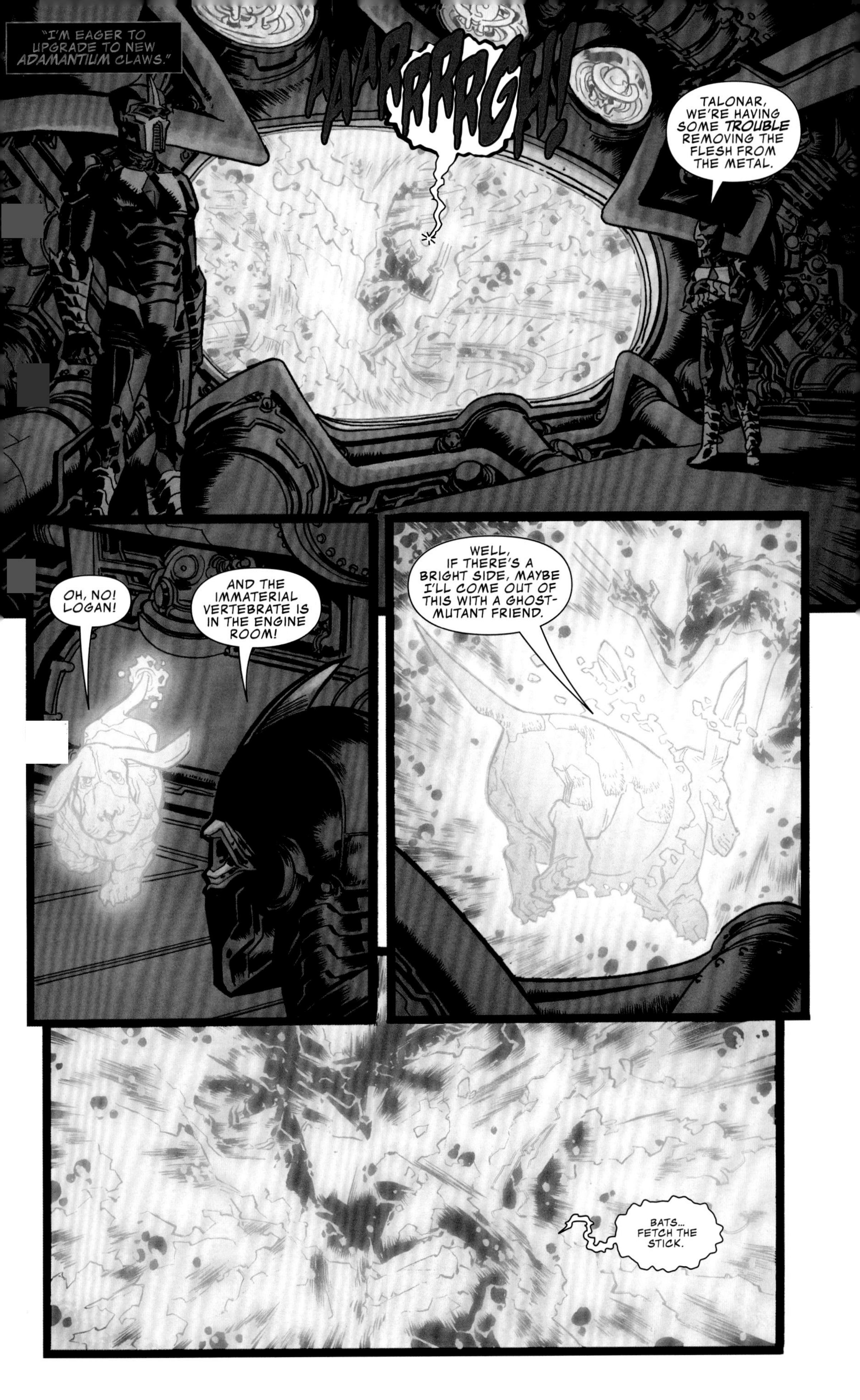
"I'M EAGER TO UPGRADE TO NEW ADAMANTIUM CLAWS."
AAARRRRGH!
TALONAR, WE'RE HAVING SOME TROUBLE REMOVING THE FLESH FROM THE METAL.
OH, NO! LOGAN!
AND THE IMMATERIAL VERTEBRATE IS IN THE ENGINE ROOM!
WELL, IF THERE'S A BRIGHT SIDE, MAYBE I'LL COME OUT OF THIS WITH A GHOST-MUTANT FRIEND.
BATS... FETCH THE STICK.

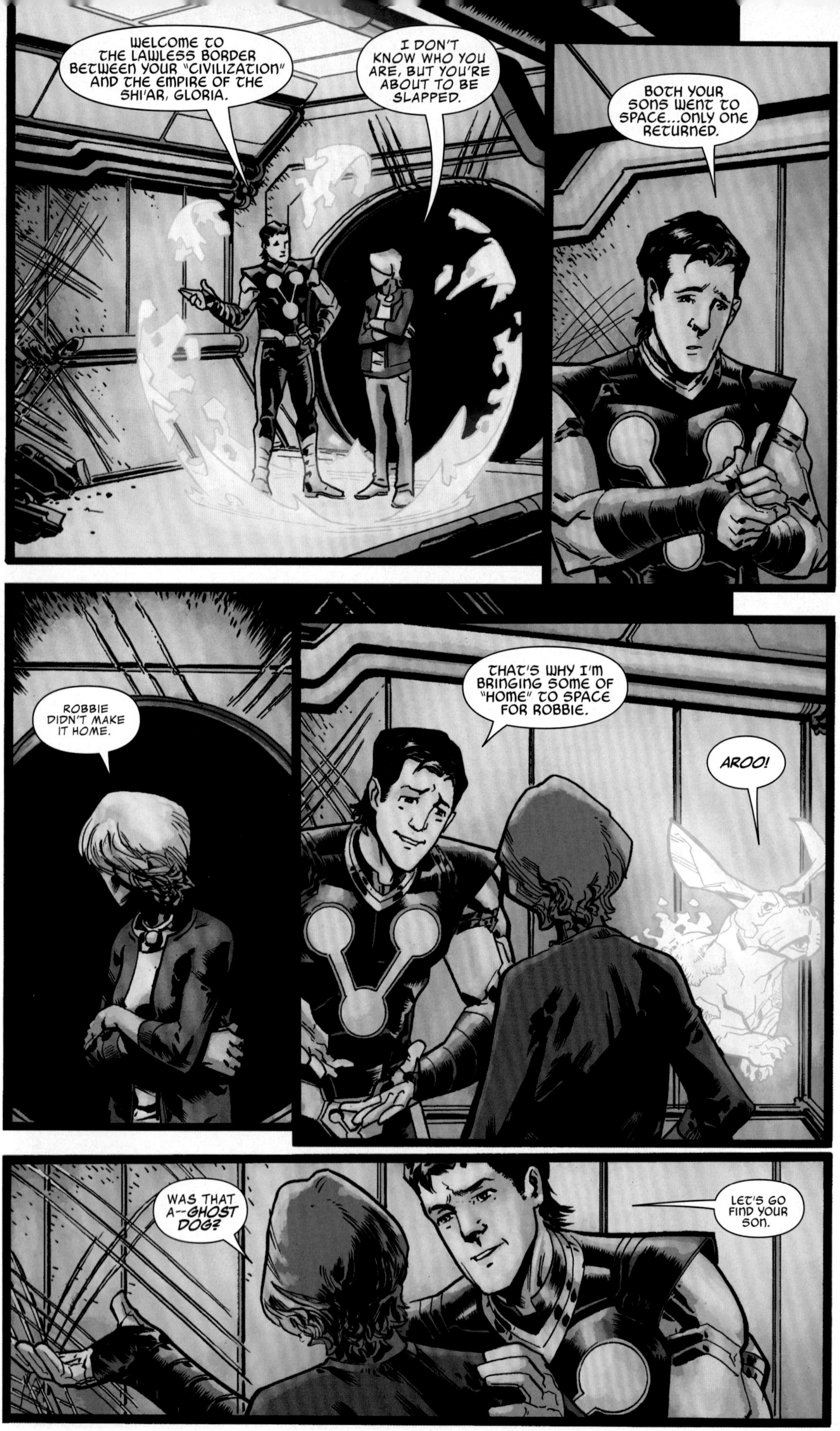

WELCOME TO THE LAWLESS BORDER BETWEEN YOUR "CIVILIZATION" AND THE EMPIRE OF THE SHI'AR, GLORIA.
I DON'T KNOW WHO YOU ARE, BUT YOU'RE ABOUT TO BE SLAPPED.
BOTH YOUR SONS WENT TO SPACE...ONLY ONE RETURNED.
ROBBIE DIDN'T MAKE IT HOME.
THAT'S WHY I'M BRINGING SOME OF "HOME" TO SPACE FOR ROBBIE.
AROO!
WAS THAT A--GHOST DOG?
LET'S GO FIND YOUR SON.

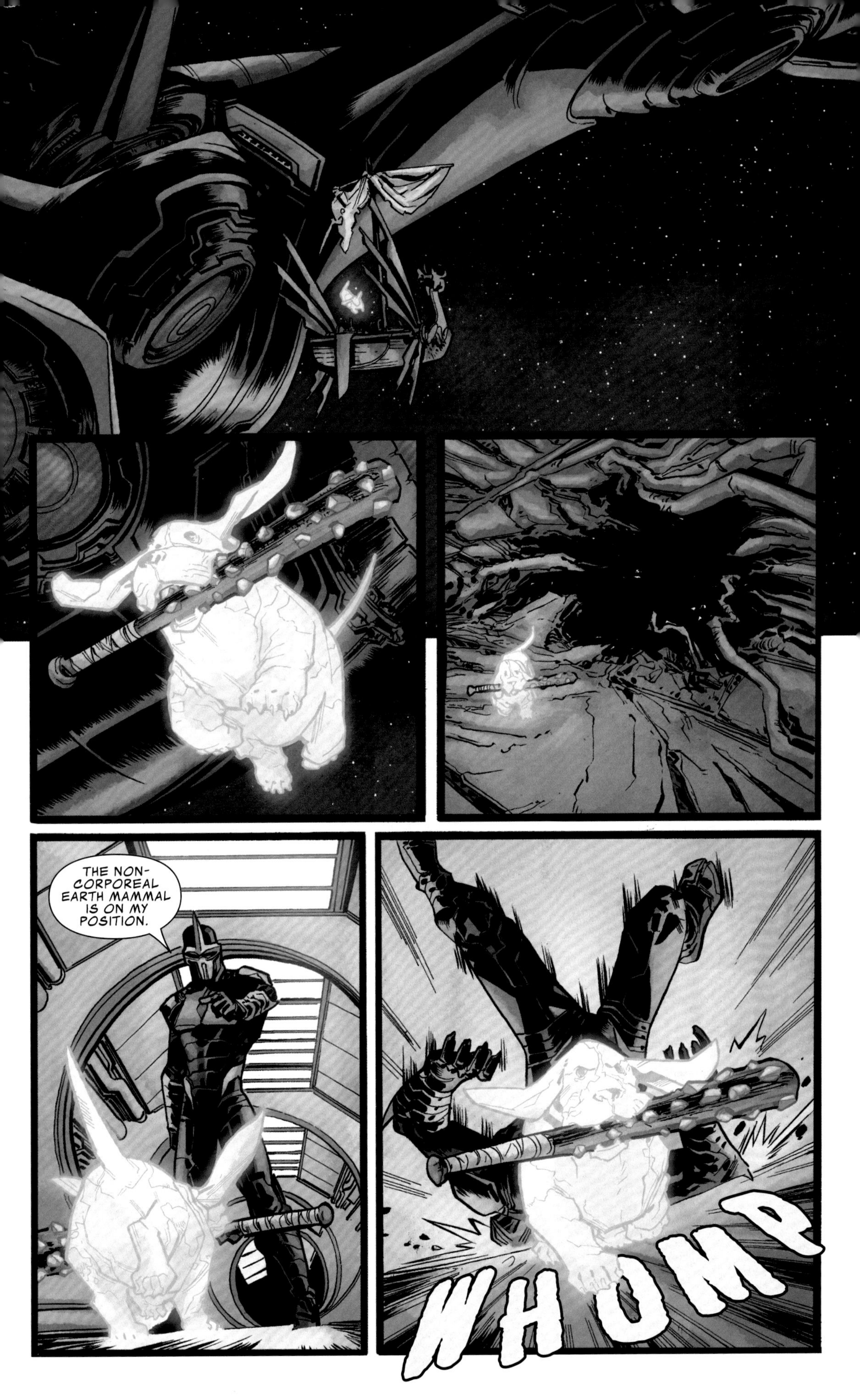
THE NON-CORPOREAL EARTH MAMMAL IS ON MY POSITION.
WHOMP

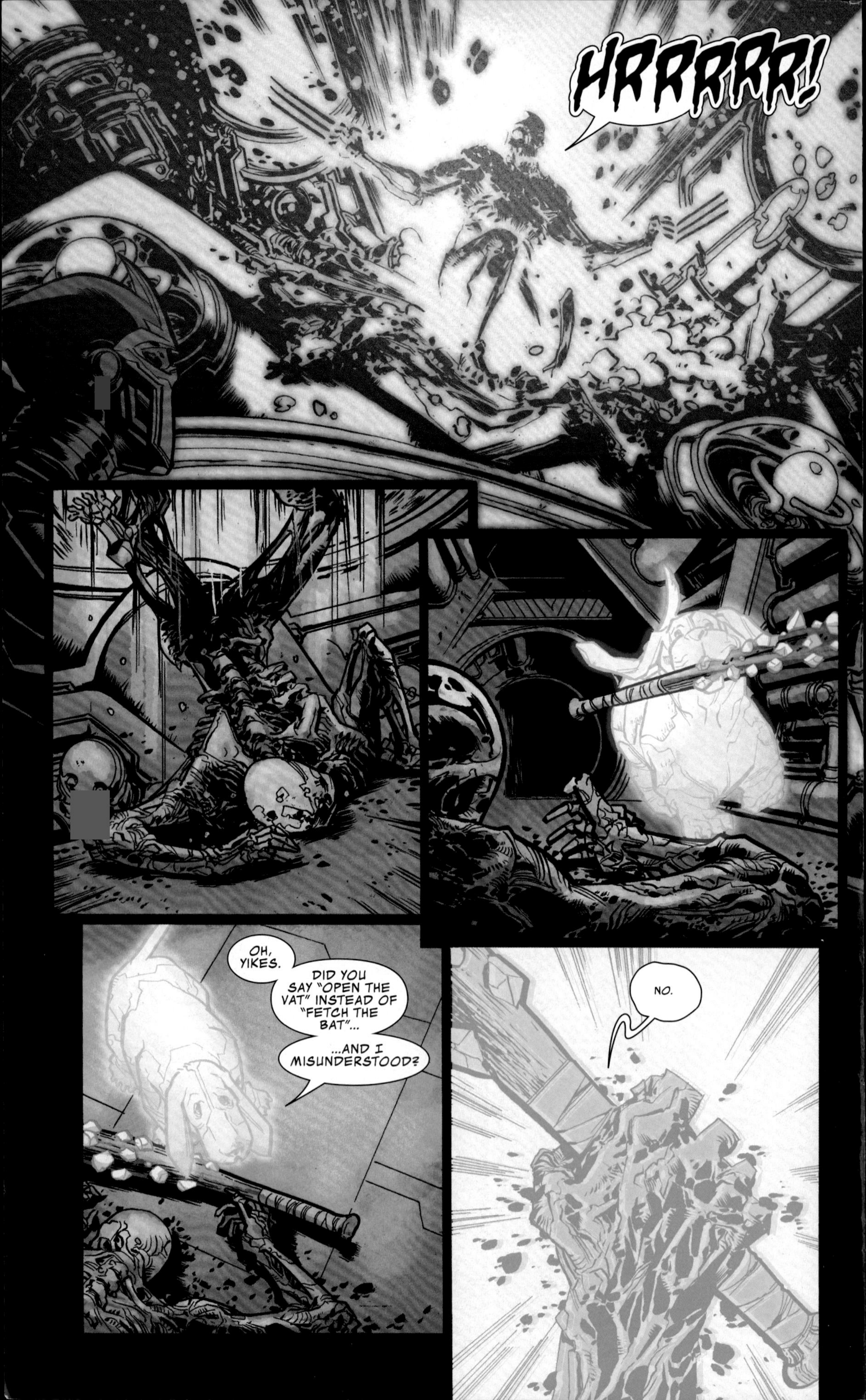
HRRRRR!
OH, YIKES.
DID YOU SAY "OPEN THE VAT" INSTEAD OF "FETCH THE BAT"...
...AND I MISUNDERSTOOD?
NO.

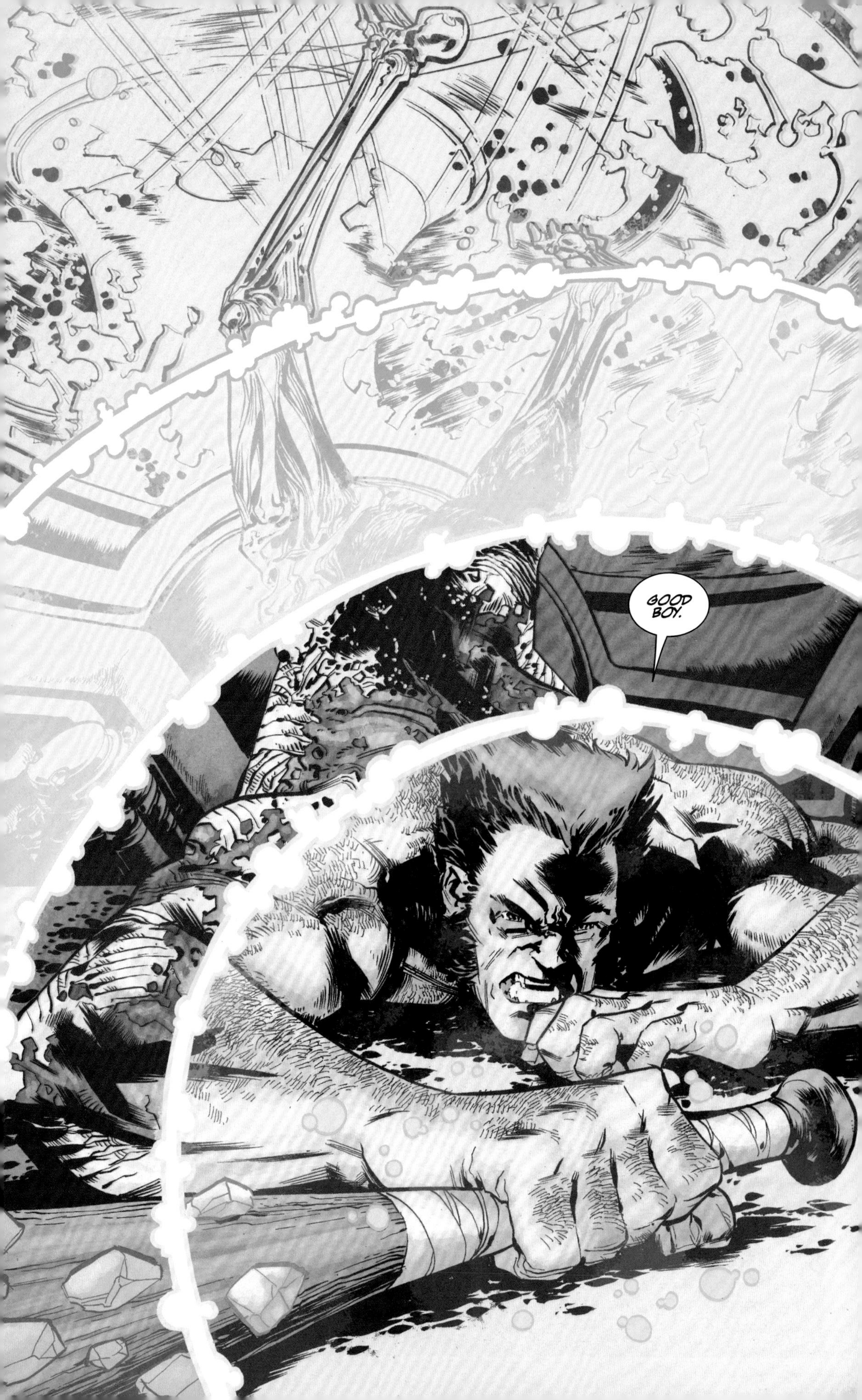
GOOD BOY.

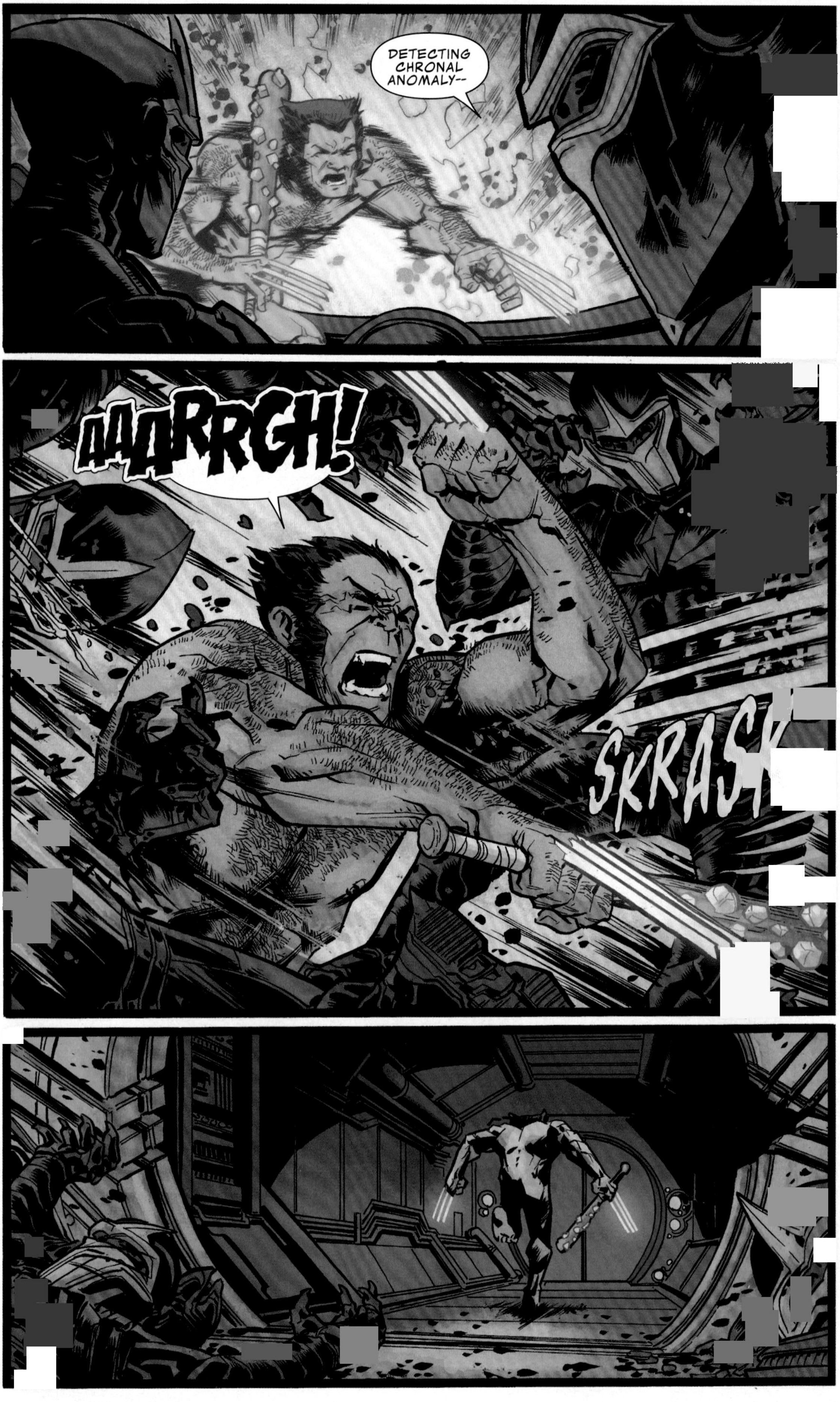
DETECTING CHRONAL ANOMALY--
AAARRRGH!
SKRASK

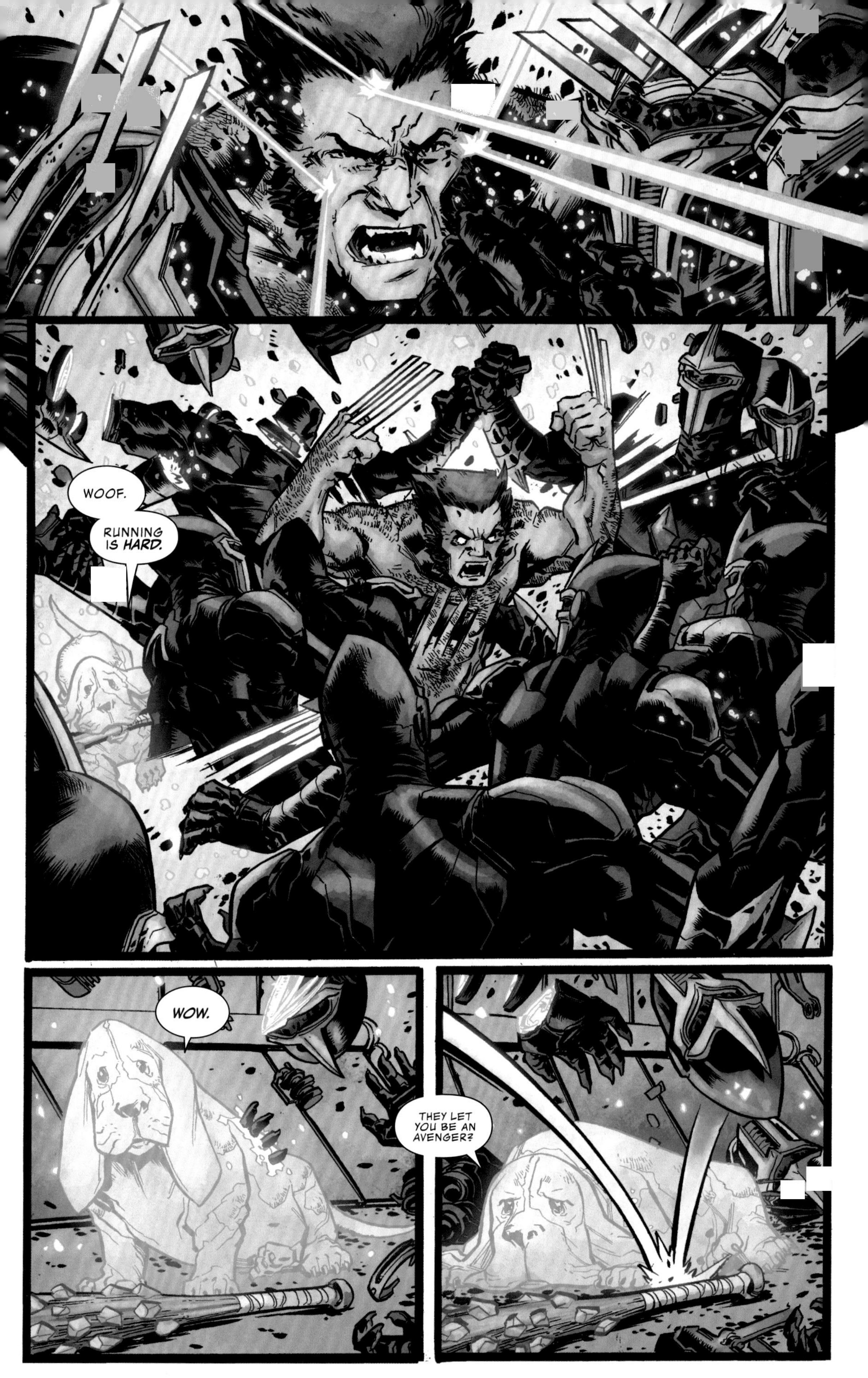
WOOF.
RUNNING IS HARD.
WOW.
THEY LET YOU BE AN AVENGER?

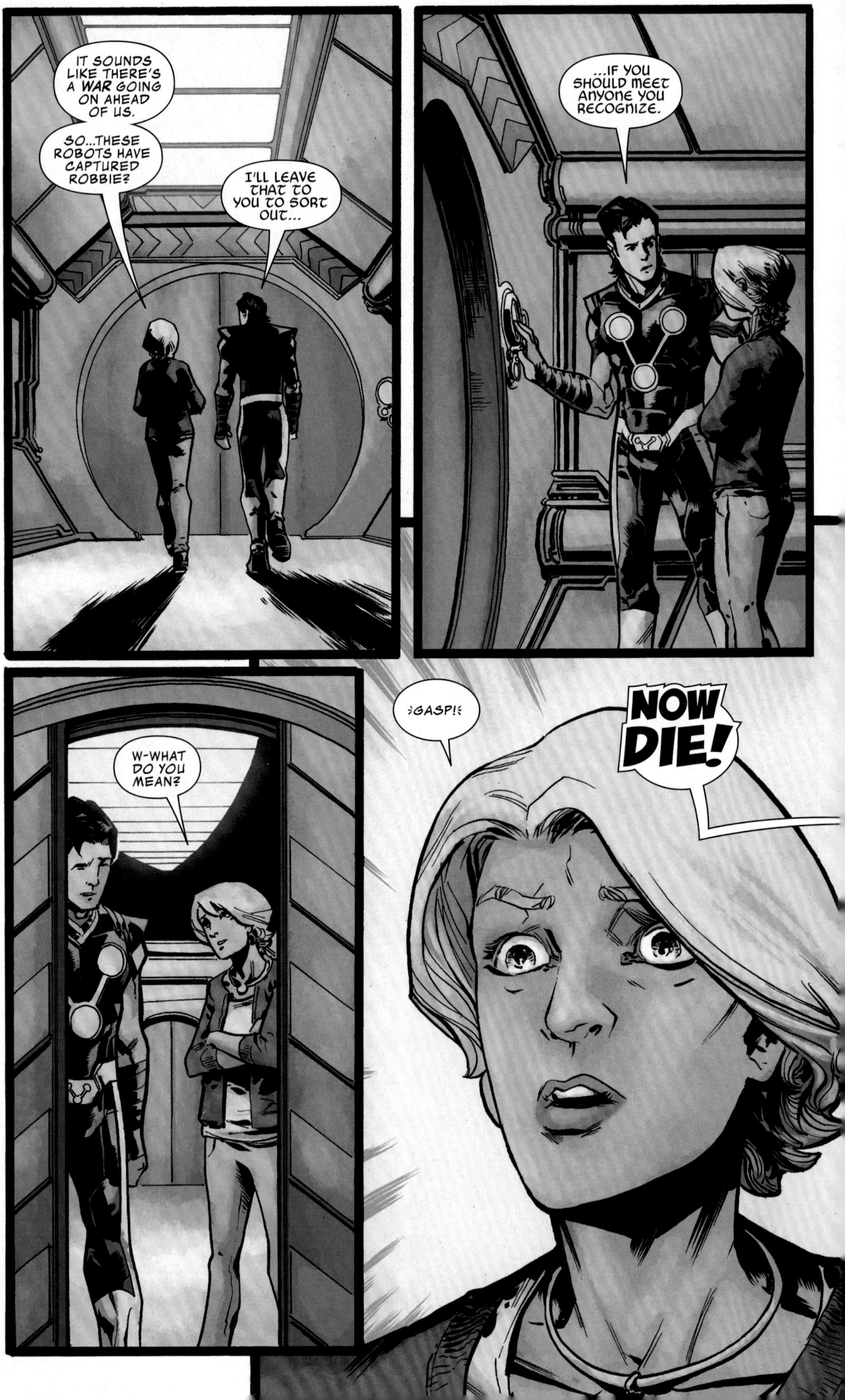
IT SOUNDS LIKE THERE'S A WAR GOING ON AHEAD OF US.
SO...THESE ROBOTS HAVE CAPTURED ROBBIE?
I'LL LEAVE THAT TO YOU TO SORT OUT...
...IF YOU SHOULD MEET ANYONE YOU RECOGNIZE.
W-WHAT DO YOU MEAN?
GASP!
NOW DIE!

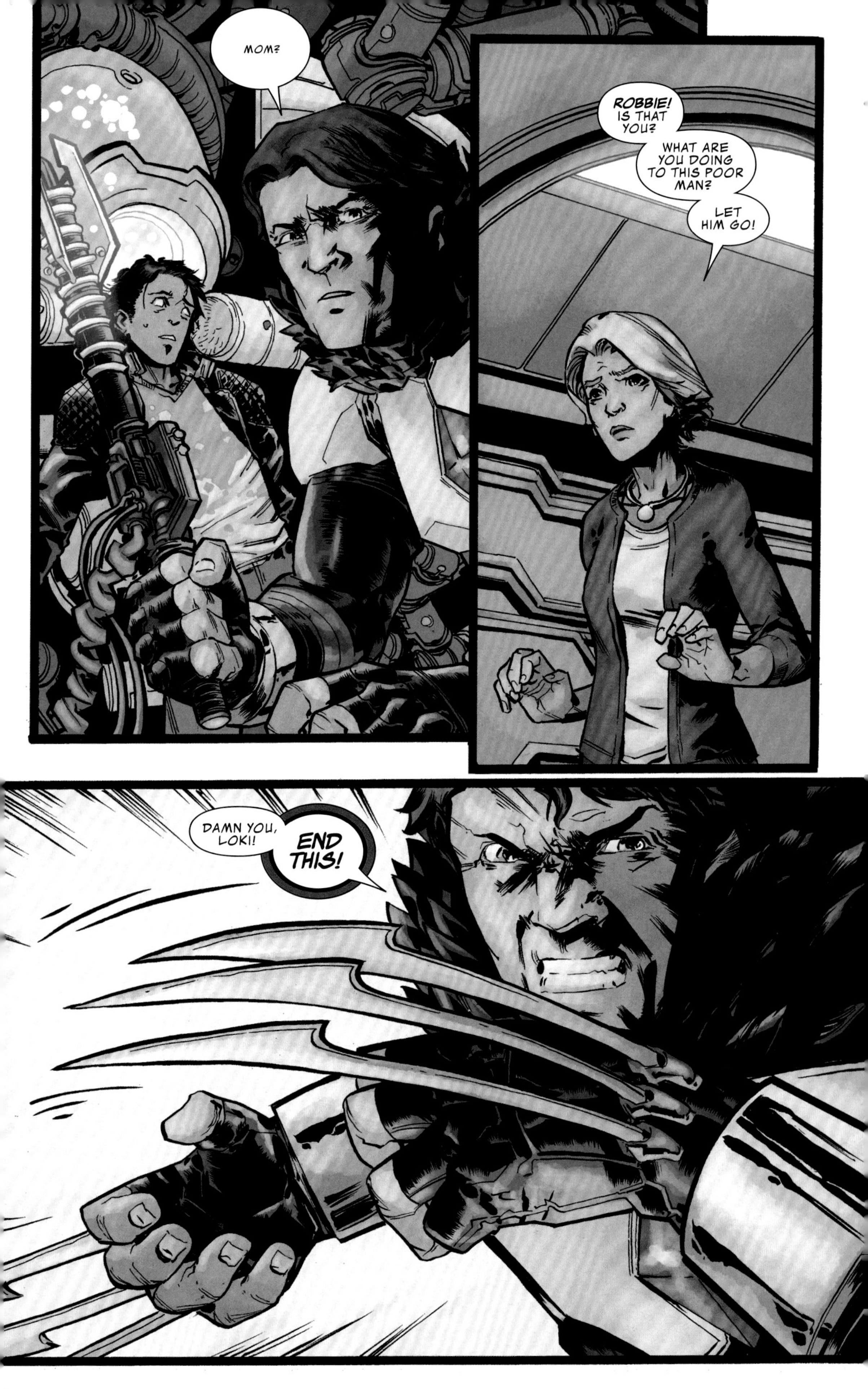
MOM?
ROBBIE! IS THAT YOU?
WHAT ARE YOU DOING TO THIS POOR MAN?
LET HIM GO!
DAMN YOU, LOKI!
END THIS!

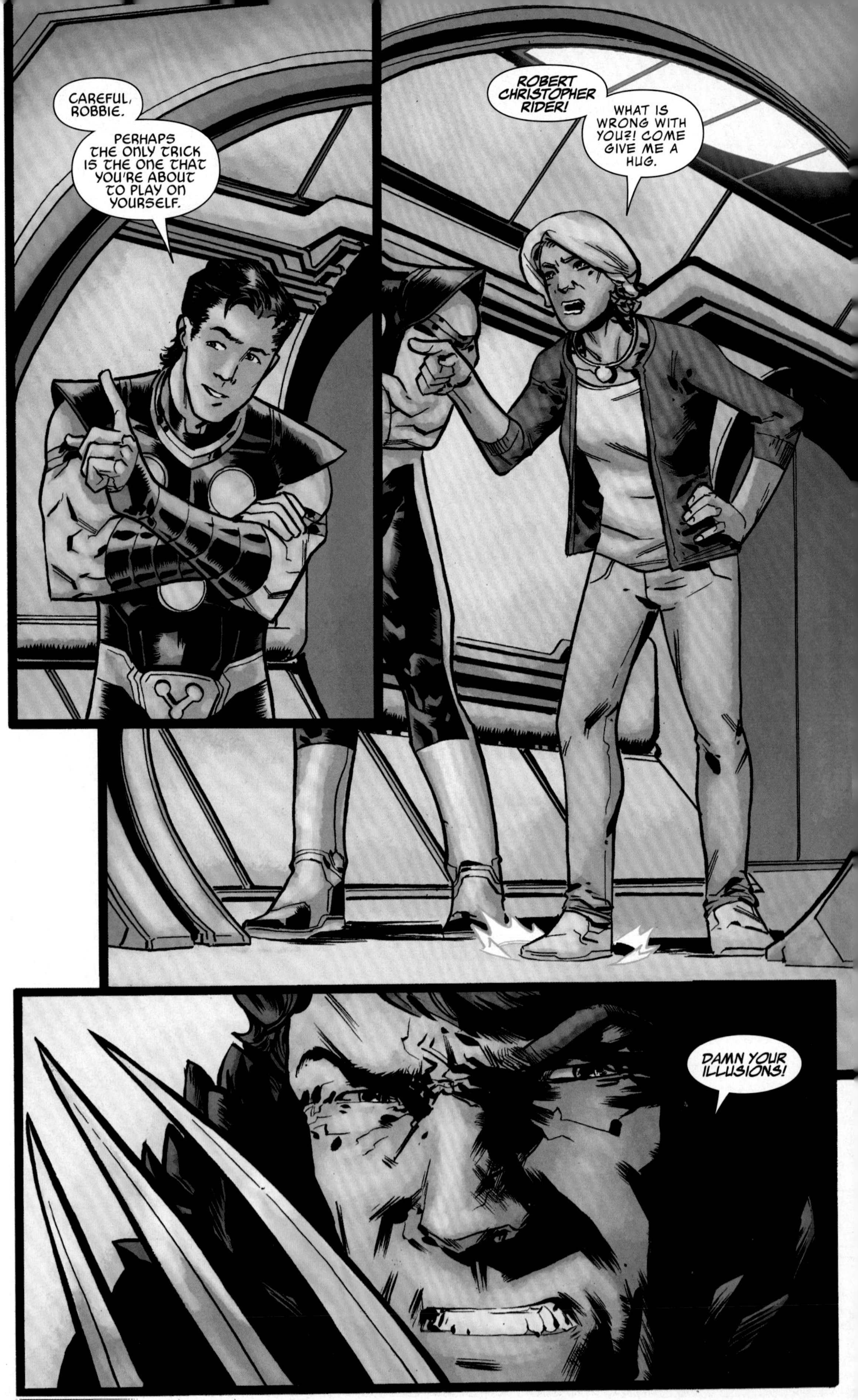
CAREFUL, ROBBIE.
PERHAPS THE ONLY TRICK IS THE ONE THAT YOU'RE ABOUT TO PLAY ON YOURSELF.
ROBERT CHRISTOPHER RIDER!
WHAT IS WRONG WITH YOU?! COME GIVE ME A HUG.
DAMN YOUR ILLUSIONS!

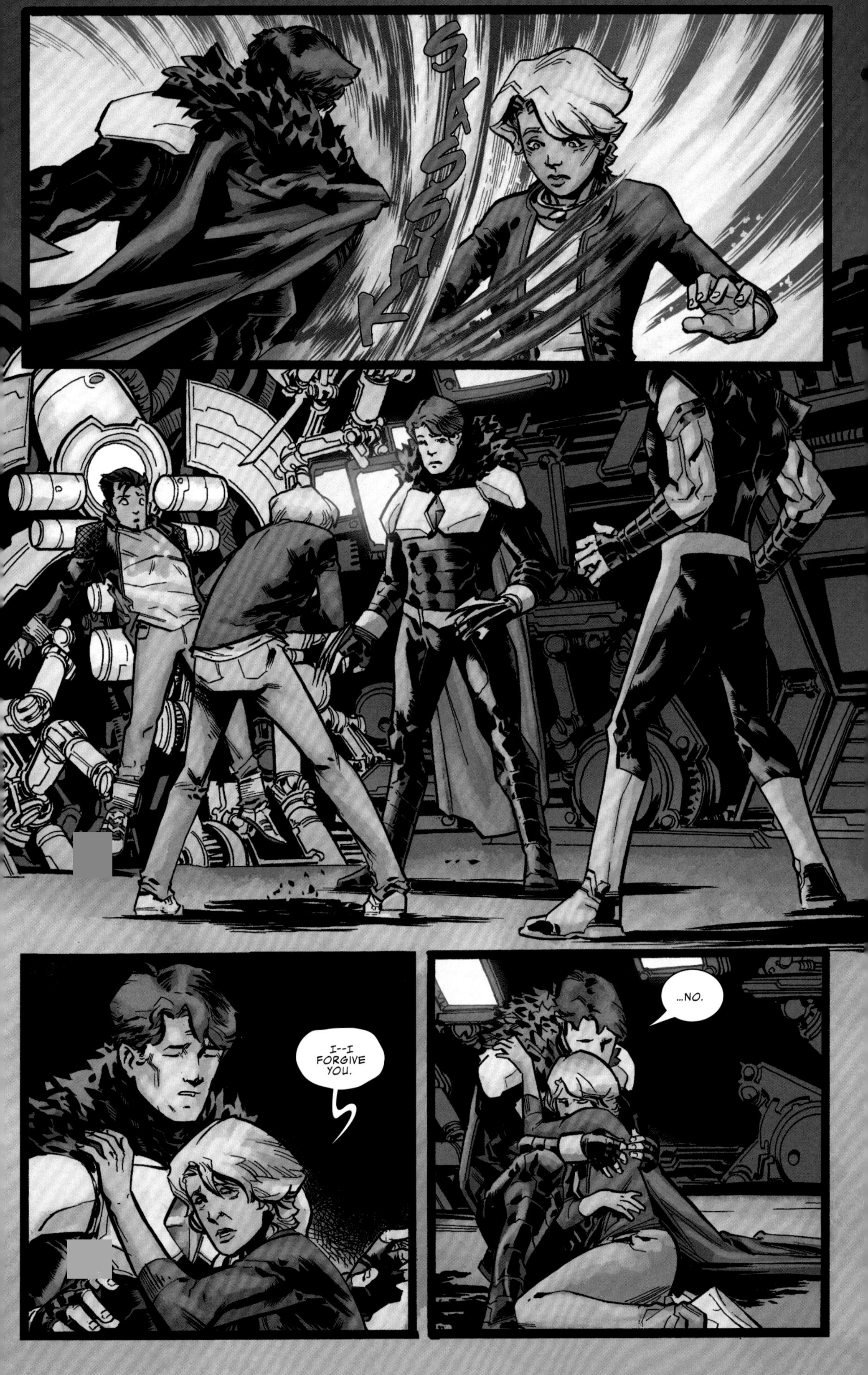
SHASHK
I--I FORGIVE YOU.
...NO.

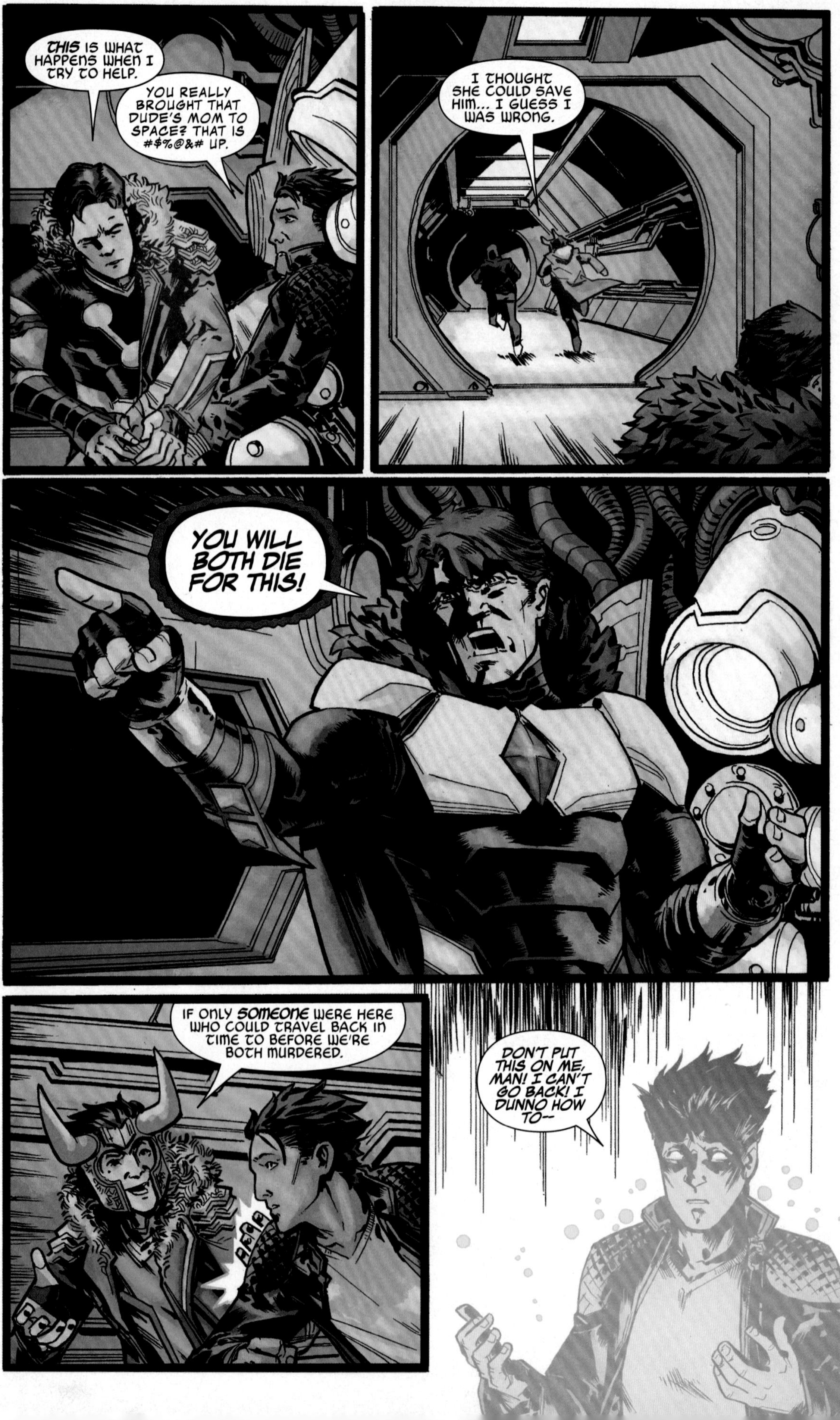
THIS IS WHAT HAPPENS WHEN I TRY TO HELP.
YOU REALLY BROUGHT THAT DUDE'S MOM TO SPACE? THAT IS #$%@&# UP.
I THOUGHT SHE COULD SAVE HIM... I GUESS I WAS WRONG.
YOU WILL BOTH DIE FOR THIS!
IF ONLY SOMEONE WERE HERE WHO COULD TRAVEL BACK IN TIME TO BEFORE WE'RE BOTH MURDERED.
DON'T PUT THIS ON ME, MAN! I CAN'T GO BACK! I DUNNO HOW TO--

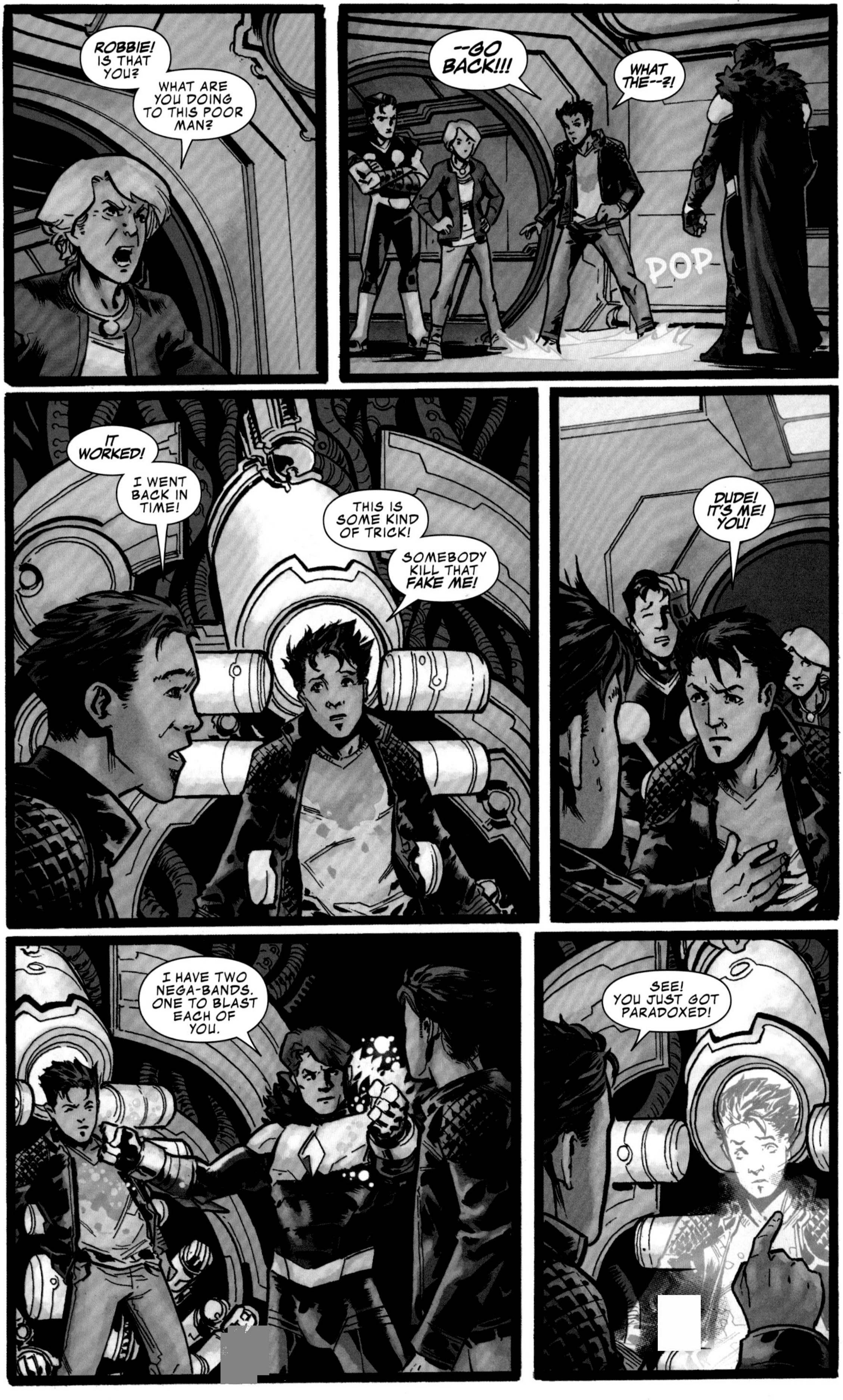
ROBBIE! IS THAT YOU?
WHAT ARE YOU DOING TO THIS POOR MAN?
--GO BACK!!!
WHAT THE--?!
POP
IT WORKED!
I WENT BACK IN TIME!
THIS IS SOME KIND OF TRICK!
SOMEBODY KILL THAT FAKE ME!
DUDE! IT'S ME! YOU!
I HAVE TWO NEGA-BANDS. ONE TO BLAST EACH OF YOU.
SEE! YOU JUST GOT PARADOXED!

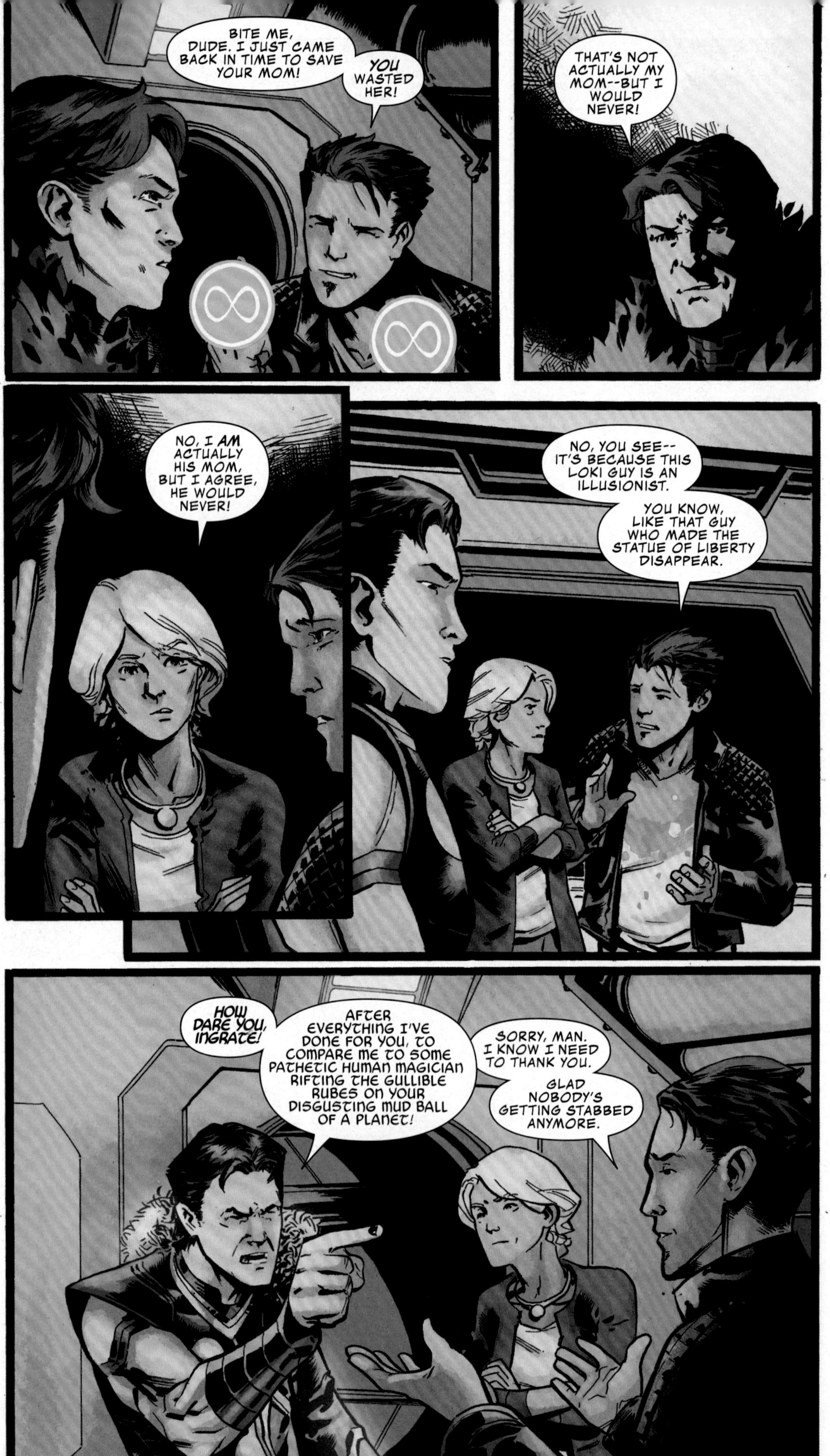
BITE ME, DUDE. I JUST CAME BACK IN TIME TO SAVE YOUR MOM!
YOU WASTED HER!
THAT'S NOT ACTUALLY MY MOM--BUT I WOULD NEVER!
NO, I AM ACTUALLY HIS MOM, BUT I AGREE, HE WOULD NEVER!
NO, YOU SEE-- IT'S BECAUSE THIS LOKI GUY IS AN ILLUSIONIST.
YOU KNOW, LIKE THAT GUY WHO MADE THE STATUE OF LIBERTY DISAPPEAR.
HOW DARE YOU, INGRATE!
AFTER EVERYTHING I'VE DONE FOR YOU, TO COMPARE ME TO SOME PATHETIC HUMAN MAGICIAN RIFTING THE GULLIBLE RUBES ON YOUR DISGUSTING MUD BALL OF A PLANET!
SORRY, MAN. I KNOW I NEED TO THANK YOU.
GLAD NOBODY'S GETTING STABBED ANYMORE.

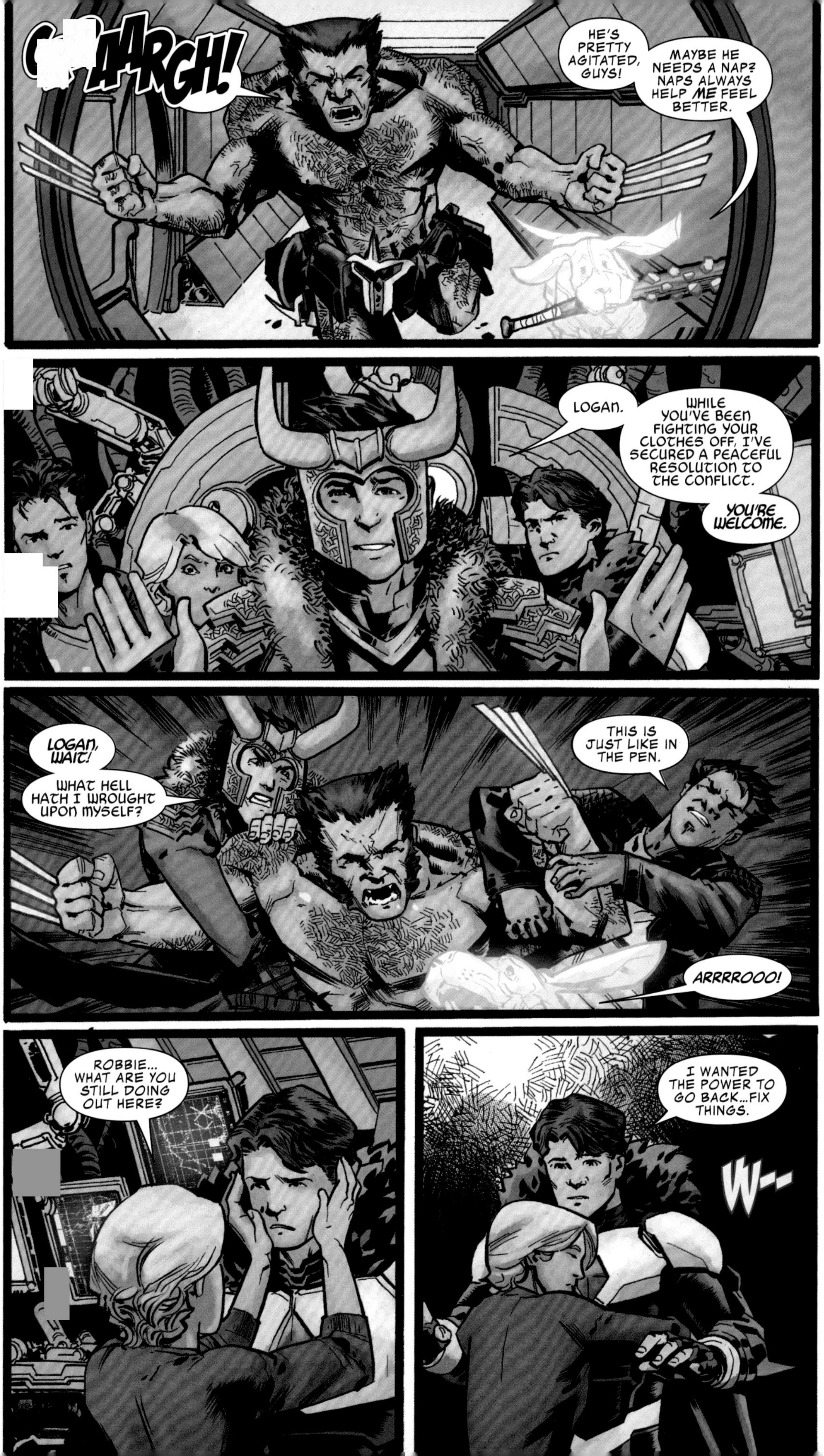
AARGH!
HE'S PRETTY AGITATED, GUYS!
MAYBE HE NEEDS A NAP? NAPS ALWAYS HELP ME FEEL BETTER.
LOGAN.
WHILE YOU'VE BEEN FIGHTING YOUR CLOTHES OFF, I'VE SECURED A PEACEFUL RESOLUTION TO THE CONFLICT.
YOU'RE WELCOME.
LOGAN, WAIT!
WHAT HELL HATH I WROUGHT UPON MYSELF?
THIS IS JUST LIKE IN THE PEN.
ARRRROOO!
ROBBIE... WHAT ARE YOU STILL DOING OUT HERE?
I WANTED THE POWER TO GO BACK...FIX THINGS.
W--

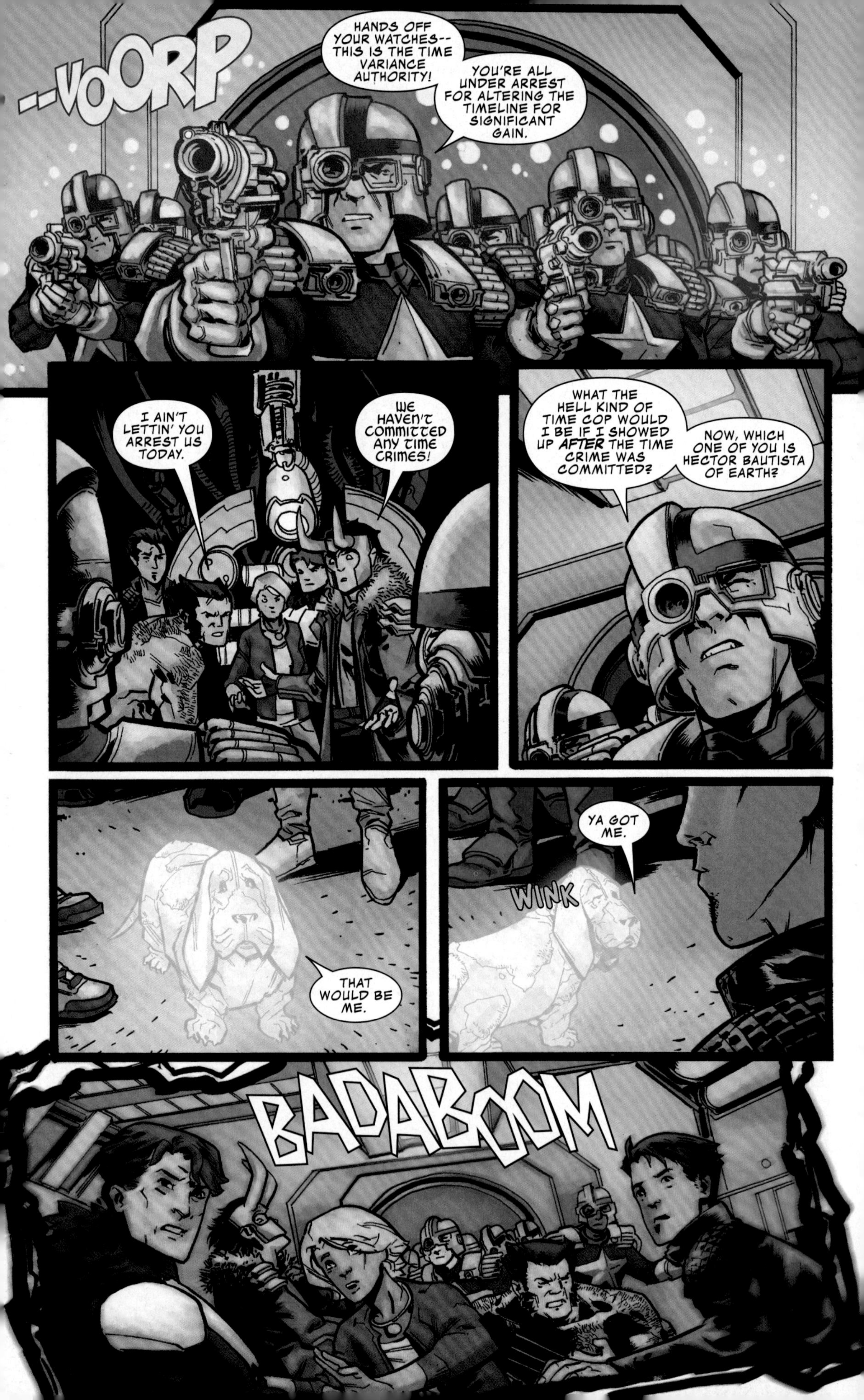
--VOORP
HANDS OFF YOUR WATCHES-- THIS IS THE TIME VARIANCE AUTHORITY!
YOU'RE ALL UNDER ARREST FOR ALTERING THE TIMELINE FOR SIGNIFICANT GAIN.
I AIN'T LETTIN' YOU ARREST US TODAY.
WE HAVEN'T COMMITTED ANY TIME CRIMES!
WHAT THE HELL KIND OF TIME COP WOULD I BE IF I SHOWED UP AFTER THE TIME CRIME WAS COMMITTED?
NOW, WHICH ONE OF YOU IS HECTOR BAUTISTA OF EARTH?
THAT WOULD BE ME.
WINK
YA GOT ME.
BADABOOM

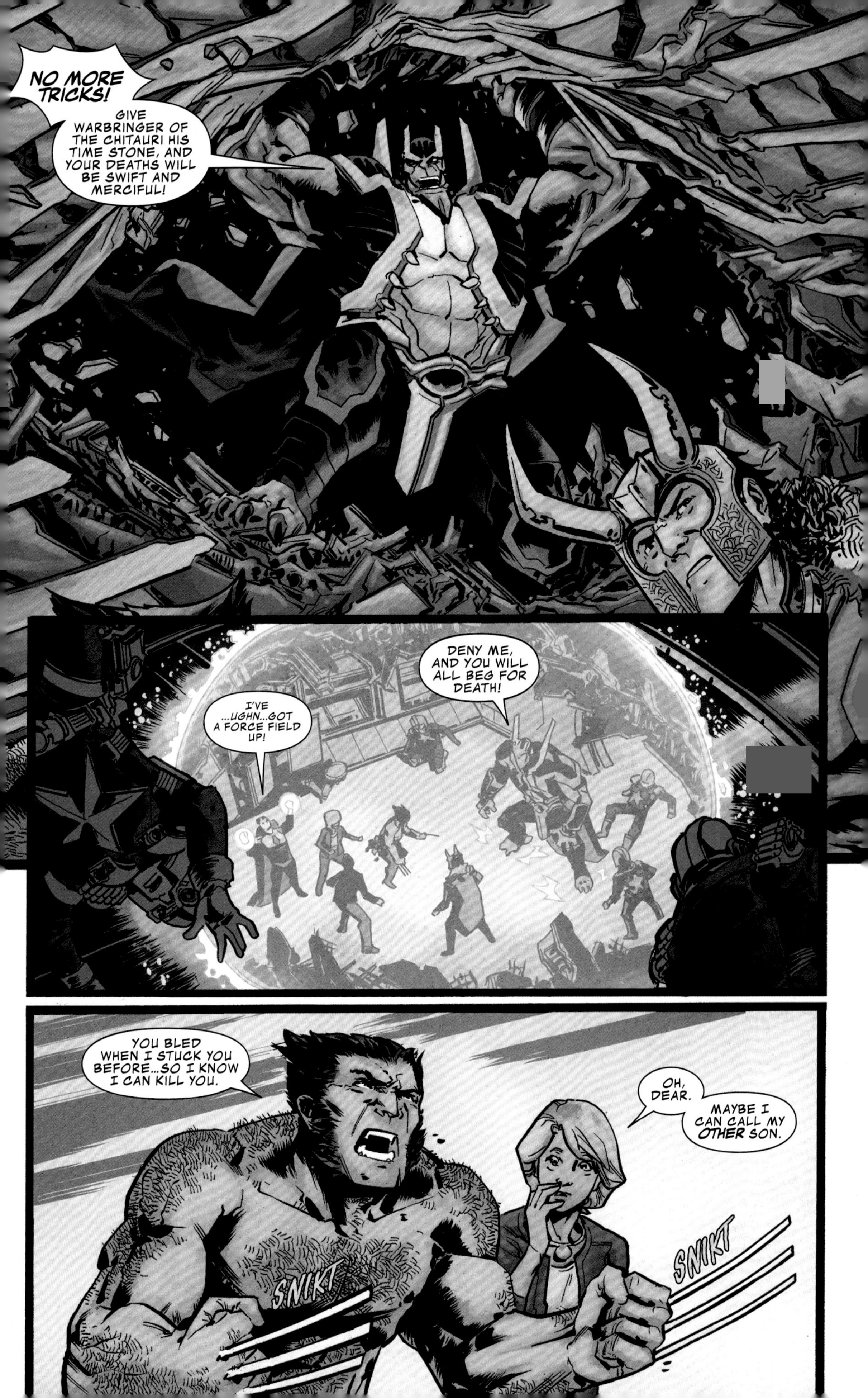
NO MORE TRICKS!
GIVE WARBRINGER OF THE CHITAURI HIS TIME STONE, AND YOUR DEATHS WILL BE SWIFT AND MERCIFUL!
DENY ME, AND YOU WILL ALL BEG FOR DEATH!
I'VE ...UGHN...GOT A FORCE FIELD UP!
YOU BLED WHEN I STUCK YOU BEFORE...SO I KNOW I CAN KILL YOU.
OH, DEAR.
MAYBE I CAN CALL MY OTHER SON.
SNIKT
SNIKT

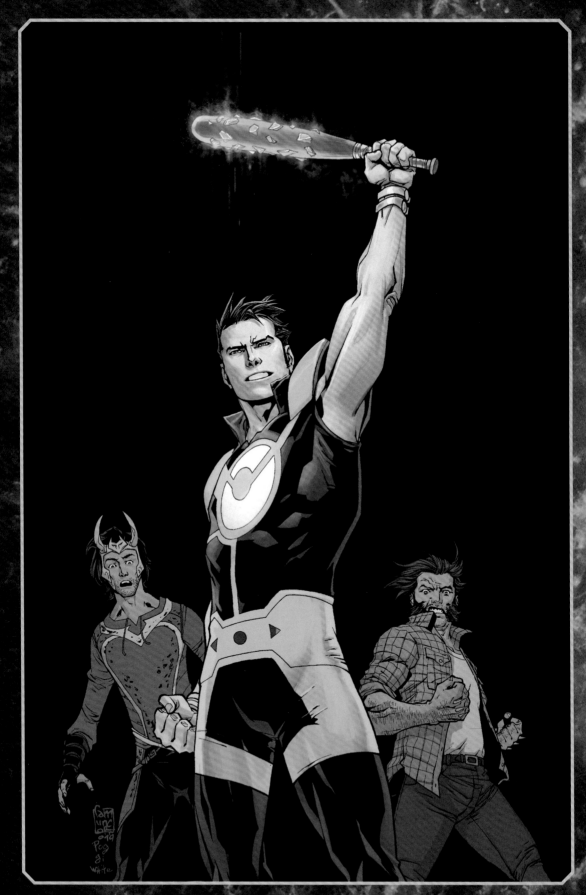

FIVE

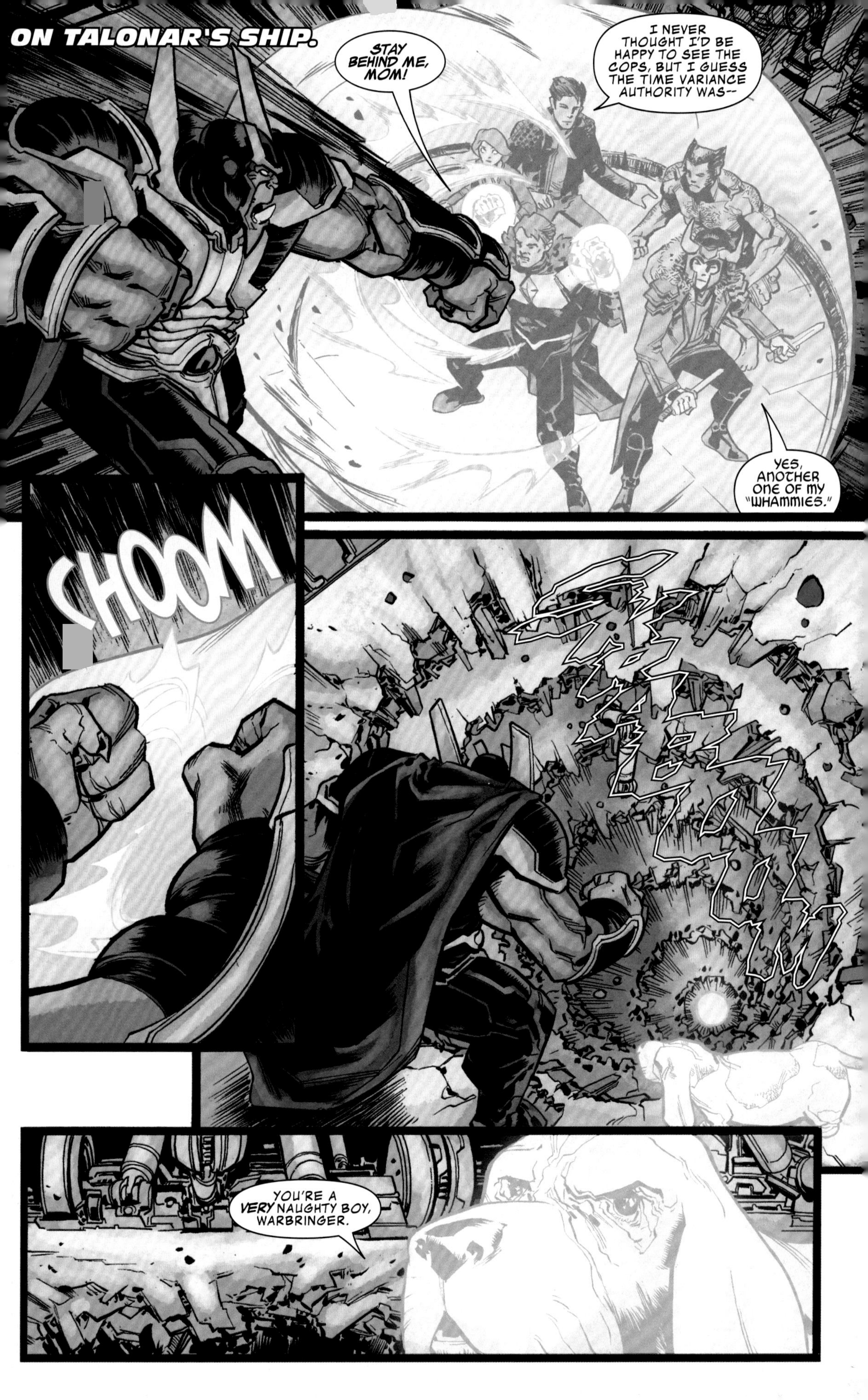
ON TALONAR'S SHIP.
STAY BEHIND ME, MOM!
I NEVER THOUGHT I'D BE HAPPY TO SEE THE COPS, BUT I GUESS THE TIME VARIANCE AUTHORITY WAS--
YES, ANOTHER ONE OF MY "WHAMMIES."
CHOOM
YOU'RE A VERY NAUGHTY BOY, WARBRINGER.

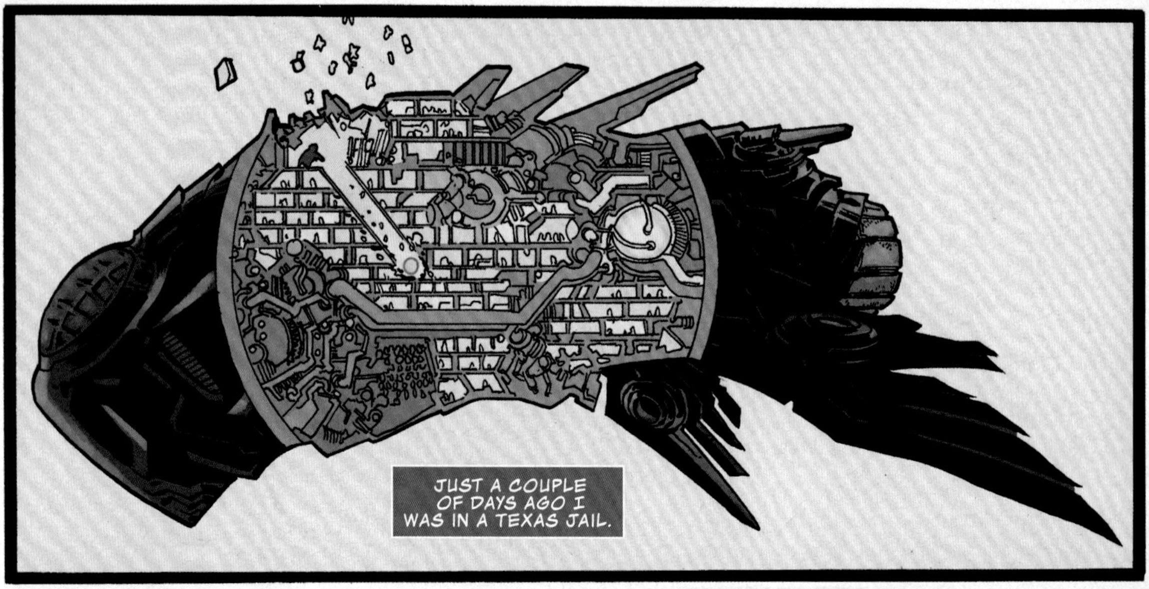
JUST A COUPLE OF DAYS AGO I WAS IN A TEXAS JAIL.

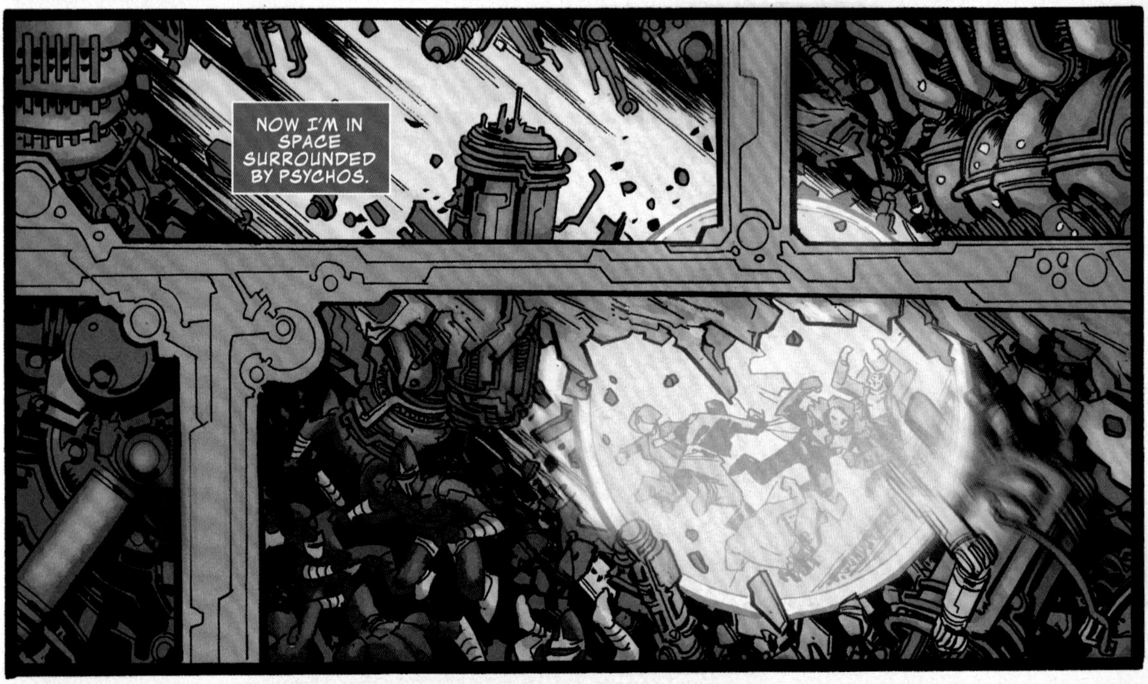
NOW I'M IN SPACE SURROUNDED BY PSYCHOS.

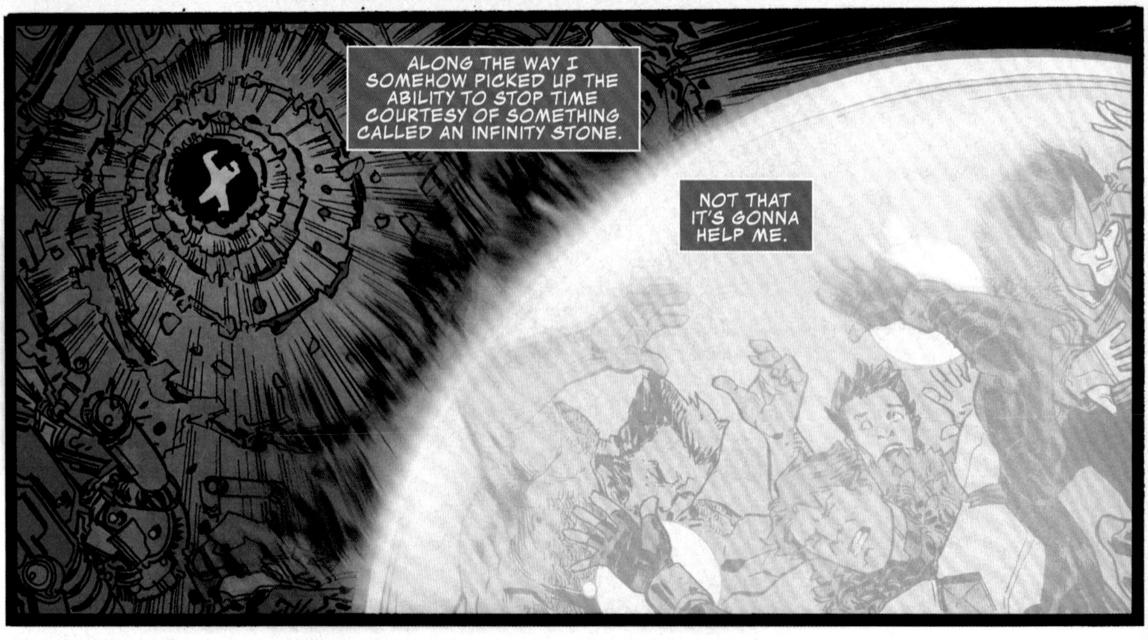
ALONG THE WAY I SOMEHOW PICKED UP THE ABILITY TO STOP TIME COURTESY OF SOMETHING CALLED AN INFINITY STONE.
NOT THAT IT'S GONNA HELP ME.

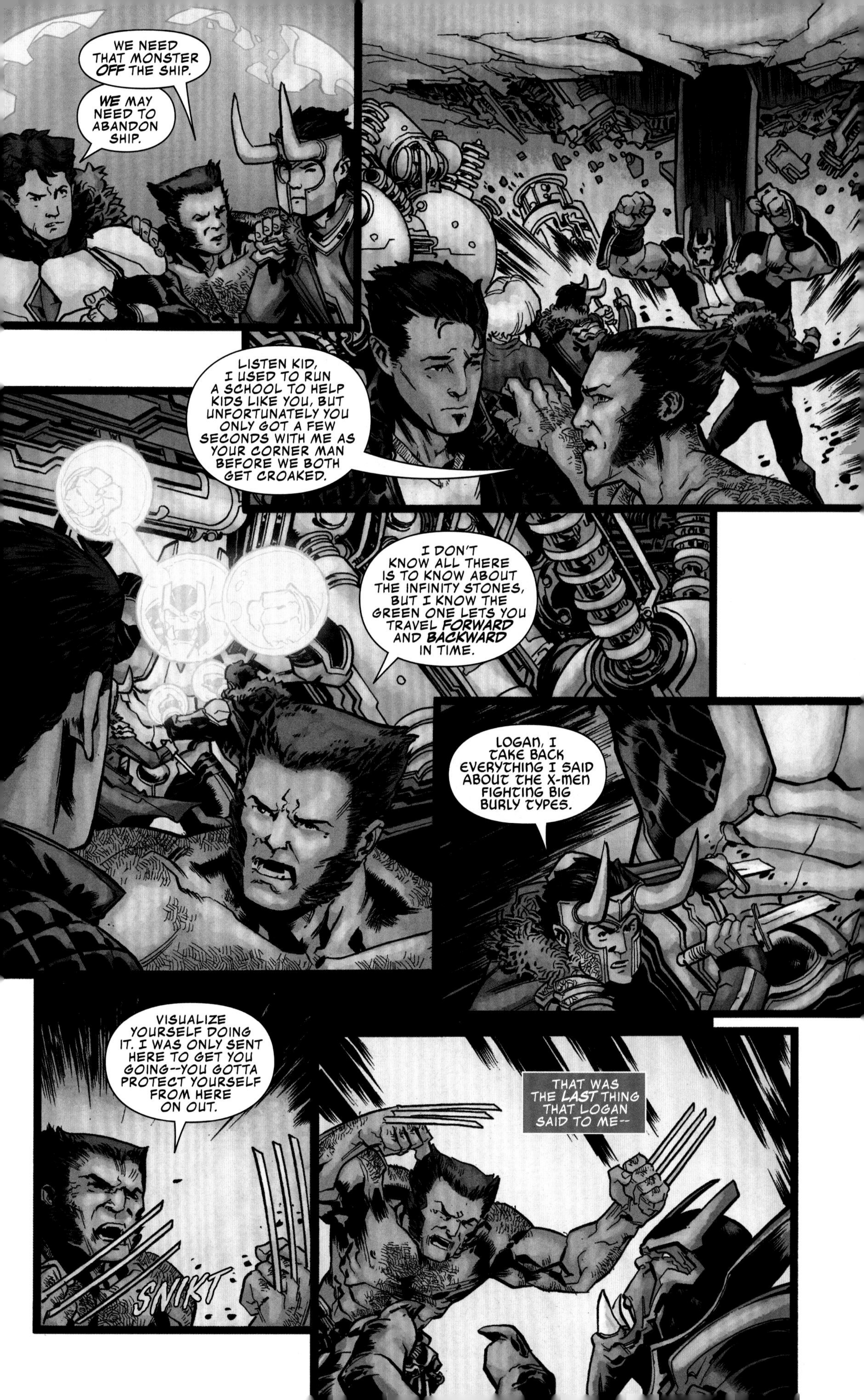
WE NEED THAT MONSTER OFF THE SHIP.
WE MAY NEED TO ABANDON SHIP.
LISTEN KID, I USED TO RUN A SCHOOL TO HELP KIDS LIKE YOU, BUT UNFORTUNATELY YOU ONLY GOT A FEW SECONDS WITH ME AS YOUR CORNER MAN BEFORE WE BOTH GET CROAKED.
I DON'T KNOW ALL THERE IS TO KNOW ABOUT THE INFINITY STONES, BUT I KNOW THE GREEN ONE LETS YOU TRAVEL FORWARD AND BACKWARD IN TIME.
LOGAN, I TAKE BACK EVERYTHING I SAID ABOUT THE X-MEN FIGHTING BIG BURLY TYPES.
VISUALIZE YOURSELF DOING IT. I WAS ONLY SENT HERE TO GET YOU GOING--YOU GOTTA PROTECT YOURSELF FROM HERE ON OUT.
SNIKT
THAT WAS THE LAST THING THAT LOGAN SAID TO ME--

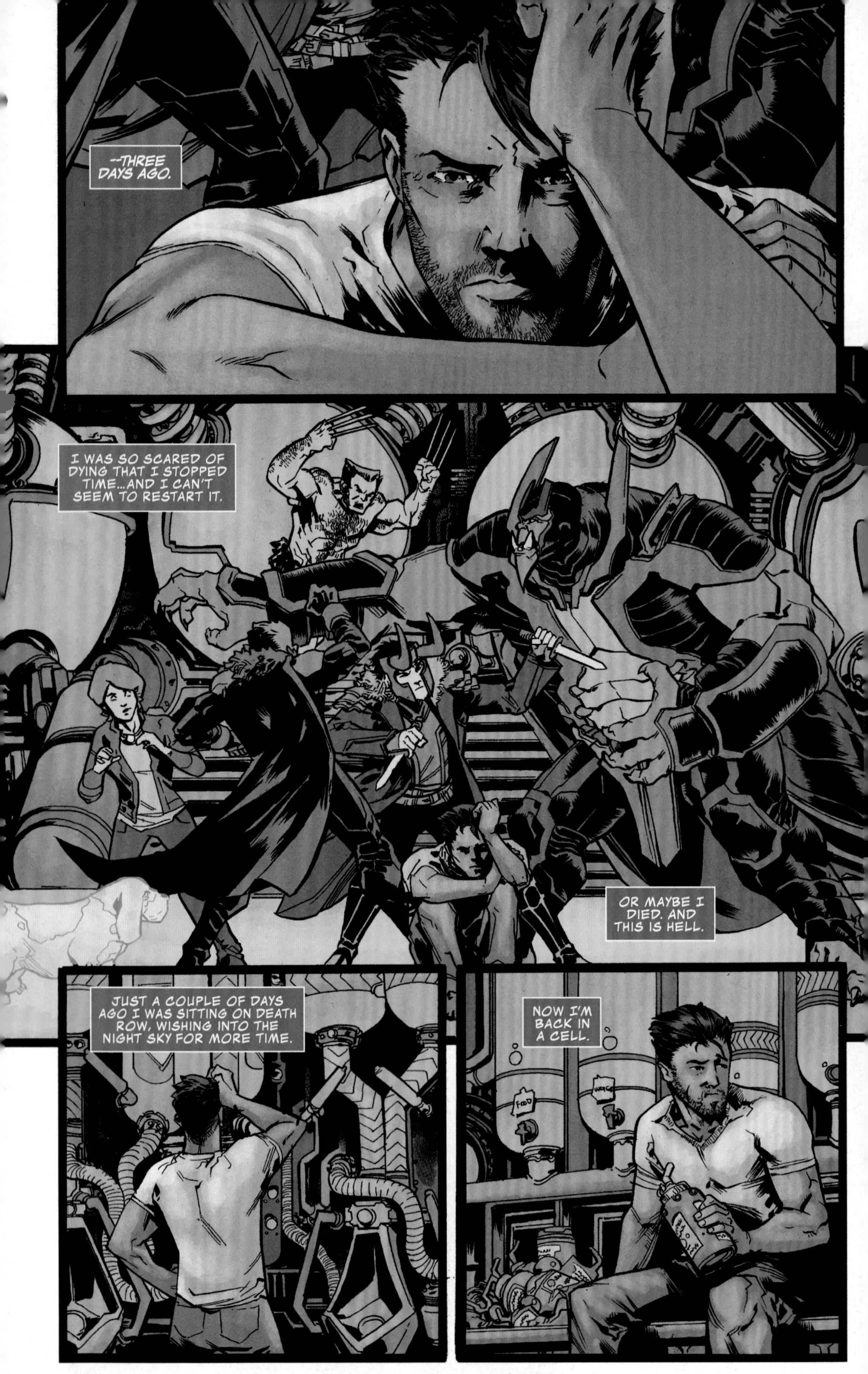
--THREE DAYS AGO.
I WAS SO SCARED OF DYING THAT I STOPPED TIME...AND I CAN'T SEEM TO RESTART IT.
OR MAYBE I DIED. AND THIS IS HELL.
JUST A COUPLE OF DAYS AGO I WAS SITTING ON DEATH ROW, WISHING INTO THE NIGHT SKY FOR MORE TIME.
NOW I'M BACK IN A CELL.
FOOD

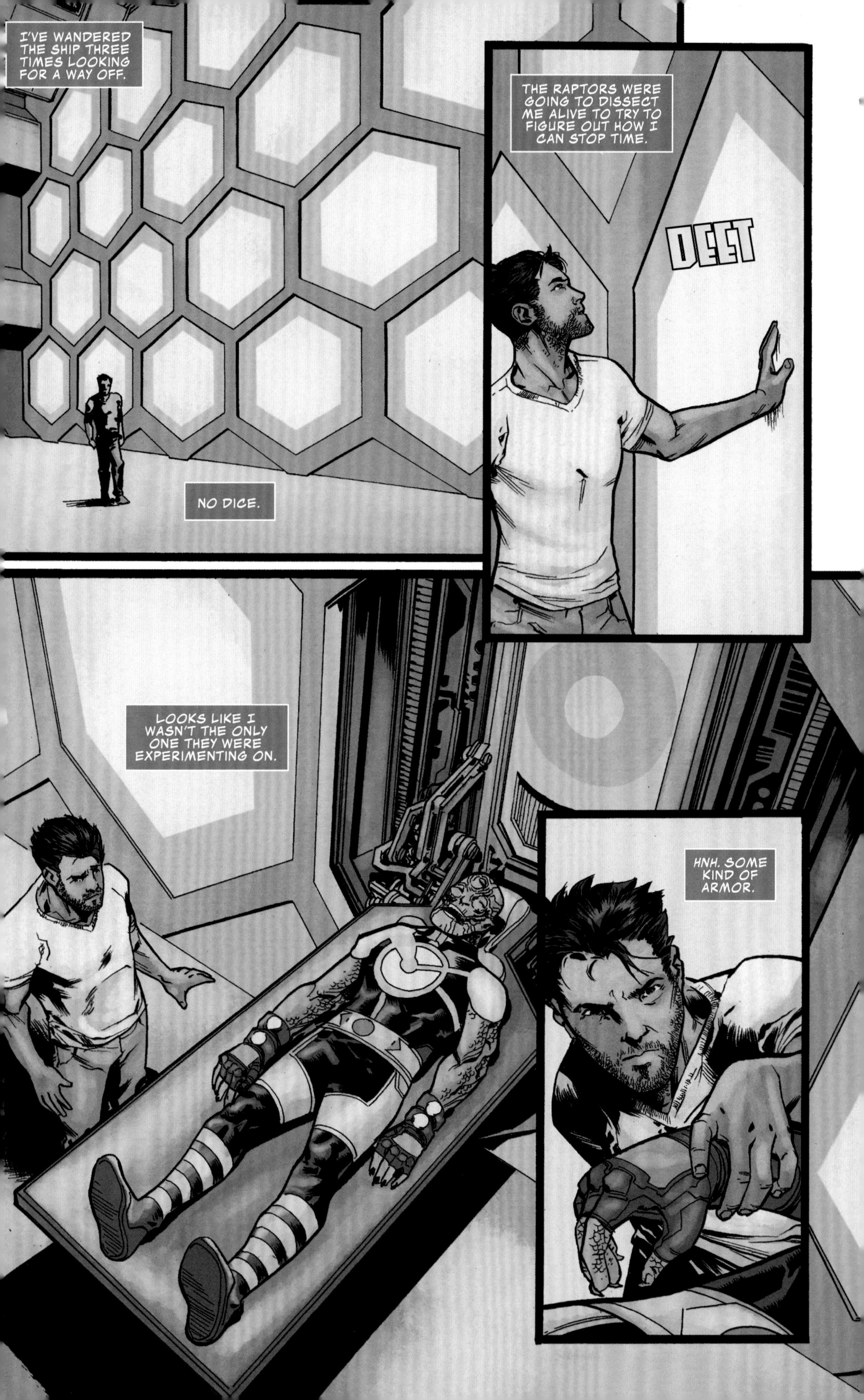
I'VE WANDERED THE SHIP THREE TIMES LOOKING FOR A WAY OFF.
NO DICE.
THE RAPTORS WERE GOING TO DISSECT ME ALIVE TO TRY TO FIGURE OUT HOW I CAN STOP TIME.
DEET
LOOKS LIKE I WASN'T THE ONLY ONE THEY WERE EXPERIMENTING ON.
HNH. SOME KIND OF ARMOR.

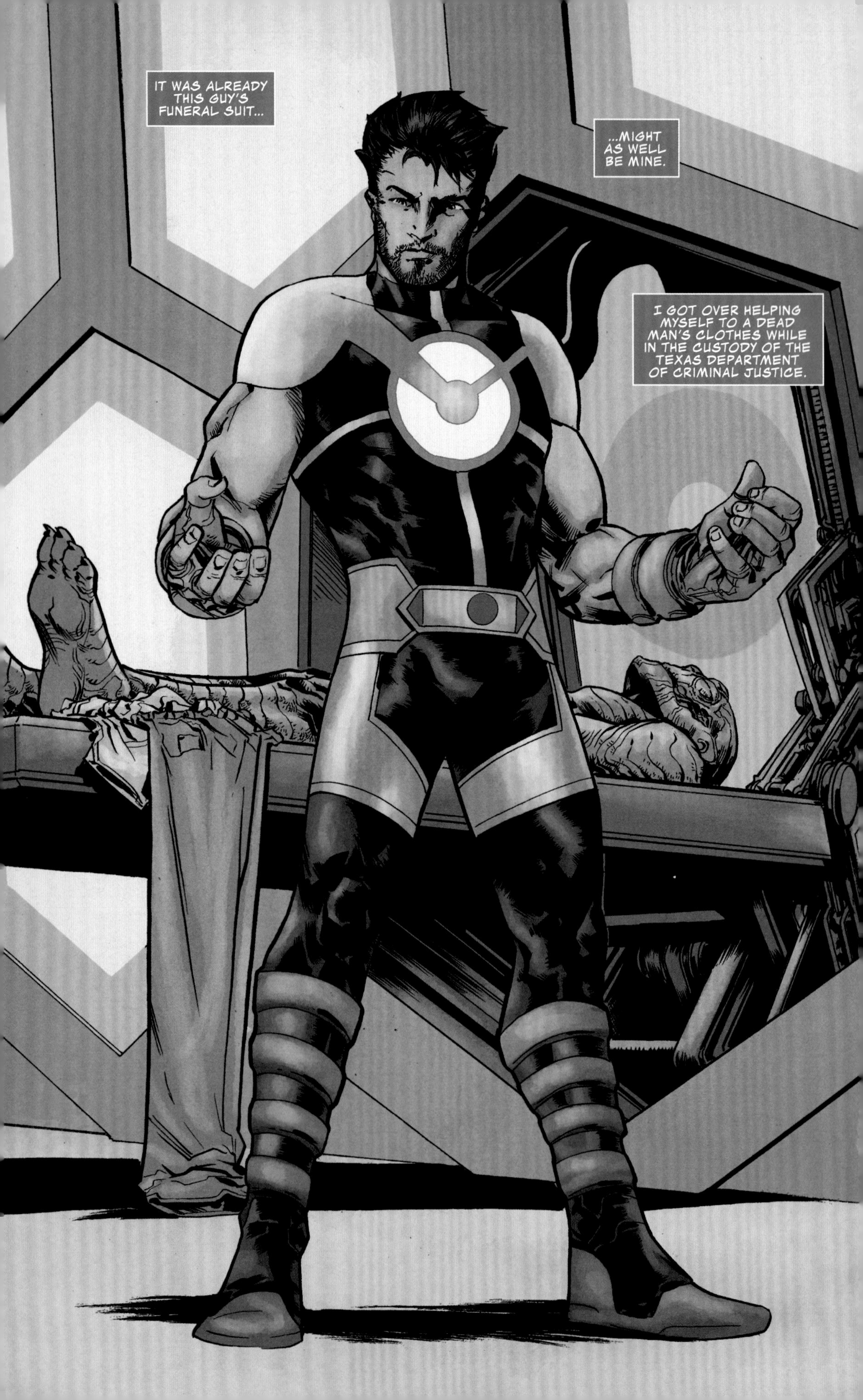
IT WAS ALREADY THIS GUY'S FUNERAL SUIT...
...MIGHT AS WELL BE MINE.
I GOT OVER HELPING MYSELF TO A DEAD MAN'S CLOTHES WHILE IN THE CUSTODY OF THE TEXAS DEPARTMENT OF CRIMINAL JUSTICE.

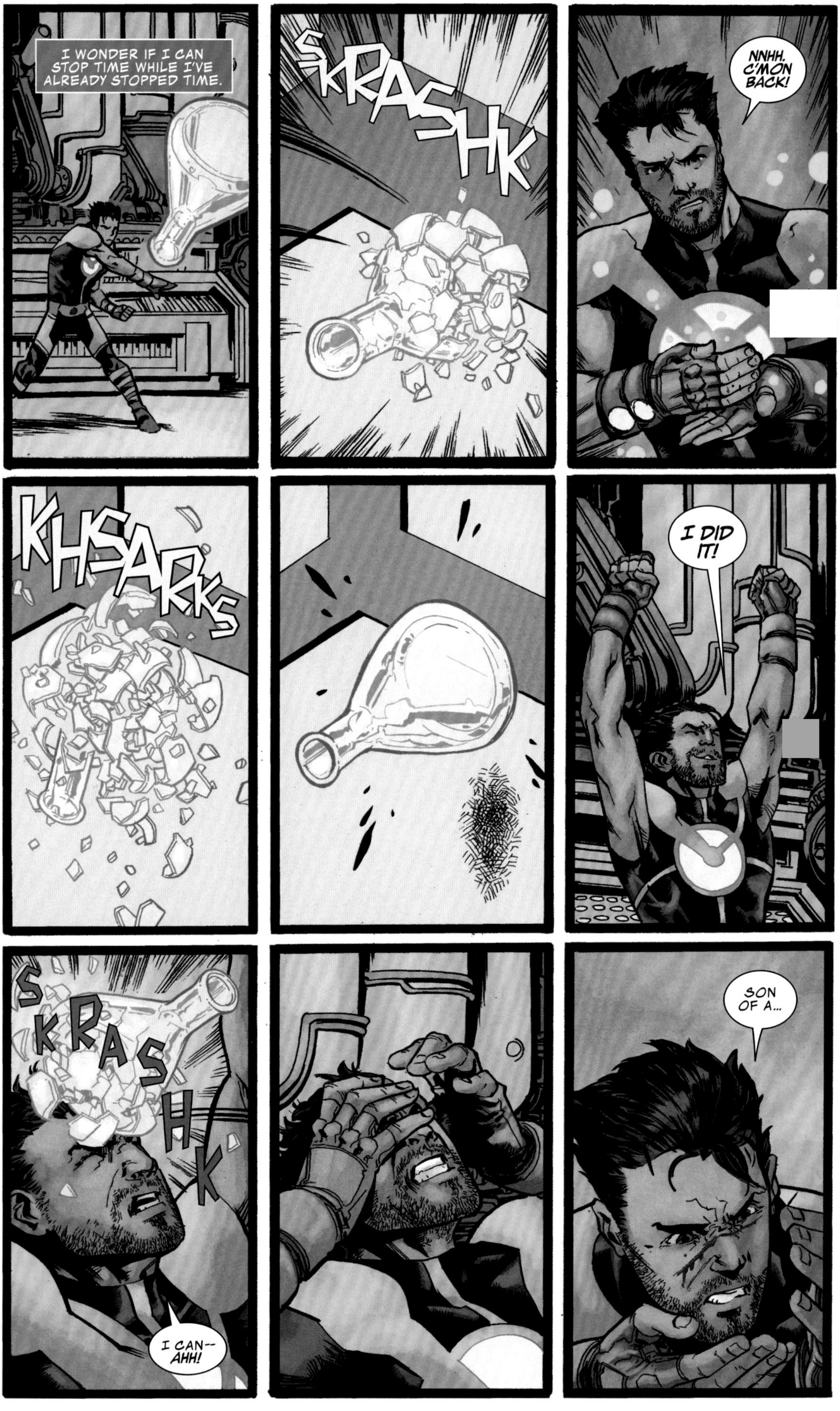
I WONDER IF I CAN STOP TIME WHILE I'VE ALREADY STOPPED TIME.
SKRASHK
NNHH. C'MON BACK!
KHSARKS
I DID IT!
SKRASHK
I CAN-- AHH!
SON OF A...

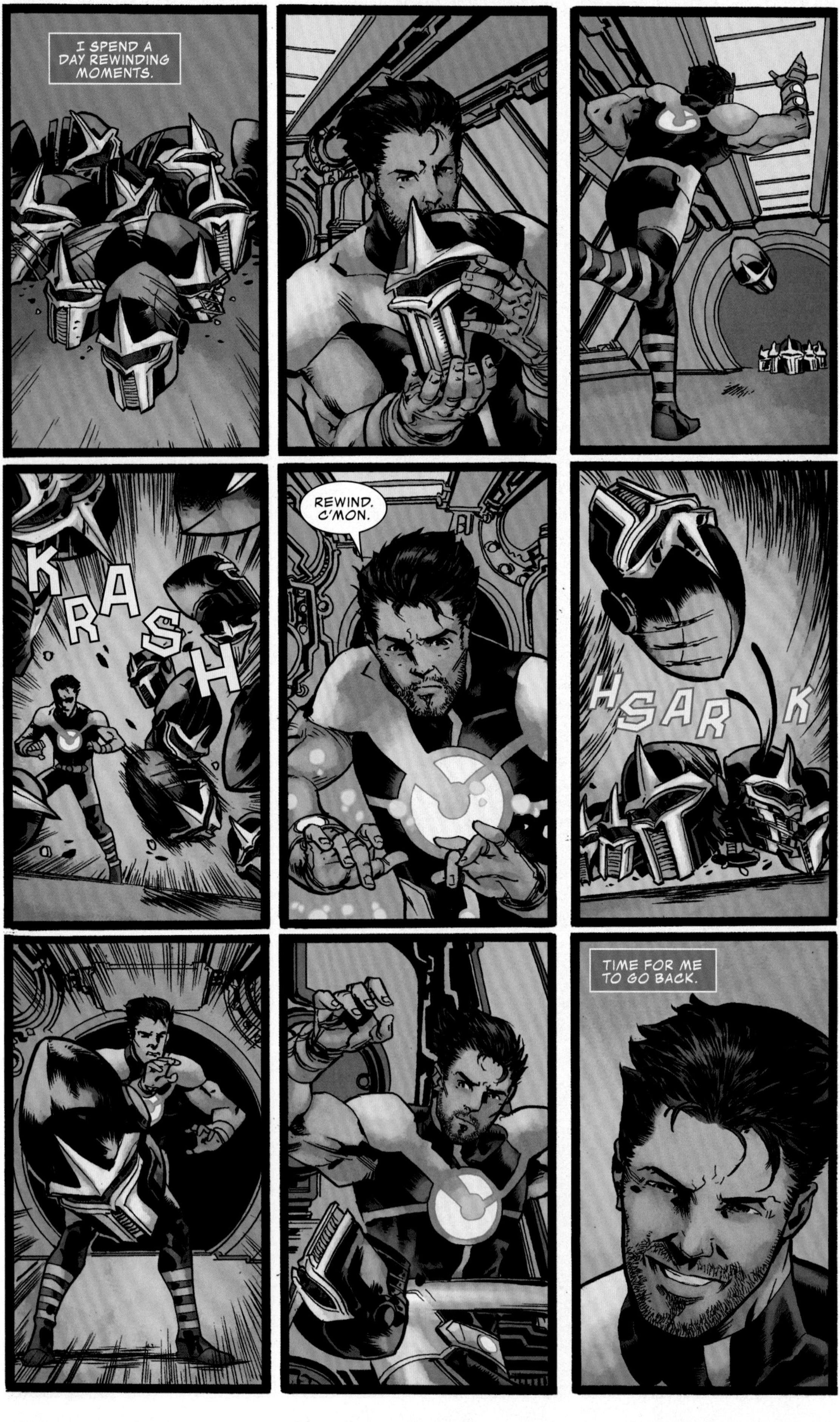
I SPEND A DAY REWINDING MOMENTS.
KRASH
REWIND. C'MON.
HSARK
TIME FOR ME TO GO BACK.

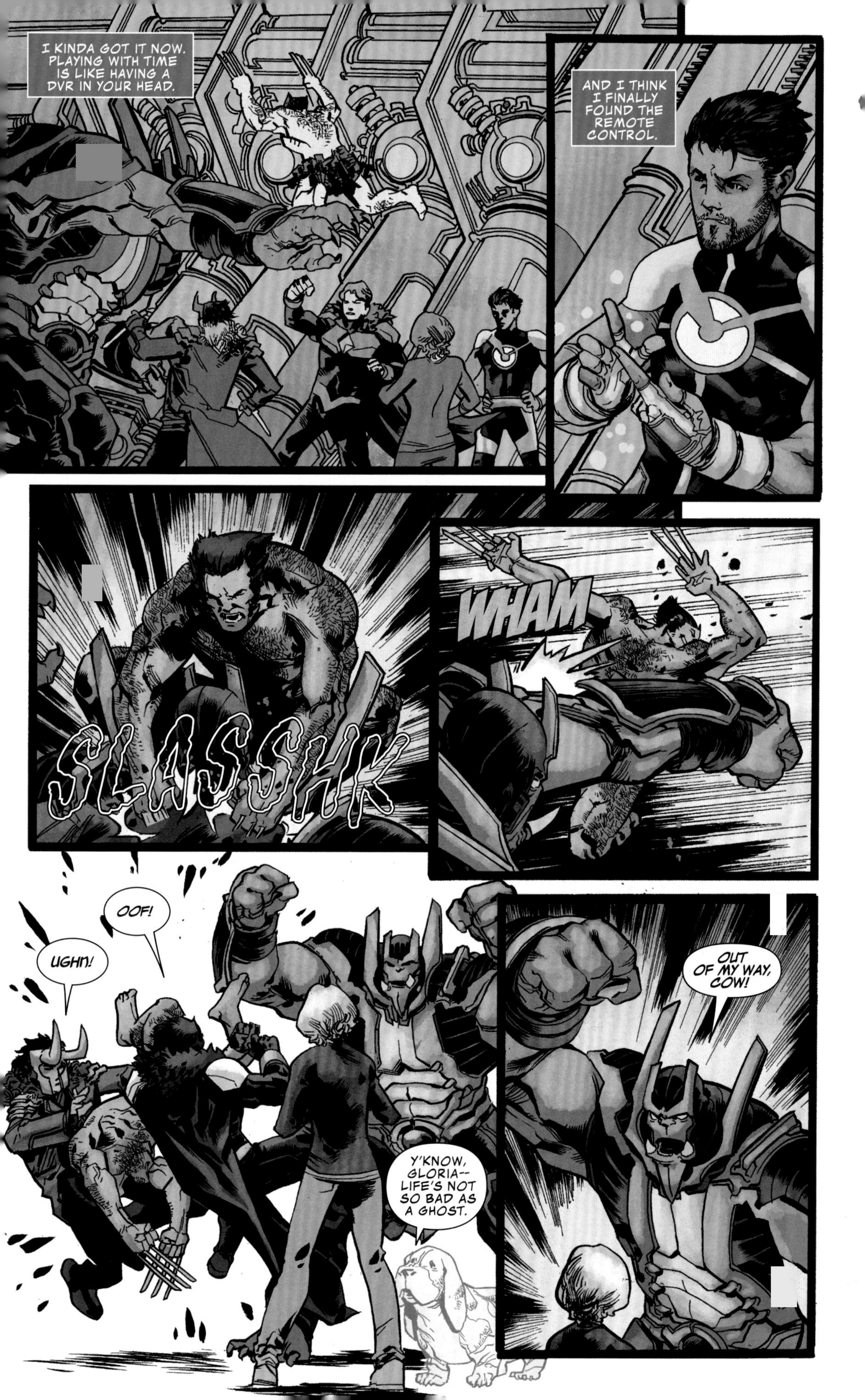
I KINDA GOT IT NOW. PLAYING WITH TIME IS LIKE HAVING A DVR IN YOUR HEAD.
AND I THINK I FINALLY FOUND THE REMOTE CONTROL.
SLASSHK
WHAM
UGHN!
OOF!
OUT OF MY WAY, COW!
Y'KNOW, GLORIA-- LIFE'S NOT SO BAD AS A GHOST.

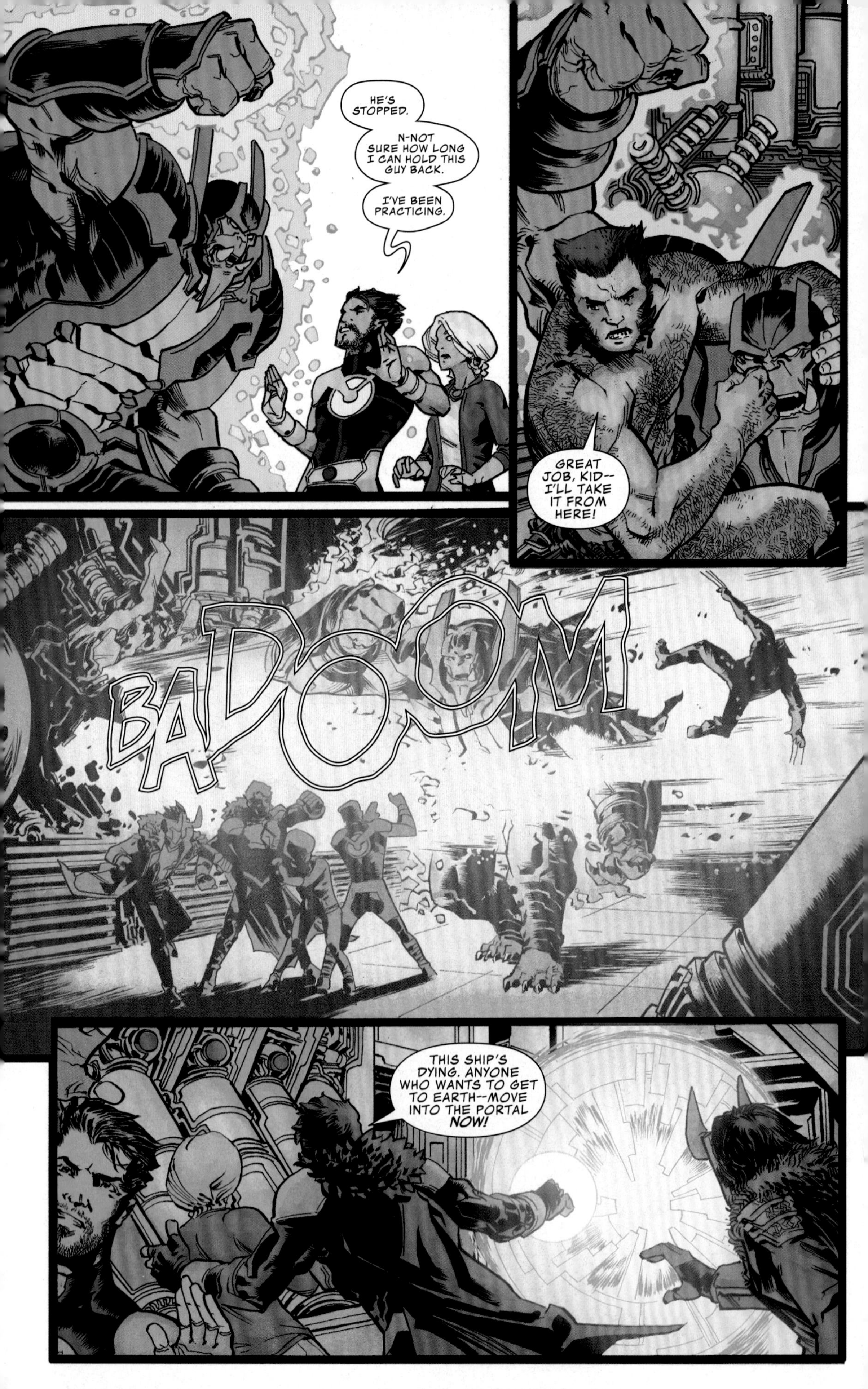

HE'S STOPPED.
N-NOT SURE HOW LONG I CAN HOLD THIS GUY BACK.
I'VE BEEN PRACTICING.
GREAT JOB, KID-- I'LL TAKE IT FROM HERE!
BADOOM
THIS SHIP'S DYING. ANYONE WHO WANTS TO GET TO EARTH--MOVE INTO THE PORTAL NOW!

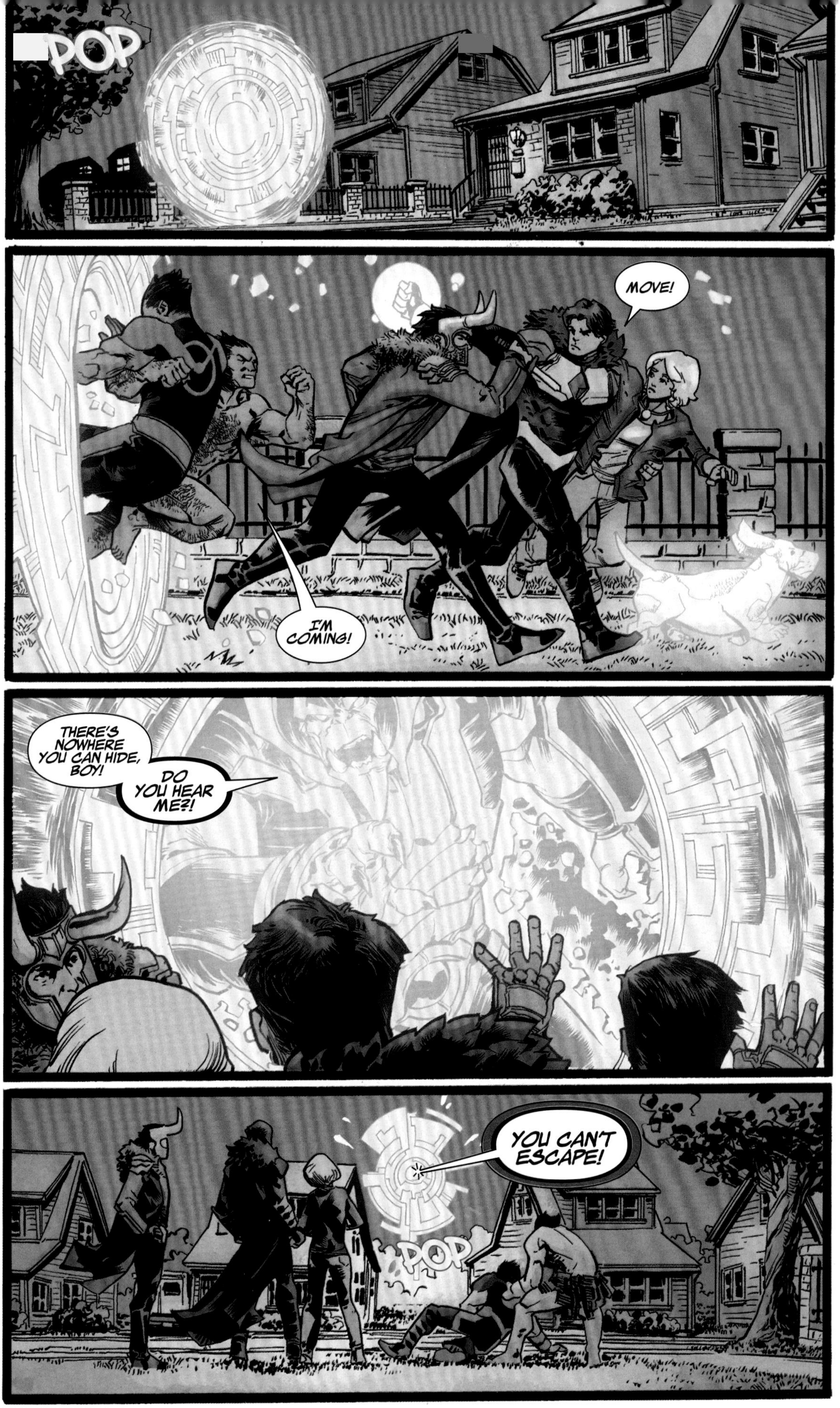
POP
MOVE!
I'M COMING!
THERE'S NOWHERE YOU CAN HIDE, BOY!
DO YOU HEAR ME?!
YOU CAN'T ESCAPE!
POP

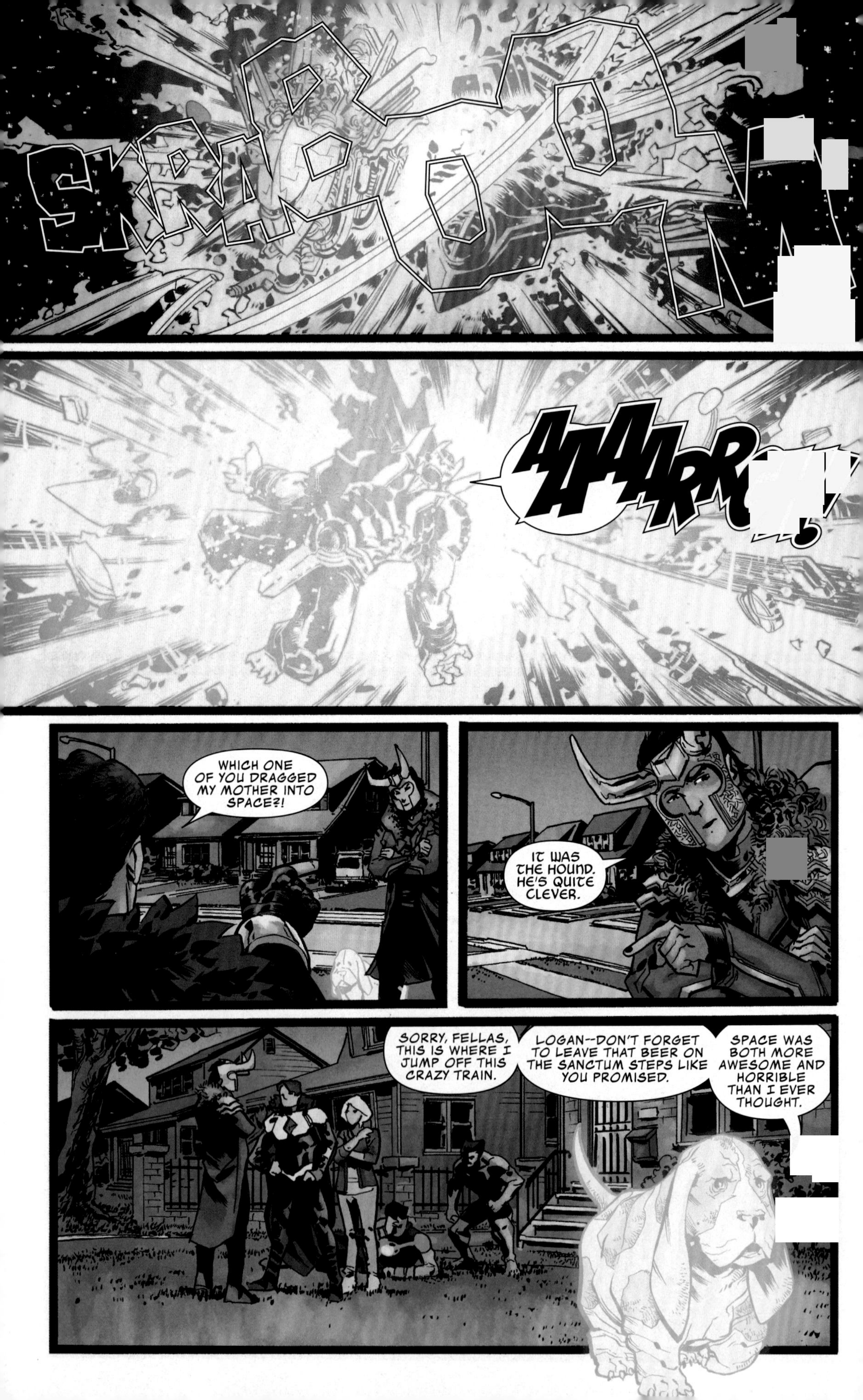
WHICH ONE OF YOU DRAGGED MY MOTHER INTO SPACE?!
IT WAS THE HOUND. HE'S QUITE CLEVER.
SORRY, FELLAS, THIS IS WHERE I JUMP OFF THIS CRAZY TRAIN.
LOGAN--DON'T FORGET TO LEAVE THAT BEER ON THE SANCTUM STEPS LIKE YOU PROMISED.
SPACE WAS BOTH MORE AWESOME AND HORRIBLE THAN I EVER THOUGHT.

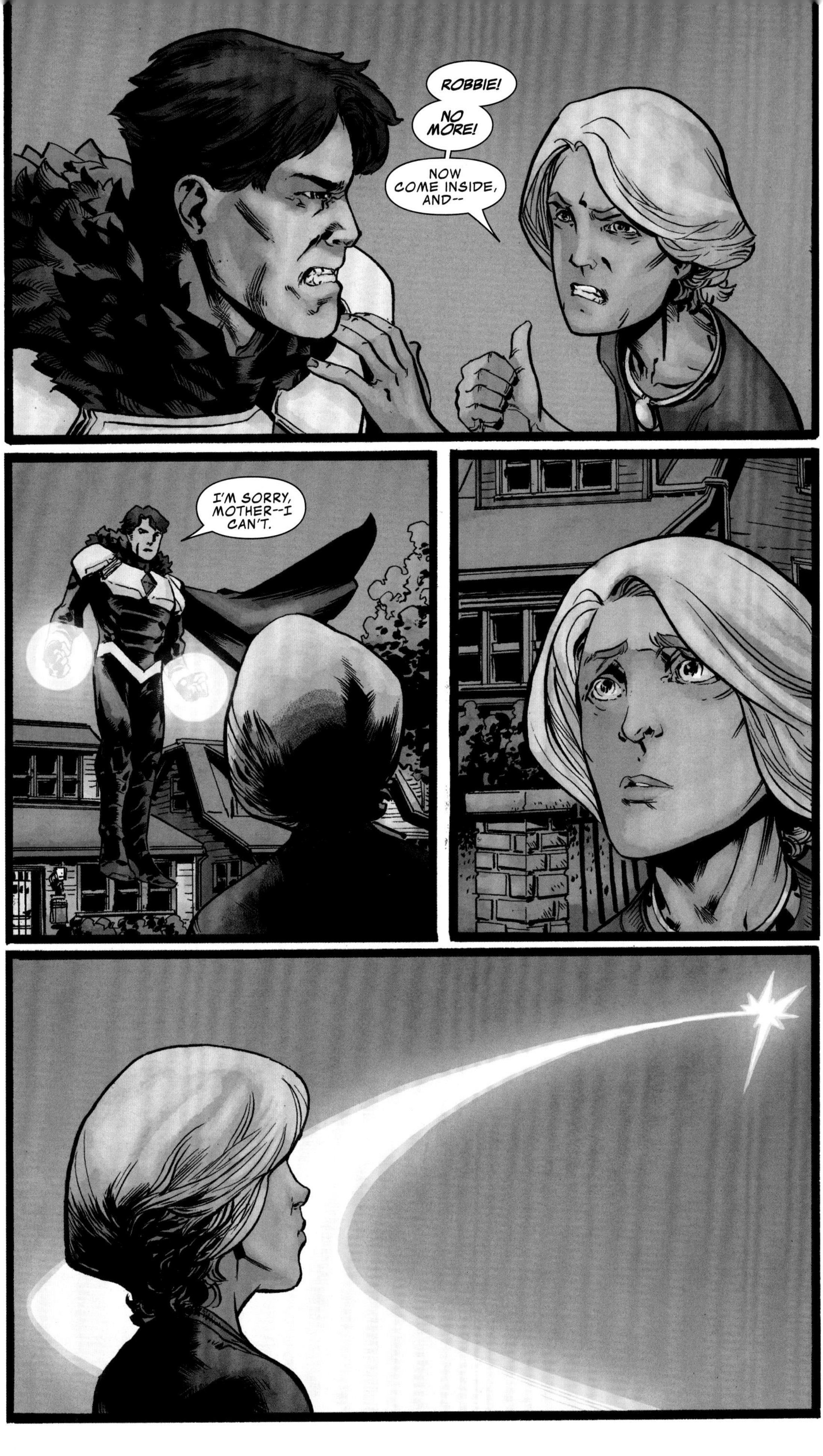
ROBBIE!
NO MORE!
NOW COME INSIDE, AND--
I'M SORRY, MOTHER--I CAN'T.

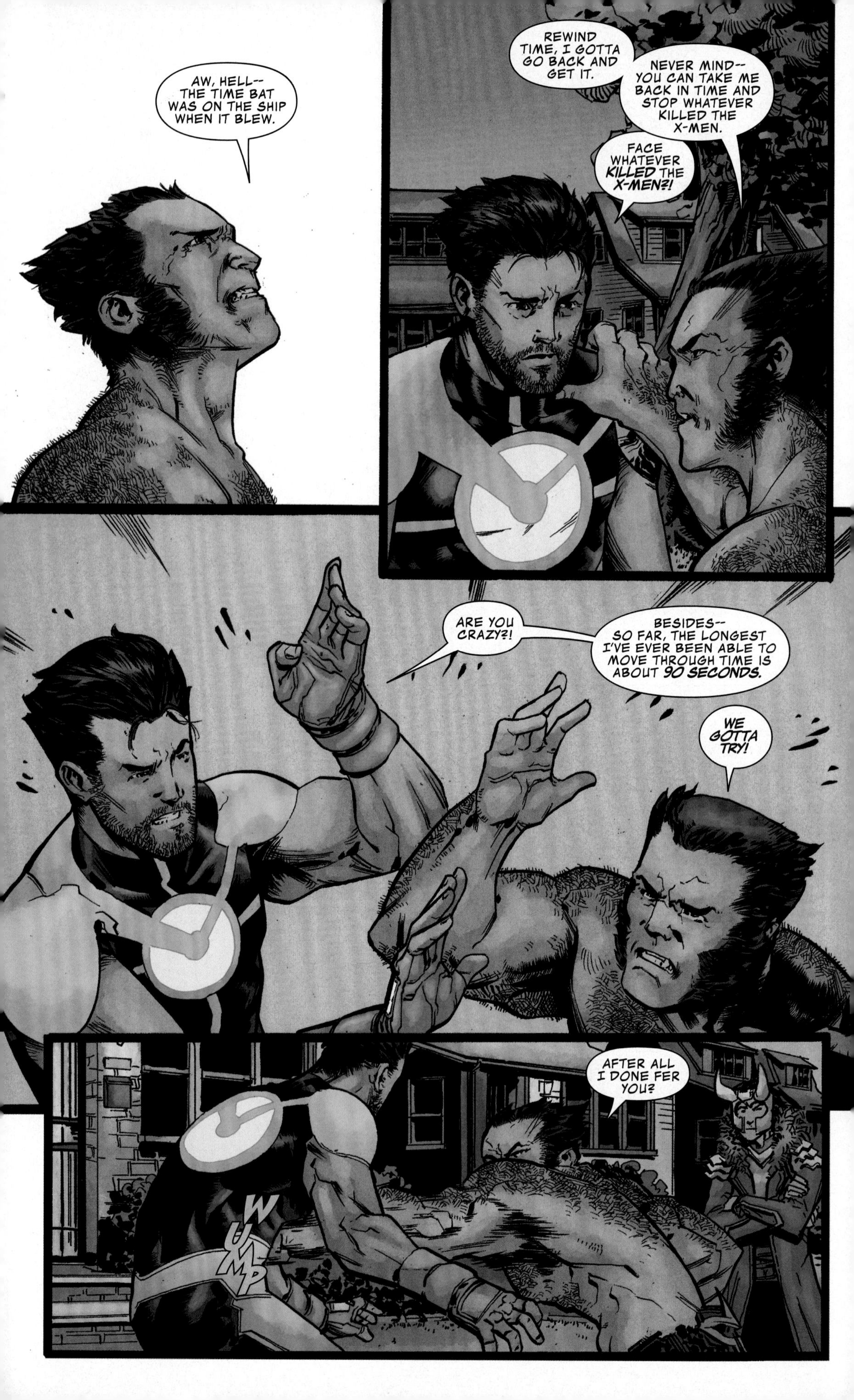
AW, HELL-- THE TIME BAT WAS ON THE SHIP WHEN IT BLEW.
REWIND TIME, I GOTTA GO BACK AND GET IT.
NEVER MIND-- YOU CAN TAKE ME BACK IN TIME AND STOP WHATEVER KILLED THE X-MEN.
FACE WHATEVER KILLED THE X-MEN?!
ARE YOU CRAZY?!
BESIDES-- SO FAR, THE LONGEST I'VE EVER BEEN ABLE TO MOVE THROUGH TIME IS ABOUT 90 SECONDS.
WE GOTTA TRY!
AFTER ALL I DONE FER YOU?
WUMP

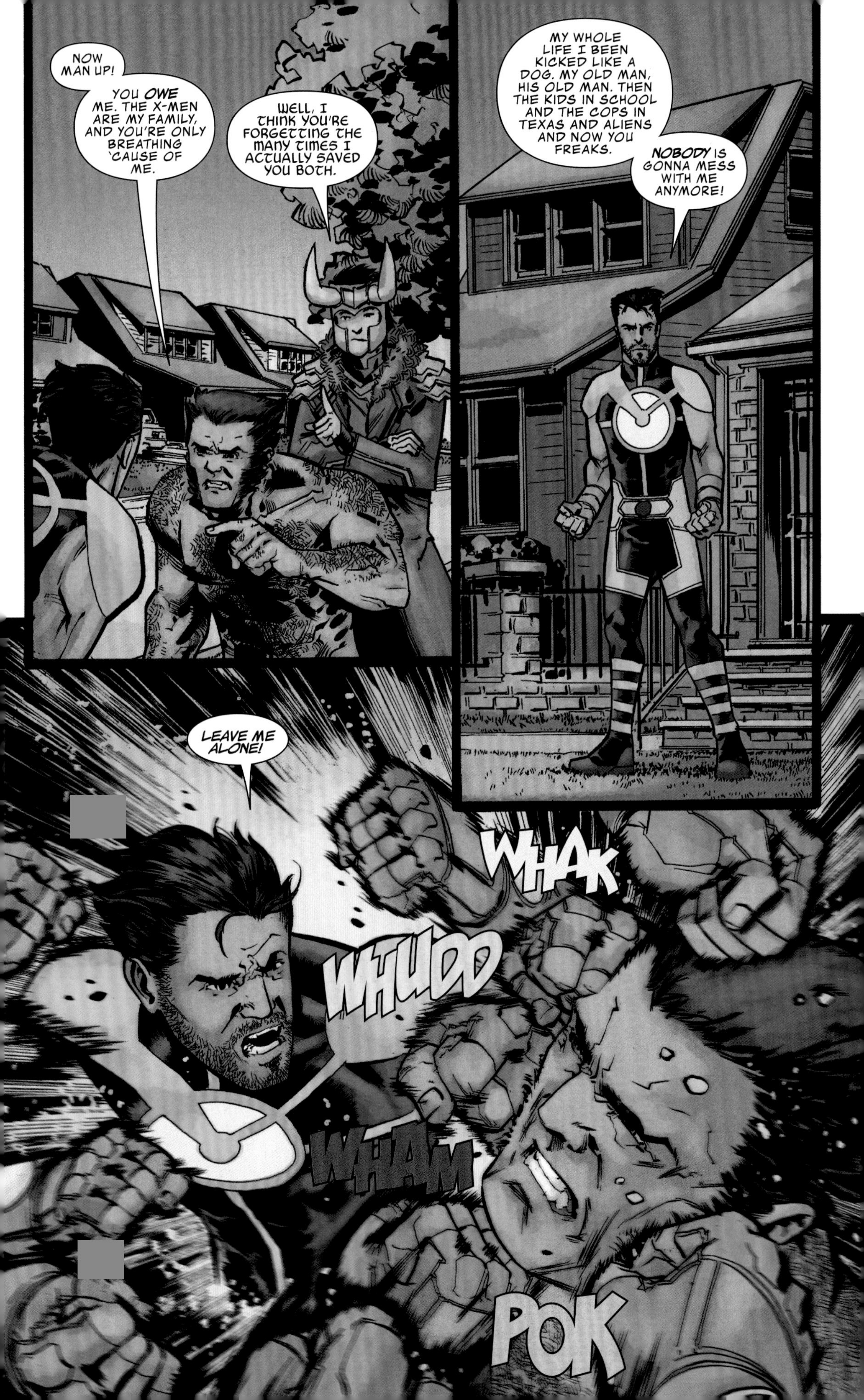
NOW MAN UP!
YOU OWE ME. THE X-MEN ARE MY FAMILY, AND YOU'RE ONLY BREATHING 'CAUSE OF ME.
WELL, I THINK YOU'RE FORGETTING THE MANY TIMES I ACTUALLY SAVED YOU BOTH.
MY WHOLE LIFE I BEEN KICKED LIKE A DOG. MY OLD MAN, HIS OLD MAN. THEN THE KIDS IN SCHOOL AND THE COPS IN TEXAS AND ALIENS AND NOW YOU FREAKS.
NOBODY IS GONNA MESS WITH ME ANYMORE!
LEAVE ME ALONE!
WHAK
WHUDD
WHAM
POK

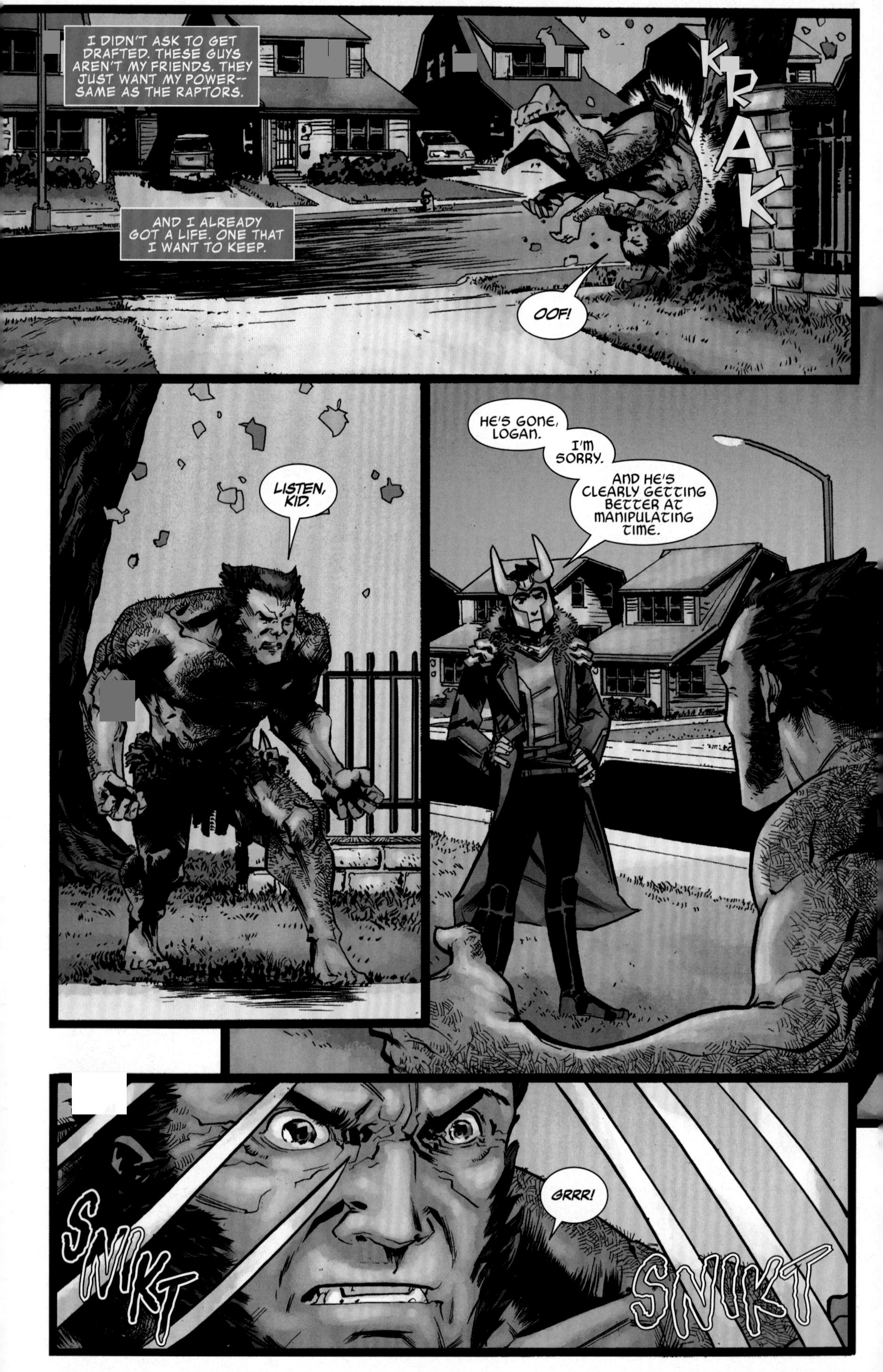
I DIDN'T ASK TO GET DRAFTED. THESE GUYS AREN'T MY FRIENDS. THEY JUST WANT MY POWER-- SAME AS THE RAPTORS.
AND I ALREADY GOT A LIFE. ONE THAT I WANT TO KEEP.
KRAK
OOF!
LISTEN, KID.
HE'S GONE, LOGAN.
I'M SORRY.
AND HE'S CLEARLY GETTING BETTER AT MANIPULATING TIME.
SNIKT
GRRR!
SNIKT

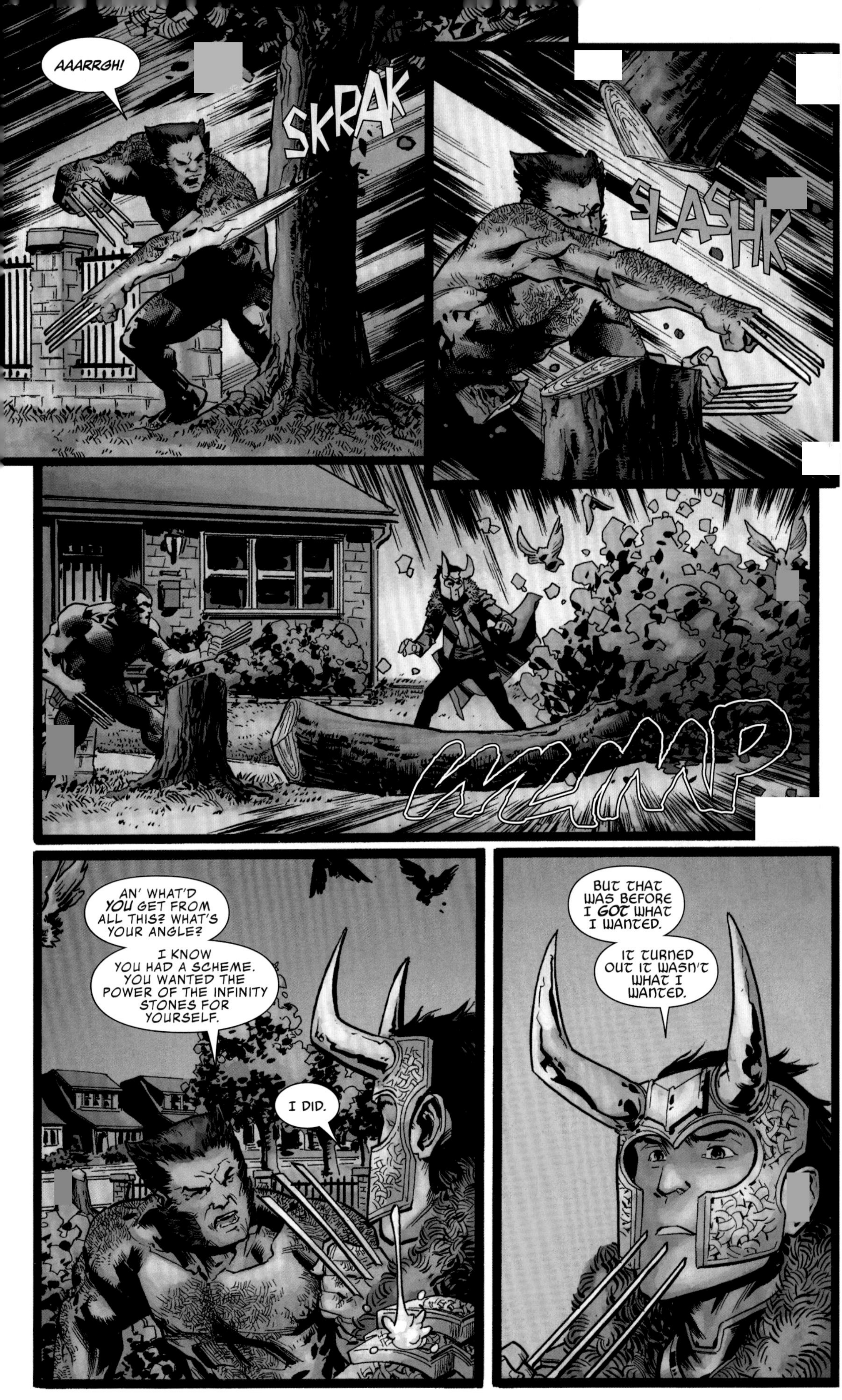
AAARRGH!
SKRAK
SLASHK
AN' WHAT'D *YOU* GET FROM ALL THIS? WHAT'S YOUR ANGLE?
I KNOW YOU HAD A SCHEME. YOU WANTED THE POWER OF THE INFINITY STONES FOR YOURSELF.
I DID.
BUT THAT WAS BEFORE I *GOT* WHAT I WANTED.
IT TURNED OUT IT WASN'T WHAT I WANTED.

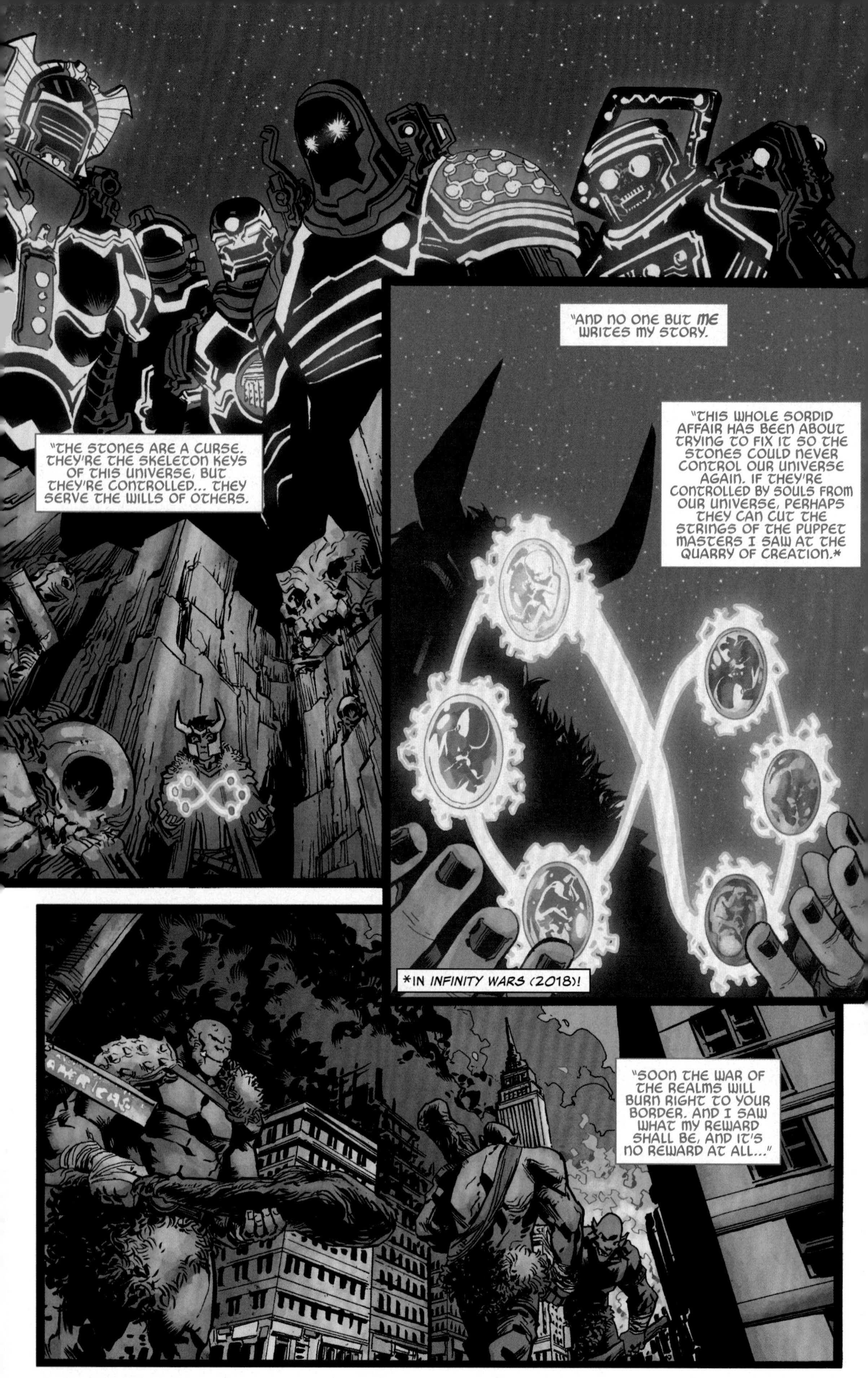
"THE STONES ARE A CURSE. THEY'RE THE SKELETON KEYS OF THIS UNIVERSE, BUT THEY'RE CONTROLLED... THEY SERVE THE WILLS OF OTHERS.
"AND NO ONE BUT *ME* WRITES MY STORY.
"THIS WHOLE SORDID AFFAIR HAS BEEN ABOUT TRYING TO FIX IT SO THE STONES COULD NEVER CONTROL OUR UNIVERSE AGAIN. IF THEY'RE CONTROLLED BY SOULS FROM OUR UNIVERSE, PERHAPS THEY CAN CUT THE STRINGS OF THE PUPPET MASTERS I SAW AT THE QUARRY OF CREATION.*
*IN *INFINITY WARS* (2018)!
"SOON THE WAR OF THE REALMS WILL BURN RIGHT TO YOUR BORDER. AND I SAW WHAT MY REWARD SHALL BE, AND IT'S NO REWARD AT ALL..."

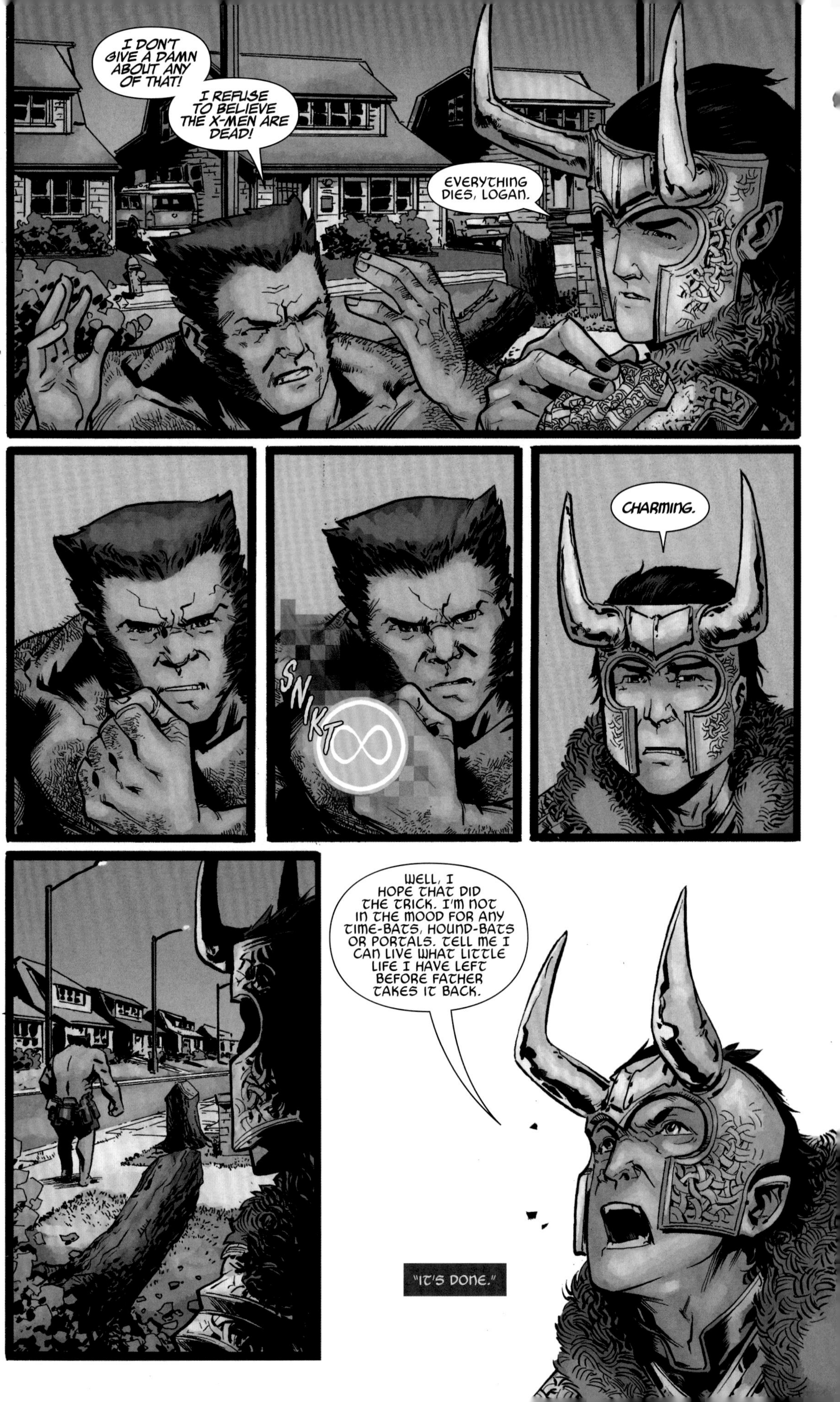
I DON'T GIVE A DAMN ABOUT ANY OF THAT!
I REFUSE TO BELIEVE THE X-MEN ARE DEAD!
EVERYTHING DIES, LOGAN.
SNIKT
CHARMING.
WELL, I HOPE THAT DID THE TRICK. I'M NOT IN THE MOOD FOR ANY TIME-BATS, HOUND-BATS OR PORTALS. TELL ME I CAN LIVE WHAT LITTLE LIFE I HAVE LEFT BEFORE FATHER TAKES IT BACK.
"IT'S DONE."

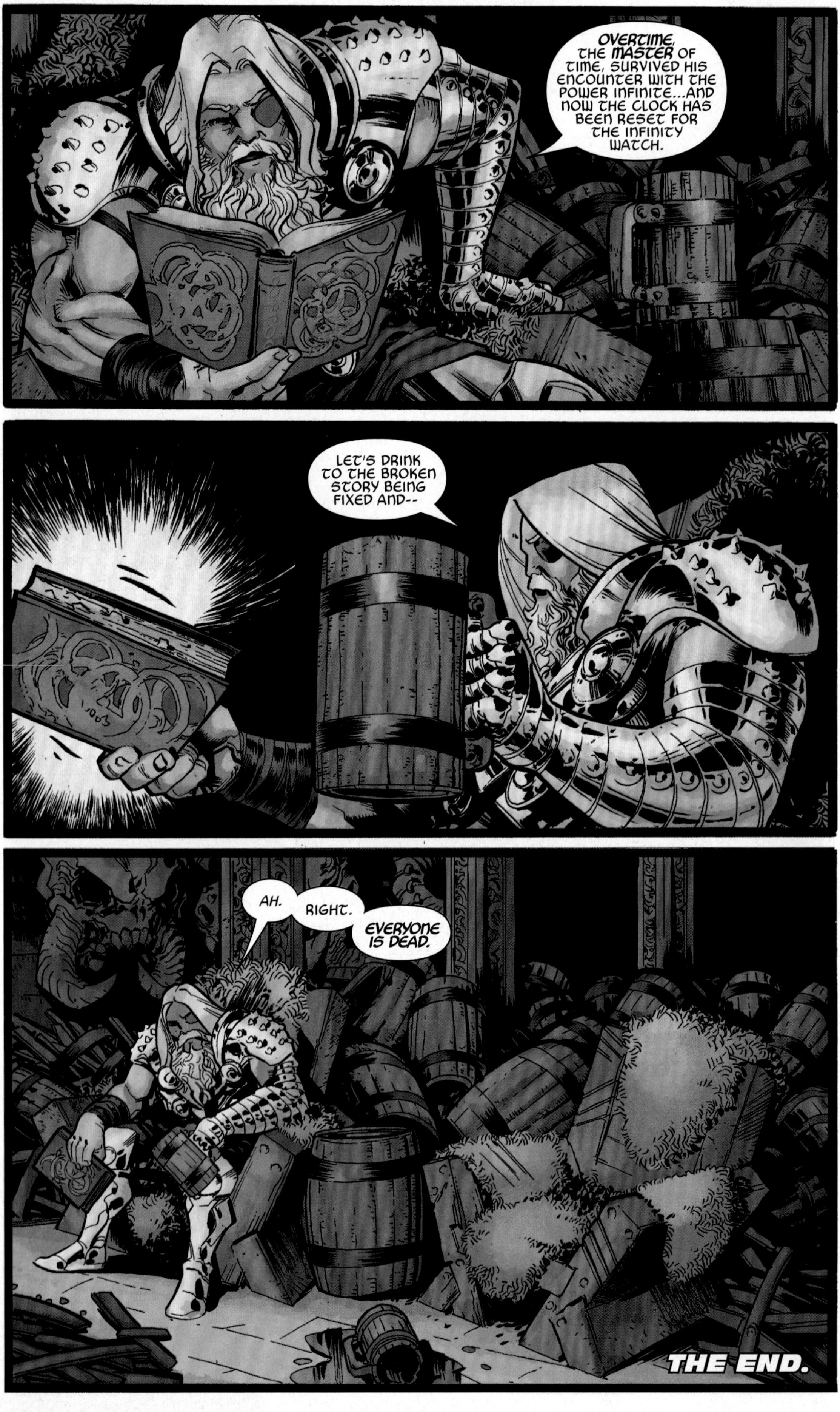

OVERTIME, THE MASTER OF TIME, SURVIVED HIS ENCOUNTER WITH THE POWER INFINITE...AND NOW THE CLOCK HAS BEEN RESET FOR THE INFINITY WATCH.
LET'S DRINK TO THE BROKEN STORY BEING FIXED AND--
AH.
RIGHT.
EVERYONE IS DEAD.
THE END.

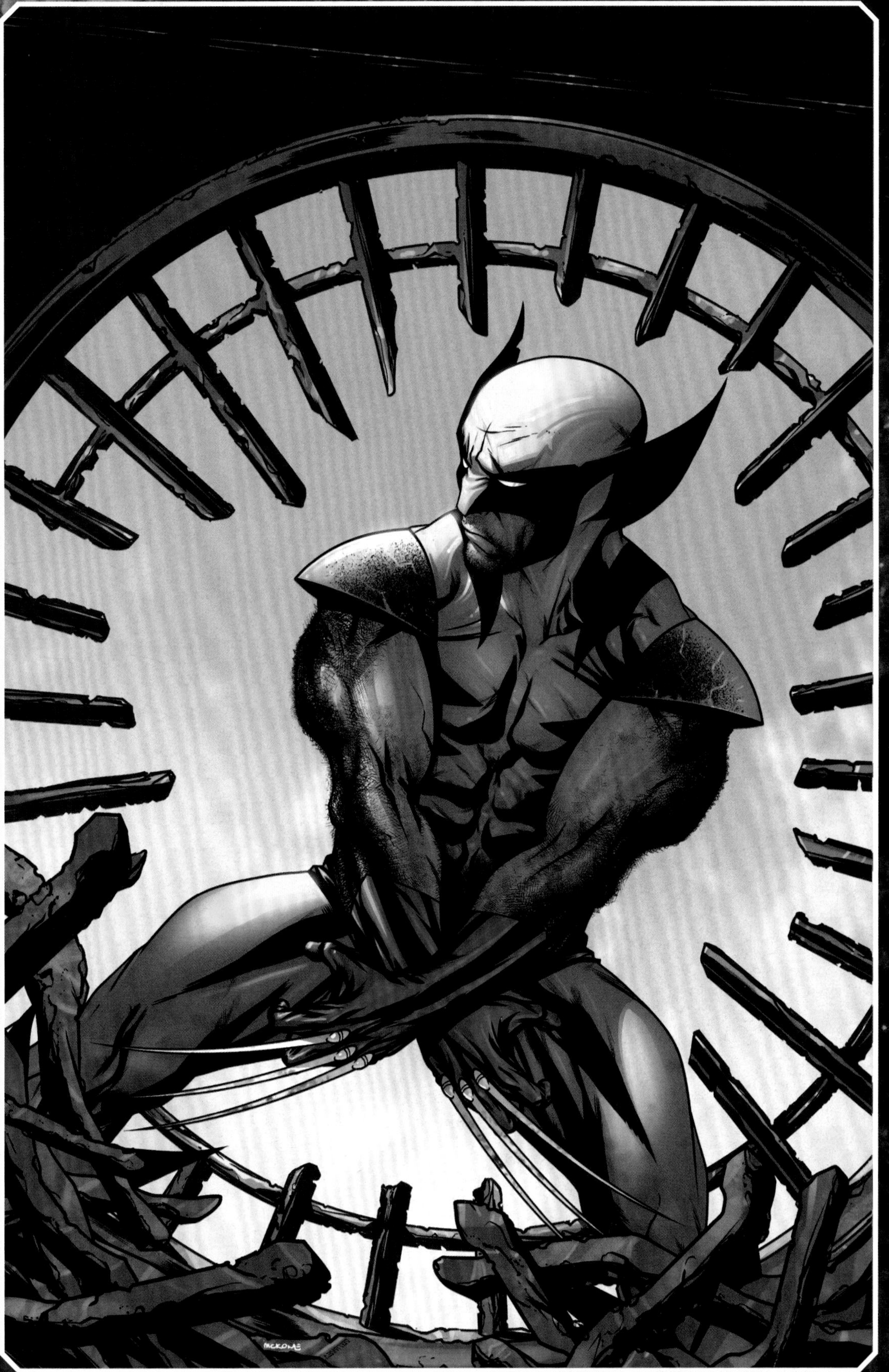

ONE VARIANT

MIKE McKONE & JESUS ABURTOV

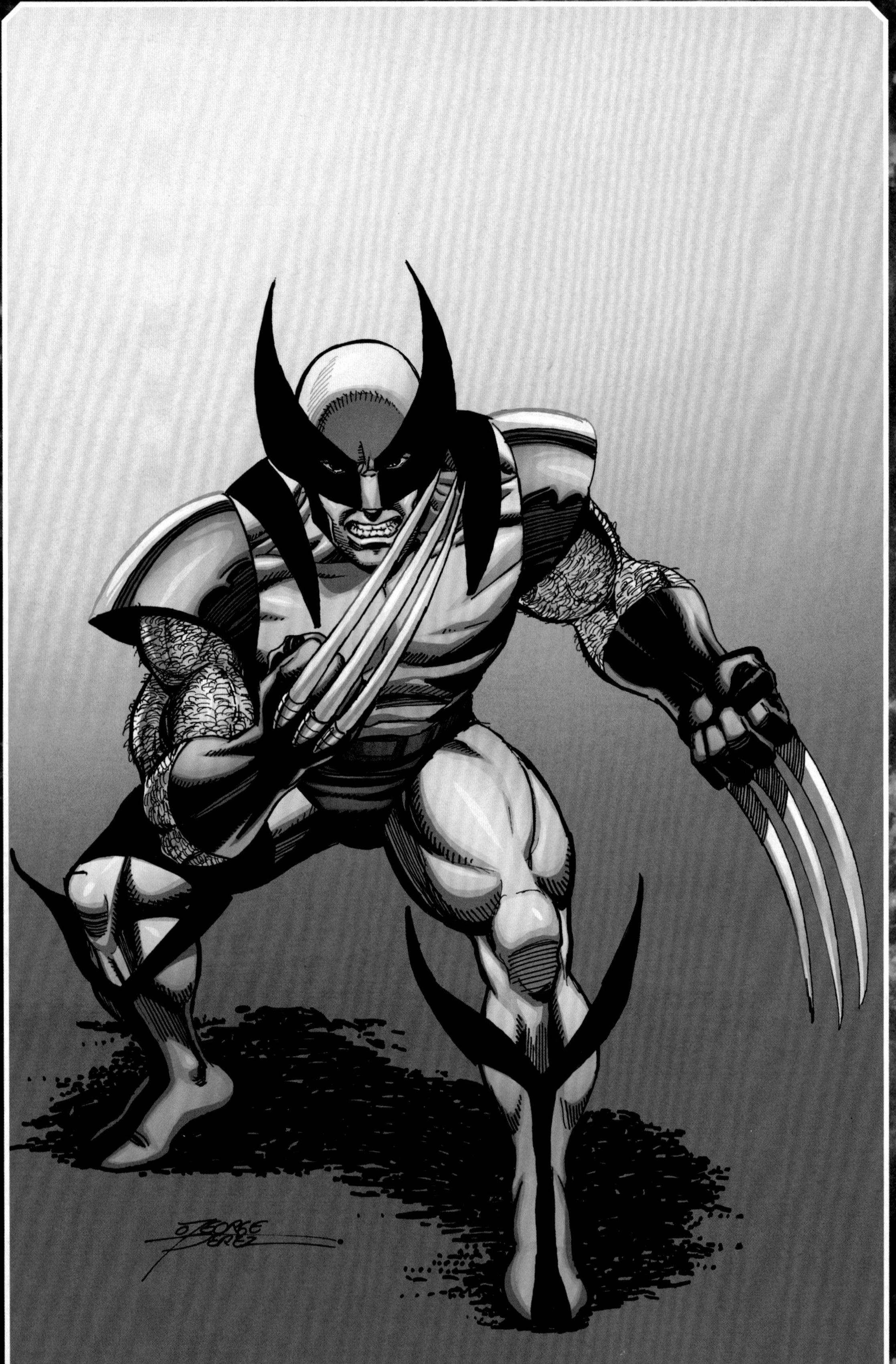

ONE VARIANT
GEORGE PÉREZ & DAVE McCAIG

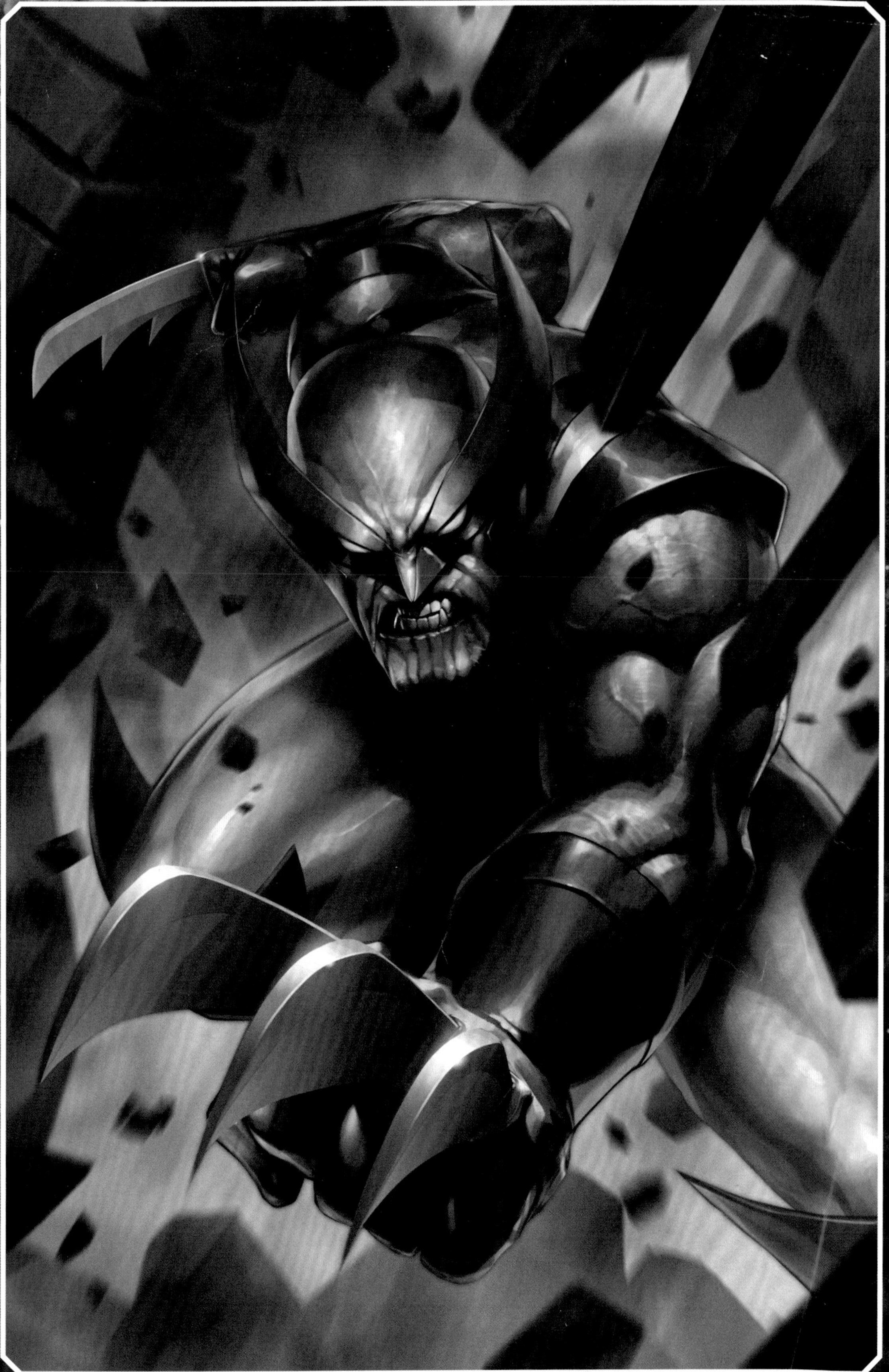

ONE SKRULLS VARIANT
JEEHYUNG LEE

5

TWO CAT VARIANT
NAO FUJI